FIGHTER

FIGHTER

Military Aircraft From World War I To The Present Day
Technology › Facts › History

Ralf Leinburger

Bath · New York · Cologne · Melbourne · Delhi
Hong Kong · Shenzhen · Singapore · Amsterdam

CONTENTS

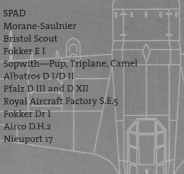

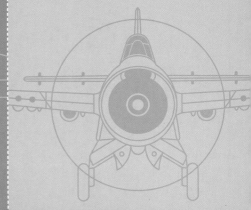

THE SECOND WORLD WAR 116

POSTWAR FIGHTERS 206

INTRODUCTION

Conquering the skies

On December 17, 1903, the Wright brothers achieved the first manned, controlled, powered flight in front of witnesses, thereby laying the foundations for the rapid development of aviation that followed. The time was ripe for this technological leap forward and inventors in a number of other countries were also on the verge of conquering the skies. Some had already done so but couldn't claim any glory because their exploits had been inadequately documented.

The Royal Aircraft Factory S.E.5 (shown here) and the Sopwith Camel were the most successful British fighters of the First World War.

Air superiority—a new strategic goal

A logical consequence of the invention of powered flight was the use of aircraft as weapons of war. This was to have a profound influence on the way war was waged over the coming years.

Prior to the First World War, the key objective of warfare had always been to seize and control land. With this new weapon, the struggle for control was extended upwards. Air superiority became a prerequisite for military success and has remained so ever since.

To start with, the main priority of military pilots was reconnaissance. From here it was only a small step to the development of armed scout planes that sought to prevent other reconnaissance craft from carrying out their missions. These armed scout planes developed into the first fighters.

This new class of weapon superseded the cavalry units that had previously been responsible for reconnaissance. The cavalry became superfluous and it is no coincidence that many of the first military pilots were drawn from its ranks. Henceforth, scouting ceased to be the responsibility of individuals on horseback and became that of individuals in airplanes.

Flying crates

At the beginning of the First World War, military aircraft were still flimsy constructions of canvas, wire, and wooden struts, but significant developments were made over the next four years.

Having initially rejected the use of powered aircraft, the military became the main customer of the new aircraft industry. Inextricably linked with progress are the names of numerous aircraft pioneers. In France, the European home of flying, Louis Blériot made a name for himself as a designer as well as a pilot. In Germany, Dutchman Anthony Fokker developed the synchronization gear to production-readiness, thus inventing the technique of firing through the propeller. In the UK, Geoffrey de Havilland's designs were revolutionary during the pioneering years. But these three names are merely

The Albatros D II helped German pilots achieve air superiority in the First World War. Manfred von Richthofen alone scored 17 kills in this type of plane.

The Curtiss P-40 was an extremely robust aircraft. Shown here is a squadron of the American Volunteer Group, otherwise known as the "Flying Tigers."

The McDonnell Douglas F-4 Phantom became NATO's primary fighter in the 1970s and is one of the most successful military planes of all time.

advantages. The enemy would have to respond by developing a new machine and this in turn called forth a new, more advanced model from the other side.

Although some aircraft had a longer lifetime than others, no single plane stands out as the ultimate fighter of the day. The race, in other words, was never won—and remains unwon today. A classic example is the competition between the Supermarine Spitfire and the Messerschmitt Bf 109. To the present day it remains impossible to ascertain which was the better plane. Often one or other appeared to have gained the edge—but only until the other side's latest models went into production.

This is not to say that all the effort was in vain. Quite apart from the strategic value of each new fighter, every innovation and the experience gained during its development flowed into future projects and gradually made flying—civil aviation included—one of the safest of all modes of transport. Today's fighters, for example, can clock up millions of flying hours.

But the complex technology that goes into the fighters of today comes at a price. In addition to the astronomically high unit costs, the development time required for new weapons systems is many times what it used to be in the early days. Even in the Second World War, individual aircraft could be developed to production stage in a year or less whereas today this is unthinkable. Many now take more than a decade to progress from initial design stage to maiden flight—and that does not include the political decision-making process.

representative of the visionaries who abounded at this time and who were committed heart and soul to mankind's age-old dream of flight.

Worthy of the same respect are the daring pilots. It is impossible to think of the early days of military flying without bringing to mind the names of Roland Garros, the first flying ace in the history of aviation, the American Eddie Rickenbacker, and the legendary "Red Baron," Manfred Freiherr von Richthofen. And to set the bravery of the early pilots properly into context, it is important to remember that at this time more pilots were killed while training than in combat.

An arms race develops

The joint efforts of designers and pilots meant that, even in the First World War, new models had a short lifespan because new inventions or even just a significant improvement in aircraft design often conferred major tactical

Aircraft development from the pioneering days to today

The development of aeronautical technology was, on the whole, very uneven. In the early days a few individual nations led the way. Although the first powered flight in front of witnesses had taken place in the USA, it was not the USA that was at the forefront of technology during the pioneering days but France, followed by the UK and Germany. The USA closed the gap during the Second World War and came to dominate aircraft production, along with the Soviet Union and France, during the postwar period. Sweden is an exception. It is the only country of its relatively small size that perceives value in developing its own fighters—for export as well as its own use.

In addition to the ambitious projects of individual countries, the first European joint projects—such as the Alpha Jet and the multi-role Tornado fighter—also saw the light of day in the 1970s. There are many good reasons for these collaborative projects: they ease the burden of incredibly high development costs for the partner countries, the research requirement helps Europe retain its position among the world's technology leaders, and, last but not least, collaborative undertakings are extremely useful for promoting the concept of a united Europe.

This phenomenon has culminated in the construction of the Eurofighter, one of today's highest-performance combat aircraft, which will protect NATO's European airspace well into the 21st century.

Aircraft selection

The history of the fighter is extremely complex and includes far too many different types to be covered in a single book. The fighters presented here are to a certain extent representative of history. Some have been chosen because they represent the cutting-edge technology of their day, others because they are associated with famous figures, and others still because they have helped to decide a nation's victory or defeat.

The avionics of the McDonnell Douglas F-15 Eagle set new standards in the 1970s.

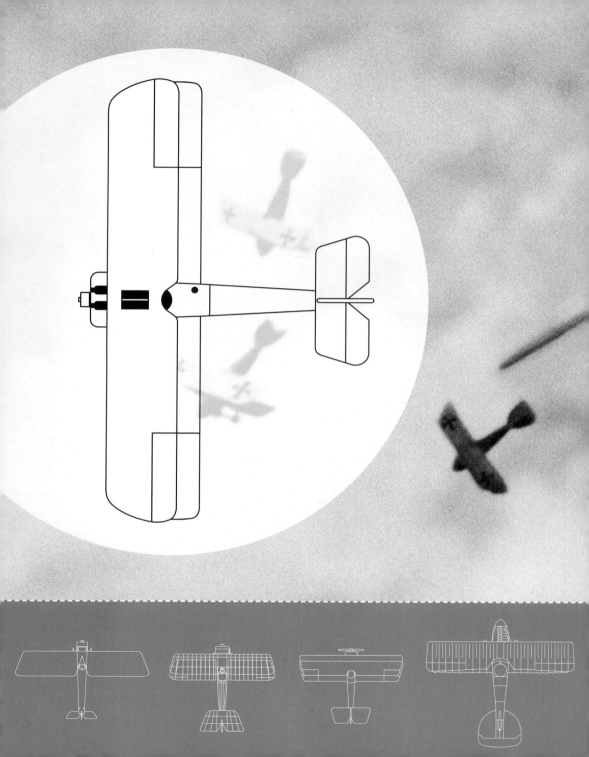

THE FIRST WORLD WAR

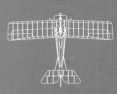

SPAD

The French SPAD S.XIII was extremely fast, powerful, and reliable. It proved outstandingly successful in combat and was built in larger numbers than any other Allied fighter of the First World War. Fighter aces from six different nations achieved their victories in this type. Although the SPAD performed most effectively in French hands—due no doubt to the specific aerial combat tactics employed—the most successful of all the SPAD aces, with 26 confirmed victories, was US ace Edward "Eddie" Rickenbacker. Over 10,000 SPADs were built in total.

SPAD S.XIII
Single-seat fighter
Wingspan: 26 ft. 6 in. (8.08 m)
Length: 20 ft. 6 in. (6.25 m)
Height: 8 ft. 6 in. (2.60 m)
Empty weight: 1,257 lb. (570 kg)
Maximum take-off weight: 1,863 lb. (845 kg)
Power plant: 1 Hispano-Suiza 8Be water-cooled inline V8, 220 hp (164 kW)
Maximum speed: 135 mph (218 km/h) at 7,218 ft. (2,200 m)
Operational ceiling: 21,818 ft. (6,650 m)
Range: 220 miles (350 km)
Armament: 2 × .303 in. (7.7 mm) Vickers machine guns

Fathers of the SPAD

The "Société pour les Appareils Deperdussin," an aircraft company founded by silk manufacturer Armand Deperdussin, went bankrupt in 1913 and was taken over the following year by renowned flying pioneer Louis Blériot. The company's former chief designer Louis Béchereau retained his position under the new ownership and remained by Blériot's side. The acronym SPAD, deriving from the company name, was kept by Blériot but now stood for "Société pour l'Aviation et ses Dérivés."

"A" Series

In 1915 the technology for shooting through the propeller was not yet fully developed. In order to be able to shoot effectively in the direction of flight without having to dispense with the tractor configuration—a front-mounted

First Lieutenant Everett Cook, Commanding Officer, US 91st Aero Squadron, standing beside his SPAD S.XIII.

propeller that "pulls" an aircraft through the air—Béchereau designed an unusual two-seater biplane fighter known as the SA.1. This so-called pulpit design accommodated the observer/gunner in a plywood gondola in front of the propeller. Five different models based on this design went into production in small numbers but SPAD soon discarded the principle. Neither the SA.1 nor its successors the SA.2-SA.5 were popular with their crews: in the event of crash-landing nose-first, the observer/gunner was certain to be killed by the engine.

SPAD stands for Société pour l'Aviation et ses Dérivés (Company for Aviation and Associated Equipment).

A replica of the two-seat SPAD biplane that went into development in 1915.

Louis Blériot

Louis Blériot was one of the pioneers of European flying. For a decade he invested all his money in aircraft development. After countless failures he finally brought his first fully developed machine, the Blériot XI monoplane, onto the market in 1909. It was in a Blériot XI—powered to a respectable 46 mph (74 km/h) by an air-cooled 25 hp engine—that he set a continuous flying record in 1909 of almost 37 minutes. This feat emboldened him to attempt the first crossing of the English Channel and attempt to win the £1,000 prize money put up by a British newspaper, the *Daily Mail*. He succeeded—to the delight of his compatriots and horror of the British, who had lost their status as inhabitants of an island fortress once and for all—on July 25, 1909, making the crossing from Calais to Dover in 37 minutes.

This pioneering exploit brought Blériot some much-needed business success. He sold around 800 of his Blériot XI aircraft, which remained in service on the Front as a scout plane until 1915.

The French elite Groupe de Combat 12 *unit gave itself the nickname "Les Cigognes" (The Storks) and adopted the elegant bird as its squadron emblem.*

Edward "Eddie" Rickenbacker—the leading US ace

Eddie Rickenbacker came to flying in a roundabout way: via motor racing. In 1917, when the USA entered the war, the successful racing driver was 27 years old and over the age limit for pilot training. He volunteered nevertheless, and in recognition of his previous occupation was posted as a driver to the staff of the commander of the US forces, General John "Black Jack" Pershing, attached initially to aviation pioneer Colonel Billy Mitchell.

Rickenbacker managed to switch to a flying role on Mitchell's personal recommendation, eventually joining the 94th Aero Squadron with its "hat in the ring" insignia.

Here he was able to put his talents as a racing driver to good use. In the few months that remained until the Armistice (November 11, 1918), he became the USA's number

one ace, achieving 26 combat victories. On September 25, 1918, Captain Rickenbacker attacked seven German aircraft—two reconnaissance planes escorted by five Fokker D VII fighters—and shot down two of them. This feat earned him the US Medal of Honor for valor although he had to wait until after Armistice to be presented with it.

SPAD S.VII

A new fighter was needed to replace the Nieuport 17, and in August 1916 combat units took delivery of their first SPAD S.VII C1s. The abbreviation C1 stood for single-seat fighter (*chasseur* in French). By this time the technical obstacles to synchronized shooting through the propeller with a fixed machine gun had been removed. Under this system of "controlled" shooting, the firing mechanism was only activated when there was no propeller blade in front of the muzzle.

Around 5,500 S.VIIs were built in France alone—not including licensed production elsewhere. The new Hispano-Suiza 8Ab V8 inline engine introduced in spring 1917 delivered 180 hp, in other words 30 hp more than the previously used Hispano-Suiza 8Aa power plant. The 8Ab enabled the S.VII to achieve a maximum speed of 118 mph (190 km/h) at an altitude of 6,562 ft. (2,000 m). The S.VII was flown by nearly all of France's allies and it is on this model that the fame of the SPAD fighter rests.

SPAD S.XII/XIII

Only a few units were built of the S.XII, a development of the "VII." It was armed with a Hotchkiss 1.5 in. (37 mm) single-shot cannon. Mounted in the V-shaped cylinder block of the new Hispano-Suiza 8C engine—equipped with reduction gear—this gun fired through the hollow propeller hub. Its breechblock projected deep into the cockpit between the knees of the pilot. Aiming was difficult and reloading almost impossible. Furthermore, powder gas filled the cockpit whenever the gun was fired.

The first S.XIII, a wooden-framed, wire-braced, fabric-covered biplane, was delivered to the Front in 1917. Very similar in construction to the SPAD S.VII, its wing assembly was also braced by a single set of struts supplemented, in line with common practice, by auxiliary struts to anchor the bracing wires. Another feature to be retained was that only the upper wings had ailerons. When the aircraft went into series production, the rounded wingtips were changed to a straighter profile that significantly improved the plane's handling.

Instead of a cannon, the SPAD S.XIII was armed with two synchronized Vickers .303 in. (7.7 mm) machine guns. It was powered by various models of the 220 hp Hispano-Suiza V8 engine and benefited from aerodynamic improvements. Fighter aces such as American Eddie Rickenbacker, Irishman William Cochran-Patrick, and Frenchmen Guynemer and Fonck scored numerous combat victories in the S.XIII,

making it famous throughout the world. Over 8,400 of the S.XIII were ordered, although by the time production ended in 1919 only 7,300 or so had actually been delivered.

Immediately after the First World War, a number of SPAD S.XIIIs were exported to countries including Czechoslovakia, Poland, Greece, Spain, Turkey, Brazil, Argentina, and Siam, and a repeat order was supplied to Belgium. A few isolated examples remained in active service until 1935.

The SPAD S.XIII, which had a flying time of two hours, was one of the most-produced aircraft of its day with over 7,000 built.

An A.2, one of SPAD's "pulpit" models, of the Imperial Russian Air Force.

MORANE-SAULNIER

Had it not been for the Morane... Although originally designed for civilian rather than military use, the Morane was brought into service as a scout plane and later armed. It is thought to have been the immediate stimulus for Germany's development of synchronized shooting through the propeller. Its appearance at the Front marked the birth of a new weapon, the fighter plane, and thus the beginning of combat between armed aircraft.

MORANE-SAULNIER TYPE N
Single-seat fighter
Wingspan: 27 ft. 3 in. (8.30 m)
Length: 22 ft. (6.70 m)
Height: 8 ft. 2 in. (2.5 m)
Empty weight: 816 lb. (370 kg)
Maximum take-off weight: 1,124 lb. (510 kg)
Power plant: 1 × Le Rhône 9J 9-cylinder air-cooled rotary, 110 hp (82 kW)
Maximum speed: 90 mph (145 km/h)
Operational ceiling: 13,123 ft. (4,000 m)
Range: 140 miles (225 km)
Armament: 1 × .303 in. (7.7 mm) Vickers or Hotchkiss .311 in. (7.9 mm) machine gun

Morane-Saulnier Type L

The Morane L was the first aircraft to be fitted with a fixed machine gun and thus the first fighter in history.

The Morane-Saulnier Type L played a decisive role in the history of aerial warfare. It is regarded as the first military plane in the world and thus the forefather of all fighters.

Its history with the French Air Service exemplifies the way the role of aircraft developed during the First World War. Its deployment as a fighter was accidental rather than deliberate. It was initially flown as an unarmed scout or reconnaissance

The system of struts holding its wing in place mark the Morane L out as a "parasol wing" design.

plane and only later equipped with a machine gun. This weapon, fixed in a forward-facing position, fired .315 in.-caliber (8 mm) solid copper projectiles through an obstacle that stood in its direct line of fire—its own propeller arc! To avoid damaging the propeller blades during firing, Raymond Saulnier and Roland Garros developed a synchronizer. As this was unreliable, and optimum synchronization of propeller position and machine-gun fire was difficult to achieve, Garros turned to a more straightforward solution. Being a brave sort, he simply covered the slender propeller blades with steel deflectors, causing any bullets that did not pass between the blades to ricochet away. Using this primitive—and for him personally highly dangerous—weapon system, Garros scored three aerial victories in quick succession before being forced to make an emergency landing behind German lines on April 19, 1915. Having tried unsuccessfully to destroy his aircraft by setting fire to it as per orders, he was taken prisoner and the remains of his plane were commandeered by the enemy. The secret of his combat success was now out and the German Air Service commissioned Anthony Fokker to develop an improved system of synchronized shooting through the propeller arc.

The Type N was nicknamed the "Bullet" by the Royal Flying Corps because of its conical propeller spinner.

Roland Garros—the first fighter ace

Conquering the skies was the biggest adventure of the early 20th century. In France, flying attracted abundant enthusiasts from early on. By 1910 there were already 30 registered aircraft and 52 military pilots licensed by the Aero Club. The entire European aircraft industry was decisively influenced by developments in France, and many manufacturers began life building French-designed flying machines—as they were still then called—under license.

Roland Garros, a music student from a comfortable background, was one of those who succumbed to the flying bug. He abandoned his studies and taught himself how to fly using a flimsy bamboo craft called the "Demoiselle." After acquiring his flying license in 1910, he entered a number of races and competitions, initially earning himself the nickname "Eternally Second." The turning point came with his victory in the *Grand Circuit d'Anjou*, after which he launched himself on an all-out quest to break records. In 1913 he crossed the Mediterranean from France to North Africa in just under eight hours.

It was in the French Air Service that Garros finally became a national hero. The first true fighter pilot, he also became the first ace in history with three confirmed victories.

On April 19, 1915, he was hit by defensive fire while bombing a railway station and forced to make an emergency landing behind German lines. He spent three years as a prisoner of war until he succeeded in escaping to Belgium, from where he made it back to France, at the beginning of 1918. After a few hours' flying practice he returned to the Front and continued to serve as a fighter pilot.

Roland Garros was killed in October 1918 during an air battle near Vouziers in the Ardennes. His native country paid due tribute to this great aviation pioneer and fighter pilot and later named a tennis tournament—also known as the French Open—after him. The island of Réunion immortalized him in the name of its airport.

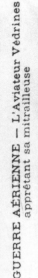

A French pilot loads a rigid ammunition clip into his Morane's Maxim gun.

Morane-Saulnier Type N

Another aircraft built by the Morane-Saulnier company, the Type N, is regarded as the first "real" fighter developed specifically for the role. This model was also flown by Russian and British pilots. It was nicknamed the "Bullet" by the Royal Flying Corps because of the shape of its propeller spinner.

The Type N was not especially popular and was unsuitable for beginners. Designed for speed, it also had a high landing velocity, which demanded a considerable level of skill from the pilot. It is known from contemporary sources that after dangerous aerial combat, the tricky landing represented an enormous psychological burden for pilots.

Wing warping

It is important to remember that the first, tentative attempts to fly had been made only a few years before the beginning of the First World War and that the pioneering days were by no means over. Controlling a plane using adjustable flaps known as ailerons and elevators was far from universal. In a number of early aircraft, changes of direction were effected by means of "wing warping."

Moving the joystick to the left, for example, would warp the port wing negatively and the starboard wing positively—a similarity with bird flight was still clearly recognizable. One arrangement that did become firmly established in the early days, however, and is still in place today, was the principle of controlling the ailerons and elevator with the joystick and the rudder with foot pedals.

Details

The Morane-Saulnier Type L "Parasol" was constructed of a wooden frame covered with canvas. It was a typical parasol-design high-wing monoplane with the wing supported above the fuselage on struts.

One technical peculiarity was its "wing warping" system of roll control using bracing cables and pulleys.

The Morane-Saulnier Type N, designated the MS.5C.1 by the French flying corps, was also built of wood but was a mid-wing design. The circular cross-section of its fuselage combined with its "casercle" propeller hub gave the aircraft its characteristic streamlined appearance. The plane's fuselage and wings were fabric-covered and the tail assembly was of cantilever design with a split rudder.

April 19, 1915—an emergency landing with serious consequences

Raymond Saulnier applied for a patent for his synchronization gear early in 1914. It was actually a well-conceived design—the weak link in the chain was the Hotchkiss machine gun, which had a tendency to fire unevenly and was generally rather unreliable. Together with Roland Garros, Saulnier tried a new arrangement incorporating triangular steel bullet deflectors. After a few teething troubles, Roland Garros took off for his first combat miss on in his Morane-Saulnier fitted with the new weapon system on April 1, 1915. He spotted a German observation plane, attacked without a moment's hesitation, and shot the enemy plane down in flames. This was the first air combat victory in military history achieved with a machine gun shooting through the propeller arc. Two weeks later he scored a second victory, and on April 18 a third. The following day, while descending from 6,500 ft. (2,000 m) to 2,300 ft. (700 m) in order to drop bombs on a railway station, he flew into German defensive fire, took a hit to the engine, and was captured after making an emergency landing.

The Morane-Saulnier Type P—a larger and more powerful successor to the Type L.

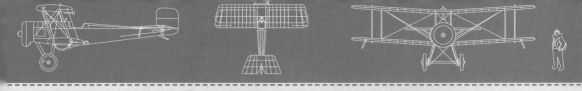

BRISTOL SCOUT

The Bristol and Colonial Aeroplane Company, which became known simply as Bristol, had started building aircraft in 1910. One of its first models was the Boxkite, a further development of the French Farman biplane.

A Bristol Scout with British Home Defence. Over 5,000 Scouts were built, including 1,600 of the F.2B alone.

BRISTOL SCOUT D
Single-seat scout
Wingspan: 24 ft. 7 in. (7.49 m)
Length: 20 ft. 8 in. (6.30 m)
Height: 8 ft. 6 in. (2.59 m)
Empty weight: 761 lb. (345 kg)
Maximum take-off weight: 1,199 lb. (544 kg)
Power plant: 1 × Le Rhône 9C rotary, 80 hp (59 kW)
Maximum speed: 100 mph (161 km/h)
Operational ceiling: 13,999 ft. (4,267 m)
Range: 199 miles (320 km)
Armament: 1 × Lewis or Vickers machine gun

Bristol Scout

The Scout made a name for itself in 1914, four years after the development of the Boxkite. This single-seat biplane was small—so small in fact that it also became known as the Bristol "Baby"—but maneuverable. It had a good rate of climb—10,000 ft. (3,050 m) in 18 minutes

One of the weapon options, the machine gun, was fixed in place on the fuselage in front of the cockpit.

30 seconds—and was the equal of any German plane of the day. Initially unarmed, the Scout was equipped at airfields near the Front with every weapon going, including revolvers, rifle grenades, and a Lee-Enfield rifle with its stock sawn off which was fixed to the fuselage and fired past the propeller at a 45-degree angle. Captain Lanoe Hawker of No. 6 Squadron, Royal Flying Corps, achieved seven confirmed victories with these relatively modest weapons during the summer of 1915 and was awarded the Victoria Cross, the highest British decoration for valor.

The first model to be fitted with weapons in the factory was the Scout D. Equipped with a fixed Lewis or Vickers machine gun that fired through the propeller arc, the Scout D was delivered to the Front from the beginning of 1916.

The Bristol F.2A Fighter, nicknamed the "Brisfit"

The maiden flight of the F.2A Fighter, designed by Captain Frank Barnwell, took place on September 9, 1916. The technical progress made in the intervening period is evident from the figures: its Rolls-Royce V12 Falcon engine powered the two-seater—which was almost three times as heavy as the Scout—to a maximum speed of nearly 125 mph (200 km/h).

An unarmed Bristol Scout in its original role as a reconnaissance plane.

The biplane—why build planes with two wings?

Construction
In order to restrict weight to a minimum, the lightest available materials were used, but combining lightness and strength is no easy matter. The bracing against each other of two wing surfaces that would not be able to support the aircraft's weight singly substantially increases strength and rigidity. The wires absorb the tractive and the struts the compressive forces.

Handling
The wing loading—the ratio of wing surface area to weight—is the same for monoplanes, biplanes, and triplanes. What changes is wingspan. For the same surface area, the wingspan of a biplane is substantially less than that of a monoplane. The shorter wings facilitate tighter banking and thus good maneuverability. During the transitional phase from biplane to monoplane, many pilots favored the biplane for this reason.

The big disadvantage
The bracing wires, spars, and struts between the wings increased the resistance of the biplane to such an extent that it was said—correctly—that this design of airplane came with its own in-built headwind. It may be hard to imagine but a wire with a round cross-section generates so much turbulence and thus air resistance on its lee side that its braking effect is several times that of a streamlined airfoil of the same thickness.

Regardless of how powerful an engine was fitted, this restricted the extent to which performance could be improved and by the end of the 1930s the days of the biplane were all but over.

Pitch-roll-yaw

Three main perpendicular axes meet at the gravitational center of an aircraft. With relation to the aircraft in a level or horizontal position, these are the longitudinal axis, the lateral axis, and the vertical axis.

Rotation around the lateral axis is called "pitch." Pitch is controlled using the elevators located on the trailing edges of the tailplane. Adjusting the elevators changes the angle of attack of the aircraft's wings. Rotation around the longitudinal axis is called "roll." Roll is controlled by adjusting the ailerons—in contrary directions—which will cause the aircraft to bank or straighten out again.

Rotation around the vertical axis is called "yaw" and is controlled by adjusting the rudder or ailerons. This affects the direction of flight.

More important than its actual performance, however, was the tactical knowledge gained from this machine. The plane's maiden combat flight in early April 1917 ended in disaster. Of the six Bristols that took off, only two made it back from an encounter over Douai with a flight of Albatros D IIIs from Manfred von Richthofen's fighter squadron. One reason for their failure was that they were flying in strict formation at the same height. Protection was provided by the observer, armed with a swiveling machine gun, in the rear cockpit. This strict battle formation made it very easy for the maneuverable German fighters to take aim and hit the British aircraft. The Royal Flying Corps learned its lesson and changed tactics, deploying the Bristol in the same manner as single-seat fighters with a forward-facing machine gun as the main weapon and the observer as additional insurance.

The "Brisfit" in the Royal Flying Corps

The improved F.2A had its maiden flight in September 1916. Just a few months later, in mid-April 1917, deliveries began of the F.2B. In February, No. 48 Squadron Royal Flying Corps had become the first flying unit to be equipped

Hucks Starter

Ground crews equipped with a Hucks Starter vehicle were lucky, as this made the task of starting aircraft engines significantly easier. The Hucks Starter consisted of a linkage and crankshaft mounted, as a rule, on a Model T Ford. The starter vehicle would be driven up to the nose of the airplane and the shaft connected to the propeller hub with a claw coupling. When the engine fired, the coupling would be disengaged and the next aircraft started—no muscle power required!

A Bristol Scout after a difficult landing. Take-off and landing have always been the most dangerous phases of a flight.

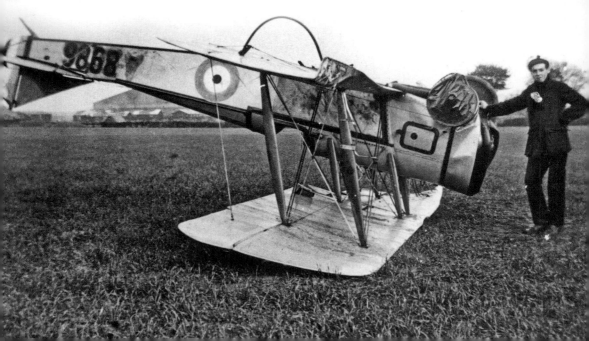

Because it was so small, the Bristol Scout was also known as the "Baby."

with the Bristol F.2 and the aircraft saw its first—disastrous—action (described above) a month later during the Battle of Arras. After the initial difficulties, the aircraft developed into an effective weapon. It was eventually flown by fourteen Royal Flying Corps squadrons and after the war remained in service with the Royal Air Force—in which it found a role at the end of its life as a liaison aircraft—until 1932 and with the Royal New Zealand Air Force (RNZAF) until 1936.

The starter motor

Starter motors were extremely rare in First World War aircraft.

Turning the propeller by hand was—and for those same models still is—the only way to start a plane's engine. The mechanic or member of the ground crew would turn the propeller a few times with the ignition switched off in order to pump a combustible fuel mixture into the cylinders. The ignition was then switched on and a sharp eighth turn was usually enough to start the engine.

As engine performance improved—and with it compression and mass—hand starting became increasingly laborious. A technique known as the rope and glove method was developed to make the task easier. A sheath of firm canvas (the glove) with a rope attached would be slipped over a propeller blade and the rope pulled by the starting team, drawing the propeller through a near-180-degree turn and firing the engine.

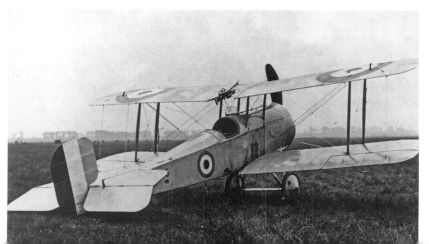

The most inconvenient of all weapon configurations required the pilot to stand up in order to aim properly.

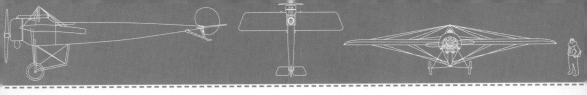

FOKKER E I

The Fokker E I occupies a unique place in history as the world's first mass-produced fighter, the weapon of famous aces such as von Richthofen, Boelcke, and Immelmann, and a milestone in aeronautical engineering. Thanks to Fokker's synchronization gear, the German Air Service achieved such comprehensive air superiority in 1916 that Entente pilots spoke of a "Fokker Scourge."

FOKKER E I
Single-seat fighter
Wingspan: 29 ft. 4 in. (8.95 m)
Length: 22 ft. 2 in. (6.75 m)
Height: 10 ft. 3 in. (3.12 m)
Empty weight: 794 lb. (360 kg)
Maximum take-off weight: 1,246 lb. (565 kg)
Power plant: 1 × Oberursel U o rotary, 80 hp (60 kW)
Maximum speed: 82 mph (132 km/h)
Operational ceiling: 10,171 ft. (3,100 m)
Range: 199 miles (320 km)
Armament: 1 × fixed .312 in. (7.92 mm) synchronized machine gun firing through the propeller arc

The first fighters

When people think of First World War fighter planes, the image that springs to many minds is that of the famous Fokker Dr I triplane with the "Red Baron" at the controls. Manfred Freiherr von Richthofen—known in Germany as "der rote Kampfflieger" (the Red Fighter Pilot)—joined battle wing Kampfgeschwader 2 in March 1916. When Oswald Boelcke formed the first fighter squadrons in August 1916, he selected von Richthofen for his own

Aircraft designer Anthony Fokker visiting the legendary Jagdstaffel 2, the fighter squadron commanded by Oswald Boelcke.

Jagdstaffel 2, which was to achieve legendary status as "Jagdstaffel Boelcke."

From a historical and technological point of view, however, an earlier model is of greater importance. Back in 1915 the Fokker E I had become the first mass-produced fighter aircraft in the world.

Its creator, Anthony Fokker, was Dutch by birth. Originally he had intended to study automotive engineering but his interest soon turned to flying. In 1912, at just 23 years of age, he founded his first aircraft factory in Johannisthal outside Berlin. The story goes that because of his age, it was common for customers to ask to see the boss, "Fokker Senior," upon meeting him for the first time.

Business was initially modest until in 1913 the German Army Administration ordered his "Spin III." When war broke out he was the man of the hour.

Two years later a French aircraft, a Morane-Saulnier, fell into the hands of German troops. The captured airplane was handed over to Fokker for evaluation and the insights he gained influenced his M5 designs. The resulting aircraft went down in history as the E I, and its successors the E II and E III guaranteed Germany's air superiority on the Western Front for nearly two years. German domination of the sky was so great that the British press

coined a new expression to describe it: the "Fokker Scourge."

Fighters

Why were fighters built? During the early days of military flying, aircraft were used predominantly for observation purposes and were known as "scouts." Their main task was to reconnoiter enemy positions and direct artillery fire. To start with, it was difficult to prevent enemy aircraft from doing this. Although airmen soon started to arm themselves with rifles or revolvers, these were mainly for self-defense in case they were shot down or had to make an emergency landing. It was almost impossible to pilot an aircraft while simultaneously firing from the cockpit with any degree of accuracy—in addition to concentration, flying in those days required considerable muscle power. As ground-based air defense systems were still completely inadequate, it was only natural that the idea of fighting aircraft with aircraft gradually developed. The most promising weapon was a forward-firing machine gun fitted to the fuselage directly in front of the pilot at eye level. To make it as easy as possible for pilots to aim their weapon, Fokker initially chose the air-cooled "Parabellum" Model 14 machine gun— and later the LMG 08/15 "Spandau"—with pistol grip, head support, and detachable stock.

The synchronization gear

With a weapons system of this type—a machine gun mounted on the front of the

The Fokker E I went down in aviation history as the first plane to be fitted with a properly synchronized machine gun that could fire through the propeller arc.

Ailerons were not in widespread use during the early days of flying and aircraft were steered by "warping" the wings using control wires.

fuselage directly in front of the pilot—there was an obvious obstacle that lay in the path of fire: not a few pilots crashed as a result of literally shooting their propeller to bits. At first, this problem was circumvented by using a pusher propeller mounted behind the pilot instead of a tractor configuration with the propeller at the front of the plane.

French aviation pioneers Roland Garros and Raymond Saulnier came up with an alternative solution: a synchronization gear that interrupted fire whenever a propeller blade was aligned with the machine gun muzzle. They also fitted steel bullet deflectors to the back of the propeller blades. This system only worked with soft French copper bullets, however. The steel-jacketed German bullets blasted straight through the deflectors and propeller. A further difficulty was that the French synchronization gear was unreliable and it was impossible to properly synchronize machine gun fire and propeller. Garros and Saulnier have nevertheless been acknowledged as the first to apply this concept in practice. For a brief period, the Morane-Saulnier was the only aircraft capable of firing in the direction of flight with a fixed machine gun and was correspondingly successful in aerial combat. This changed after Garros was forced down behind German lines on April 19, 1915, and his plane fell into German hands. The synchronization gear and machine gun were carefully evaluated at the Fokker factory and the resulting intelligence applied to the M5. In just two days, Fokker came up with what was probably the most important invention of the

First World War, a mechanical system for synchronizing propeller rotation and machine gun fire—the Fokker synchronizer. This system actually worked and provided a solution to all the problems. It also turned a fairly mediocre aircraft into a flying machine gun platform and superior fighter plane, some 50 specimens of which were delivered to the German flying corps. However, as the commanders of the German Air Service did not trust the synchronizer, Fokker was asked to test the new aircraft personally in combat. As a neutral Dutchman, he naturally refused and instead embarked on a demonstration tour with two E Is, instructing around ten pilots how to fly the new single-seat fighter and operate the fixed, forward-firing, power-driven machine gun. After completing the tour, he left an E I behind in Douai with army flying unit Fliegerabteilung 62. The first confirmed aerial combat victories with the new system were

Roland Garros tries out his synchronization gear—a world first.

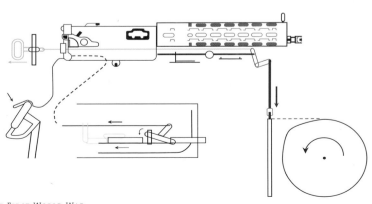

Above: a Fokker E II and crew. This model was almost identical to the E I but had a different engine. A total of 23 specimens were built.

Below: German ace Oswald Boelcke achieved numerous aerial victories in the Fokker E I. He was the commander of "Jagdstaffel 2," one of whose airmen was the "Red Baron."

AERODYNAMICS—What makes planes fly?

There are four key variables that need to be taken into account in the design and construction of "heavier-than-air" aircraft:

- Weight—aircraft plus load
- Lift—upward force capable of raising a weight into the air
- Drag—forces hindering the aircraft from achieving lift (see p.35)
- Thrust—forward driving force that has to be strong enough to cancel out the inhibiting effects of drag (see p.53).

Weight includes the empty aircraft, its load, fuel, etc. plus all crew and passengers. Lift is not quite as easy to understand because it is determined by a number of factors:

Angle of attack

If you hold your hand at an angle out of the window of a moving car, it will be forced either upwards or downwards. If the leading edge of your hand is higher than the trailing edge, the airstream will force the surface of your hand upwards and if the trailing edge is higher than the leading edge, it will be forced downwards. Acting on airfoils and control surfaces, this phenomenon is extremely important in flying. Around one-third of total lift results from this diagonal positioning, which is known as the angle of attack. If the wings are positioned at the correct angle and the aircraft is moving fast enough, the air will be deflected powerfully downwards. This produces an upward counterforce of equal strength that makes the aircraft lighter. This force alone is not enough to make the aircraft fly, however.

Bernoulli, Venturi, and their discoveries

In the 18th century, Italian physicist Giovanni Venturi and Swiss mathematician Daniel Bernoulli investigated the principles of fluid mechanics and their findings still pertain today. Bernoulli discovered the effect subsequently named after him whereby fluids and gases exert a lower pressure on their environment when in flow than when stationary. The higher the speed, the lower the pressure. This effect can be demonstrated by a simple experiment. Hold a strip of paper by one end and let the other hang down. If you now blow over the top of the strip of paper along its length from the held end, the speed of the air above will be greater than the speed of the air below, where the air is not moving. The pressure above the paper is reduced and the paper is sucked upwards.

This difference in pressure accounts for the greater part of lift. The pressure above a wing is lower than the pressure beneath it and it is the difference between the two that enables an aircraft to fly. In other words, two-thirds of total lift comes from a pressure difference that causes an aircraft to be literally sucked vertically into the air.

Wing profile

Paper airplanes prove that flight is possible even with a completely flat wing. Far more effective, however, is a wing with a domed top and a flatter or completely flat underside. This shape elongates and accelerates airflow over the top of the wing, reducing pressure above the wing even further and thus—following Bernoulli's law—generating more lift.

Lift is not the only thing an aircraft designer has to worry about, however: the overall design of an aircraft always has to be a compromise between the four main variables listed above.

Pressure differential generates lift:

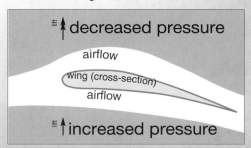

The decreased pressure above the wing generates 60 percent of lift; the increased pressure below it generates the rest

achieved in this machine by Lieutenants Immelmann and Boelcke on August 1 and 19, 1915, respectively. Ultimately, however, Fokker's synchronizer was the cause of Max Immelmann's undoing. While attacking a British flight in his E II over Sallaumines near Douai (northern France) on June 18, 1916, a burst of fire from his machine gun destroyed his propeller and the "Eagle of Lille" plunged to his death.

"Pour le Mérite"—the "Blue Max"

In 1740, King Frederick II of Prussia (Frederick the Great) transformed the royal order "Pour la Générosité" into a straightforward order of merit with which to honor military and civilian accomplishment. Not only was "Pour le Mérite" a high honor, it also conferred financial advantages. Officers awarded the medal constituted an elite order of knights and received a monthly honorarium for life. The decoration, known colloquially as the "Blue Max," was bestowed on 132 members of the German Air Service during the First World War including von Richthofen, Udet, and Immelmann.

Target acquisition for the artillery was one of the flying corps' many responsibilities during the First World War.

SOPWITH— PUP, TRIPLANE, CAMEL

The Sopwith Camel is probably the best-remembered Allied airplane of the First World War. Feared by the enemy for its excellent maneuverability, the Camel's tricky flying characteristics demanded great skill on the part of its pilots. During the war a macabre joke made the rounds of the Royal Flying Corps (RFC) to the effect that the Camel meant one of three things for its pilots: a wooden cross, the Red Cross or a Victoria Cross.

Still flying thanks to the dedication and enthusiasm of amateur pilots—a Pup today.

SOPWITH CAMEL
Single-seat fighting scout
Wingspan: 28 ft. (8.53 m)
Length: 18 ft. 9 in. (5.72 m)
Height: 9 ft. 1 in. (2.77 m)
Empty weight: 930 lb. (422 kg)
Maximum take-off weight: 1,453 lb. (659 kg)
Power plant: 1 × Clerget 9B 9-cylinder rotary (alternatively Le Rhône 9, Gnôme Monosoupape, Bentley B.R.1)
Maximum speed: 113 mph (182 km/h)
Operational ceiling: 18,996 ft. (5,790 m)
Range: 301 miles (485 km)
Armament: 2 × fixed .303 in. (7.7 mm) Vickers machine guns with 250 rounds each, four 24 lb. (11 kg) bombs under the fuselage

Sopwith Pup

Seen alongside its predecessor the 1½ Strutter, the Sopwith Scout resembled a pup with its mother giving it its nickname.

As with its predecessor, the plane's two wings were supported by one full and one half set of struts—the half struts connected the upper wing to the fuselage. Although underpowered compared to the best German fighters, this small, single-seat fighting scout made up for the modest 80 hp output of its 9-cylinder Le Rhône 9 rotary engine with superior mobility and rate of climb. The torque from its rotary engine allowed it to make two turns to the right in the time it took the Albatros to accomplish a single turn. The Pup's outstanding handling made it extremely popular with British airmen. The extreme sensitivity of its controls caused one pilot to joke that you only have to sneeze and the plane loops the loop.

In addition to the RFC, the Pup was also brought into service by the Royal Naval Air Service (RNAS). In April 1917, E.H. Dunning became the first pilot to land a Pup on cruiser HMS *Furious* after its conversion to an aircraft carrier. The cable and hook technique used today to slow down carrier aircraft while landing had not yet been invented. Officers therefore served as human arrestor hooks, literally catching the Pup by leather loops that were attached to the underside of its wings.

A typical landing accident has caused this triplane to end up in a "headstand" position.

Although built only in small numbers, the Sopwith Triplane triggered a veritable boom in three-winged aircraft.

Sopwith Triplane

In 1916 it became obvious that despite its superb flying characteristics, the Pup was no longer able to hold its own against the latest German fighters that had started being introduced to the Front. Aerial combat now required even better maneuverability and rates of climb. Experiments aimed at increasing the Pup's performance by equipping it with three slender wings were successful and the resulting triplane proved superior to German aircraft in terms of both rate of climb and maneuverability. As the RFC was in the process of re-equipping exclusively with SPADs, the entire production of Sopwith Triplanes went to the RNAS. They helped Britain survive the heavy casualties of April 1917, which became known as Bloody April. One aerial battle saw 13 Triplanes in combat with 15 German fighters. Five of the German planes were shot down for no British losses. The Canadian pilots of No. 10 Naval Squadron, the famous "Black Flight," scored a total of 87 aerial victories between May and June 1917.

Despite being manufactured in small numbers—while over 1,700 Pups were built, only 150 Triplanes ever reached the Front—the Triplane exercised an enormous influence. Even before the first wreckage of a shot-down Triplane was sent back to Germany for evaluation, Anthony Fokker had begun development of his own first triplane, the Dr I. From the beginning of 1917 onwards, nearly all German fighter manufacturers developed their own triplanes but only the Fokker Dr I entered service.

Sopwith Camel

By the end of 1916, Sopwith Aviation Co., under the direction of chief designer Herbert Smith, had developed a new, more heavily armed biplane fighter with a more powerful engine. A characteristic feature of the Sopwith F.1, as the new plane was officially known, was its humped cowling designed to deflect the eddies caused by its machine guns around the cockpit. This earned it the nickname "Camel."

The Sopwith Camel was one of the best fighters of the First World War. The example shown here is a replica.

A squadron of Triplanes at the ready. The Camel's predecessor was more maneuverable, and had a better climbing capability, than the Pup.

Thomas Sopwith—a life dedicated to flying

The story of British aviation is inextricably linked with the figure of Thomas "Tommy" Sopwith. He was born in 1888, and at the age of 22 he won a competition for the longest flight from the UK to the Continent, covering around 168 miles (270 km) in 3 hours 40 minutes. With the £4,000 prize money he leased a former ice rink in Kingston-upon-Thames, founded the Sopwith Aviation Co. and began to design aircraft with Fred Sigrist. Harry Hawker joined the company as test pilot and managing director.

Out of these small beginnings came thousands of the most important fighter aircraft of the First World War—and the famous Hawker aircraft that followed. Sopwith was one of the founders of the Hawker Siddeley Group and also retained a significant involvement with its successor British Aerospace.

In 1953 he was knighted for services to aviation in war and peace and remained true to flying for the rest of his life, continuing to work as a consultant to his by now nationalized company until the 1980s. Sir Thomas Sopwith died in 1989 at the age of 100.

Aviation pioneer and gifted designer Thomas Sopwith was knighted for his services to aviation.

This F.1 Camel was the undoing of a German Gotha in aerial combat.

The RFC took delivery of its first Camel at the end of May 1917. It is thought that at least 5,140 were eventually built. The Camel bore a strong resemblance to the Pup but mounted two synchronized machine guns rather than one.

The new biplane owed its outstanding maneuverability in part to a certain nose-heaviness resulting from the fact that the main masses—engine, pilot, fuel tank, and armament—were concentrated around its center of gravity at the front of the fuselage. The other main factor was the torque of its rotary engine. Its difficult handling characteristics demanded immense skill on the part of its pilots, however, and the accident rate was high, particularly among flying school cadets. During take-off the Camel veered to the left, requiring the pilot to counter-steer. Due to the powerful rightward torque of its rotary engine, it had a tendency to tilt forward and could quickly go into a spin. Conversely, the

A First World War air battle—a spectacular photograph whose authenticity has been questioned by modern technology.

AERODYNAMICS—drag

Drag is the third of the main variables affecting aircraft design (see pp. 29 and 53). Loosely speaking, drag is the sum of all the forces resisting the movement of an aircraft through the air in the direction of flight. These include:

Body drag

All bodies create resistance when moving through a liquid or gas. This can be experienced by holding one's arm out of the window of a moving car with the flat of the hand facing forward. This force is generally expressed as drag coefficient—designated by Cd or Cx in the English-speaking world and Cw in Germany—a term which will be familiar to many readers from vehicle specifications. In order to keep this value as low as possible, it is important to develop the most streamlined shape.

Two key examples illustrate the relative drag of different objects: at 0.08, an aircraft wing will have less than half the drag coefficient of an optimally designed car. A flat plate or panel, meanwhile, would have a Cd of around 1.2.

Frictional drag

Although air weighs very little, it nevertheless weighs something, otherwise flight would not be possible. When a solid body moves through a medium—air in this case—friction occurs at the point of contact between the two. A good example of this is the re-entry of the Space Shuttle into the Earth's atmosphere. The friction between air and the shuttle creates extreme heat. The surface of an aircraft needs to be as smooth as possible in order to reduce this friction to a minimum. Recent experiments, however, have focused on developing a rough surface akin to sharkskin, whereby friction is created not by contact between the air and the shell of the aircraft but between the air and the air surrounding the rough aircraft skin.

Induced drag

Induced drag is the term used to describe the force produced by the movement (lift) of the wing itself. One reason for induced drag is the pressure differential between the top and underside of the wing, which we have already looked at. The two pressure zones meet at the wingtip and cancel each other out, producing a vortex that the wing drags along behind it. This may sound harmless but the wake turbulence from a large aircraft is capable of tossing small planes around uncontrollably up to several minutes after its passage. This turbulence acts in the opposite direction to the direction of flight, thereby impairing performance and speed. If you have ever wondered what purpose is served by the small vertical winglets on the ends of modern commercial aircraft, the answer is that they are designed to reduce induced drag and therefore improve the plane's rate of climb, cruising speed, and handling characteristics at slow speeds.

And, finally, one last term: "glide ratio." An aircraft's glide ratio derives from the relationship between lift and drag. A theoretical unpowered aircraft with a glide ratio of 1:1 would lose a foot in altitude for every foot it moves forward (or one meter for every meter). Modern high-performance gliders can achieve glide ratios of up to 50:1, in other words they experience a reduction in altitude of one foot for every 50 feet flown (or one meter for every 50 meters).

plane tended to climb when turning to the left. Although not uncontroversial, the Camel is perhaps the most famous fighter of the First World War. In the hands of Entente pilots, the Camel destroyed more enemy aircraft—at least 1,294—than any other type. The price, though, was high: 413 airmen died in combat and 385 in accidents not involving the enemy. The most successful Camel of all was that flown by Canadian William Barker (serial number B6313), which destroyed 46 balloons and airplanes. This tally is all the more remarkable in that it was achieved within a single year in around 400 flying hours.

By mid-1918 the Camel was considered obsolete due to its relative lack of speed and modest performance at over 12,000 ft. (3,650 m). It remained in service until the signing of the Armistice, however, due to the sluggish progress being made with the development of its successor, the Sopwith Snipe. The Camel also proved its worth in a ground-attack role, and during the major German offensive of spring 1918 it inflicted heavy losses on the German troops with Hales and Cooper bombs.

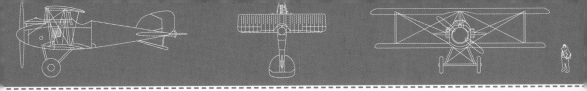

ALBATROS D I/D II

The Albatros D I single-seat fighter was almost identical to the "racing biplane" developed by Albatros for the 1913 Vienna Air Meet. Its propeller hub continued the aerodynamic lines of its beautifully rounded plywood monocoque fuselage. The slender fuselage itself tapered towards the rear in order to reduce drag and thus increase speed. Soon after the first D Is entered service in August/September 1916, German airmen were able to achieve air superiority above the battlefields of the Western Front.

ALBATROS D II
Single-seat fighter
Wingspan: 31 ft. 2 in. (9.50 m)
Length: 24 ft. 3 in. (7.4 m)
Height: 8 ft. 6 in. (2.59 m)
Empty weight: 1,411 lb. (640 kg)
Maximum take-off weight: 1,962 lb. (890 kg)
Power plant: 1 × Daimler D III inline, 160 hp (120 kW)
Maximum speed: 109 mph (175 km/h)
Operational ceiling: 18,045 ft. (5,500 m)
Range: 205 miles (330 km)
Armament: 2 × fixed .312 in. (7.92 mm) LMG 08/15 synchronized machine guns

Contemporary witnesses were thrilled by the Albatros's truly breathtaking handling as well as its engine power and firepower. But the D I was not without its faults: vision to the front and diagonally above and below was limited and in a fast dive the lower wing had a tendency to flutter and occasionally even break off. Nevertheless, the Albatros proved its worth as an extremely robust military aircraft. Its elliptical, torpedo-shaped plywood fuselage was far more capable of withstanding gunfire than the usual design of a fabric-covered wooden frame. The plane's most important innovation, however, was its twin .312 in. (7.92 mm) LMG 08/15 machine guns, fitted to the front of the fuselage in front of the pilot

The streamlined shape of the Albatros D I reveals its kinship with the racing biplane that preceded it.

Bloody April

The Albatros dominated the skies above the Western Front until well into the summer of 1917. Although no longer at the cutting edge of technology, it inflicted an exceptionally high toll on the Allies in spring 1917 thanks to the superior skill of its pilots. In March the German High Command had decided to withdraw to the section of the Hindenburg Line that extended from Arras via St. Quentin to Vailly—known in Germany as the *Siegfriedstellung*. The idea was on the one hand to gain time for the submarine war to take effect and on the other to frustrate the Allies' plans to launch an offensive along the Front between Arras and Soissons and force them to waste time taking up new positions. Thanks to German air superiority, the retreat took place undetected. But then hundreds of British aircraft attacked and as a result of the British offensive launched on April 9 at Arras, air battles of a hitherto unknown ferocity developed. The Royal Flying Corps suffered such alarming losses that this phase of the conflict went down in the history of aerial warfare as Bloody April. Jasta 11 alone, under the command of the Red Baron, Manfred von Richthofen, claimed to have shot down 89 Allied planes, and a number of British squadrons were completely annihilated. German air superiority lasted until summer 1917, when the Entente forces introduced new, higher-performance fighters that were more effective in combat. The combined elite of French and British airmen and their new machines (SPAD XIII, Bristol, Breguet, S.E.5, and Sopwith Triplane) finally succeeded in restoring at least some equilibrium in the skies.

and synchronized to shoot through the propeller arc. This system resulted in a far higher hit rate. The D I was powered by either a Benz Bz III (150 hp/110 kW) or water-cooled inline Daimler III (160 hp/120 kW).

Success at the Front was not long in coming. Oswald Boelcke, flying ace and commander of newly formed Jagdstaffel 2, achieved 11 kills in just 16 days and Manfred von Richthofen scored 48 of his 80 confirmed victories in Albatros fighters: 17 in the D II, 23 in the D III, six in the D V, and two in the D Va.

Fast on the heels of the D I came the D II. One of the changes in the new model was the lower positioning of the upper wing in order to improve upward visibility for the pilot. The

The Albatros D II, a development of the D I, had a redesigned upper wing that afforded better vision.

Albatros D IIs built under license in Austria were equipped with a more powerful Austro-Daimler engine that allowed the model to operate at higher altitudes.

Oswald Boelcke

Oswald Boelcke entered Darmstadt Flying School in 1914 at 23 years of age. After passing his pilot's exam and serving briefly with various pilot training units, he was sent to the Western Front on September 1, 1914, eventually joining Feldfliegerabteilung 62 just as Anthony Fokker was introducing his new single-seat fighter with its synchronized machine gun to the unit.

Thrilled by the new plane, Boelcke taught himself to fly it in secret and achieved his first aerial victory in it on July 6, 1915. Boelcke's most important overall contribution was to the organizational framework of the German Air Service and to the development of fighter tactics that remain relevant today. One of his lessons was that instead of seeing themselves as solitary combatants chasing individual glory, fighter pilots should focus on doing their job and contributing to the success of the team.

On January 12, 1916, Boelcke and Immelmann, having achieved eight air victories apiece, became the first airmen to win the Blue Max ("Pour le Mérite," Prussia's highest award for bravery). They were presented with their medals by Kaiser Wilhelm II in person.

On Boelcke's recommendation, the first fighter squadrons were created in August 1916. Charged with forming and commanding Jasta 2, Boelcke was able to handpick his team, and the legendary "Jagdstaffel Boelcke" became an academy for countless successful fighter pilots.

One of these was Manfred von Richthofen, then a completely unknown quantity. The extent to which the men of Jasta 2 were devoted to and respected Oswald Boelcke, a master fighter pilot and teacher but at the same time a straightforward young man who remained completely unaffected by the praise and glory he received, comes across in von Richthofen's autobiography *Der Rote Kampfflieger*. Captain Boelcke died—undefeated—on October 28, 1916, after colliding with the aircraft of his friend and comrade Erwin Böhme in battle.

The Kaiser immediately ordered that Jasta 2 be named "Jagdstaffel Boelcke" in honor of its first commander. This tradition has survived to the present day and Germany's 31st fighter-bomber squadron still bears his name.

final D-series Albatros models, the D V and D Va incorporated further—not always successful—modifications aimed at improving performance and combat effectiveness and were built in large numbers—around 1,500.

The Albatros company of Johannisthal, Berlin

Albatros Flugzeugwerke GmbH, founded in 1909 by Dr. Walter Huth and engineer Otto Wiener, is inextricably linked with the history of German aviation. Dr. Huth recognized the superiority of the French aircraft of the day and after purchasing an Antoinette monoplane and Farman biplane that same year, acquired the right to manufacture the two planes under license at his new plant.

But the company's ambitions went further than licensed production and the first aircraft of its own design was unveiled at its premises in Johannisthal-Adlershof, the birthplace of powered flight in Germany, in 1913. This was a military biplane christened the B II and was placed at the disposal of the German Air Service and its instructors. The Albatros aircraft works prospered and grew—ultimately employing

The small triangular surfaces on the elevator of the Albatros served to balance the forces acting on the control surface.

6,400 workers—and manufactured at least 20 percent of all German military aircraft during the First World War. Albatros also employed the young Ernst Heinkel—as an engineer on 200 Marks a month. Total production during the war amounted to some 67 models and over 10,000 units including one of the most feared types of the war: the D-series.

Pictured here with pilot and ground crew, the D V was one of the last variants in the D series.

Dicta Boelcke

Oswald Boelcke summarized the principles of aerial combat, which have remained relevant to the present day, as follows:

1. Secure your advantage before attacking (surprise; higher altitude; speed; numerical superiority; engage in battle above your own lines).

2. Once begun, always see an attack through (decisiveness is the crucial factor; breaking off an attack too early will bring no success).

3. Only fire from close range and only when you have your opponent firmly in your sights.

4. Keep your opponent in view at all times (never allow yourself to be taken in by ruses).

5. For all types of attack, engage your enemy from behind.

6. If your opponent attacks from above, do not try to deviate but meet him head on (the advantage in speed gained during a dive is too great for you to be able to get away).

7. Over enemy territory, never forget your line of retreat. Additional tip for squadrons: only attack in groups of four or six. When the battle disperses into one-on-one combat, never double up on an opponent.

PFALZ D III AND D XII

The fighters produced by the Eversbusch brothers' company in Speyer were overshadowed somewhat by those of Fokker and Albatros. Although forward-looking in terms of construction method and propulsion, they never achieved the performance or popularity of their competitors.

Pfalz Flugzeugwerke started life building aircraft under license and it is not difficult to see the influence of one of these aircraft in particular (the LFG "Roland") in its own designs. This was certainly true of its first model, the Pfalz D III, dating from 1916, which shared the semi-monocoque wooden fuselage design developed by LFG. This method of construction was to remain typical of both firms throughout the war.

Enemy aircraft were not always destroyed in aerial combat: the Pfalz shown here survived and was captured by the Allies.

Pfalz D III

Although this biplane was thoroughly "modern"—sporting a shorter lower wing that almost made it a sesquiplane—with its twin machine guns and inline engine, its performance in the air was on the modest side.

The D III was unique in one respect, however. In its day it was the only aircraft that could be relied upon to dive safely. In the case of all its competitors, it was luck that decided whether the wings would withstand the enormous forces generated when pulling out. Vertical attack was often the most successful method of destroying observation and barrage balloons that were protected by

Pfalz D XII

The D XII, last Pfalz to be built in significant numbers, was entered into an IdFlieg (German Air Service inspectorate) competition in May 1918. Planned as insurance and as a replacement for the Fokker D VIII, the Pfalz D XII performed well in the air and, like its predecessor, was extremely robust. It also retained the outstanding dive capability of the D III.

Although their names are lost to us, without the ground crew and mechanics there would have been no flying heroes.

Lieutenant von Alvensleben of Jagdstaffel 21 in his Pfalz D III.

heavy anti-aircraft defenses. The Pfalz was able to fire at balloons while diving from above and indeed achieved its greatest success in the role of "balloon buster."

Around 600 of this model were built. They were flown predominantly by Bavarian units. The aircraft's widespread rejection ran counter to the verdict of Allied pilots, who after evaluating a captured Pfalz D IIIa found it more maneuverable and better balanced than the Albatros D V.

Finally, it should be noted that, although the Pfalz never acquired the same aura as certain other aircraft, it nevertheless served in many squadrons alongside the Fokkers and Albatroses and had its admirers thanks to its robustness and good visibility from the cockpit. It also outlived a number of better-known aircraft on the Front, surviving in active service until August 1918.

The Pfalz on film

After the war, around 175 of the different Pfalz models were surrendered to the Allies and survived the postwar period in various museums. Two found their way into the movies.

Buck Kennel, an American who worked for US film company Paramount, came across two of these planes in 1938 and restored them. It is uncertain whether they were actually used in the film *Men with Wings* but they certainly feature in the credits. One of them is now on display at the National Air and Space Museum of the Smithsonian Institution in Washington, USA.

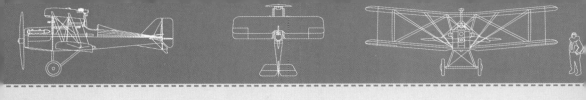

Royal Aircraft Factory S.E.5

ROYAL AIRCRAFT
FACTORY S.E.5A
Single-seat fighter
Wingspan: 26 ft. 8 in. (8.12 m)
Length: 20 ft. 11 in. (6.38 m)
Height: 9 ft. 6 in. (2.90 m)
Empty weight: 1,400 lb. (635 kg)
Maximum take-off weight: 1,955 lb. (887 kg)
Power plant: 1 × Wolseley Viper V8,
200 hp (147 kW)
Maximum speed: 138 mph (222 km/h)
Operational ceiling: 16,995 ft. (5,180 m)
Range: 300 miles (483 km)
Armament: 1 × .303 in. (7.7 mm) Vickers machine
gun, 1 × .303 in. (7.7 mm) Lewis machine gun

The S.E.5 (Scout Experimental 5) single-seat fighter was equally valued by its pilots and feared by the enemy. Along with the Sopwith Camel, it was the most successful British fighter of the First World War. The maiden flights of both planes took place within five weeks of each other and, although not as well known as its rival, the S.E.5 was far superior to the Camel in certain respects.

A difficult start

The Royal Flying Corps called for a single-seat biplane with superior weaponry and performance. One of the S.E.5's designers, Major F.W. Godden, was killed during the prototype's first flight. Structural defects were identified as the reason for the crash.

The job of testing the modified version was given to flying ace Albert Ball. Although the S.E.5 was superior in terms of performance and battle effectiveness to the Nieuport, his favorite aircraft, Ball declared himself unhappy with

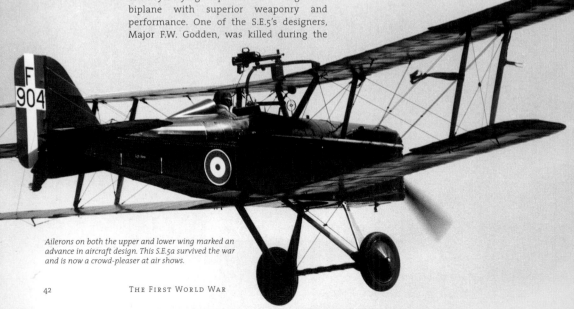

Ailerons on both the upper and lower wing marked an advance in aircraft design. This S.E.5a survived the war and is now a crowd-pleaser at air shows.

the aircraft. Despite his verdict, evidently colored by personal prejudice, the S.E.5 entered service in spring 1917.

The S.E.5 proves its worth

Pilots at the Front were thrilled by the S.E.5's outstanding performance. Delivering 150 hp (112 kW), its Hispano-Suiza 8Aa V8 inline engine was extremely powerful by contemporary standards and did not produce the dangerous gyroscopic effect of rotary engines. The S.E.5's accident statistics also speak for themselves: 207 pilots were killed in combat and "only" 70 in non-combat accidents—a significantly better ratio than that of the Camel. It was not long before Hispano-Suiza delivered a more powerful engine capable of 200 hp (147 kW), which gave rise to the S.E.5a. This power plant was not fully developed, however, and necessitated a switch to the 200 hp water-cooled Hispano-Suiza 8B V8 engine with reduction gear manufactured under license by Wolseley as the W.4a Viper V8. Thanks to its more powerful engine, the S.E.5a

Wind vanes attached to the wing struts were probably the first "instruments" from which pilots could read their direction of flight.

was more than able to make up for its reduced maneuverability. Its top speed of 138 mph (222 km/h) made it one of the leading fighters of its day. For the pilots, being able to call upon this extra power often meant the difference between life and death. If they found themselves in a tricky situation, they could always get away from the enemy with a turn of speed.

Another point in the S.E.5's favor was its endurance of 2.5 hours. As the prevailing wind on the Western Front was westerly, this gave the S.E.5 pilots more time to get back over their own lines after a patrol rather than being forced to land on the German side.

Armament

A forward-firing synchronized Vickers .303 in. (7.7 mm) machine gun was fitted to the left-hand side of the forward fuselage. To increase

The lines along the S.E.5's fuselage reveal the typical method of construction for early fighters—a wooden or metal frame covered by canvas.

The aces

Allied airmen achieved great success with the S.E.5. Edward "Mick" Mannock and Canadian William "Billy" Bishop were two of the leading aces. Another was Andrew F.W. Beauchamp-Proctor, who achieved 54 victories in this type alone. This figure includes 16 planes forced to make emergency landings and the destruction of 16 tethered balloons—the latter a British "record." Albert Ball, who had initially made disparaging remarks about the S.E.5, scored 17 of his 44 kills in one, and even by the time the Fokker VIII—probably Germany's best fighter—entered service towards the end of the war, the type was far from obsolete.

It was also a plane of this type that shot down Werner Voss, one of the First World War's most successful aces, on September 23, 1917. The German pilot had just downed his 48th opponent when he was surrounded by a flight of S.E.5s under the command of Englishman James MacCudden. Voss was eventually hit and killed after a legendary dogfight lasting more than ten minutes in which one Fokker Dr I was pitted against seven S.E.5s. Arthur Rhys Davids was credited with the victory.

The life expectancy of a fighter pilot in the First World War was incredibly short and very few returned from the Front unharmed.

Flying ace Albert Ball— loner and tinkerer

Born in Nottingham, UK, Albert Ball began his military career with the infantry (the "Sherwood Foresters"). So strong was his desire to join the flying corps that he paid for his pilot training out of his own pocket. After obtaining his flying certificate in October 1915 he immediately applied for a transfer to the Royal Flying Corps and was subsequently awarded his wings in January 1916. He was sent to the Front and, after a brief detour via an aerial reconnaissance unit, finally achieved his heart's desire on May 7, 1916, when he joined a fighter squadron—No. 56 Squadron.

Ball was a reserved and sensitive individual. He did not share the quarters of the other men but lived in a hut by himself behind his unit's end hangar. Between patrols he played the violin and spent hours tending the vegetable garden he had created. As a notorious loner, Ball set little store by formation flying and often broke away from his fellow pilots to go and hunt alone.

In combat he was relentless. His aggressiveness marked him out as one of the keenest exponents of Lanoe Hawker's philosophy of attacking every enemy aircraft he encountered. Albert Ball had a special style of attack. Whenever possible he would position himself below his opponent, pull down the breechblock of his machine gun on its Foster slide-rail and fire upwards from close proximity. While firing uninterruptedly, he would sometimes tilt his plane from side to side in order to rake the underside of the enemy aircraft with bullets. Ball was a tinkerer and had modified the controls of his plane in such a way as to enable him to fly hands-free in critical situations and operate his machine gun double-handed. He was also the first flyer to fit a rear-view mirror above his cockpit.

By the time Captain Albert Ball took off for what would be his last offensive patrol, in S.E.5 A4850, he had 44 confirmed victories under his belt and had been shot down six times. On May 7, 1917, he was part of a flight that got caught up in battle with Manfred von Richthofen's Jasta 11. He dived to the ground trailing smoke and died as a result of the injuries he sustained upon impact. His body bore no bullet wounds. It could not be established beyond doubt which German pilot had defeated him but there is a lot of evidence to suggest that it was Lothar von Richthofen, brother of the Red Baron.

the density of fire, a second machine gun, a Lewis .303 in. (7.7 mm), was located in the middle of the upper wing. This second gun was fitted to a rail known as a Foster mounting that allowed the weapon to be fired either in the direction of flight or at a vertical angle of up to nearly 90 degrees.

Another advantage of this arrangement was that to change the 97-shot ammunition drum or clear jams, the weapon could simply be pulled down to the cockpit on its rail. The system enabled a variant to be developed on the classic fighter attack—taking up a higher position and then diving towards the opponent with machine gun blazing. Now the S.E.5 could also attack from positions below the enemy. The Foster mounting proved so successful that it was retained on a number of aircraft at the end of the war.

The arrangement was not without its disadvantages, however: the Lewis gun was positioned freely in the airstream, creating significant aerodynamic drag, and was also quick to ice up. In spite of this, the S.E.5 was one of the fastest fighters of the First World War.

The weapon fixed in place in front of the windshield was supplemented by a second, movable machine gun positioned above the pilot on a Foster mounting.

FOKKER DR I

For many people, the archetypal image of the First World War fighter is a Fokker Triplane with Manfred von Richthofen at the controls. The Red Baron was responsible for increasing the fame of this aircraft beyond realistic proportions—it was in service for less than a year and total production was very small. In fact, the Dr I was almost obsolete by the time the first prototypes were delivered to von Richthofen's Jasta 11 fighter squadron at the end of August 1917 for testing under combat conditions. Production ran to 323 units and ceased in May 1918.

A supreme dogfighter

The Dr I was the only successful aircraft among eleven different Triplane models planned in response to the outstanding Sopwith Triplane.

Werner Voss was one of the first pilots to be given a Dr I for testing. The trim tabs—known as horn balances—attached to the upper wing are clearly visible here.

FOKKER DR I
Single-seat fighter
Wingspan: 23 ft. 7 in. (7.19 m) top; 20 ft. 5 in. (6.22 m) middle; 18 ft. 9 in. (5.72 m) bottom
Length: 18 ft. 11 in. (5.77 m)
Height: 9 ft. 8 in. (2.95 m)
Empty weight: 891 lb. (404 kg)
Maximum take-off weight: 1,287 lb. (584 kg)
Power plant: 1 × Oberursel UR II 9-cylinder rotary, 110 hp (82 kW)
Maximum speed: 103 mph (170 km/h) at 13,123 ft. (4,000 m)
Operational ceiling: 19,685 ft. (6,000 m)
Range: 186 miles (300 km)
Armament: 2 × fixed .312 in. (7.92 mm) LMG 08/15 machine guns with 500 rounds each

Reinhold Platz, Fokker's chief designer, had made maneuverability and rate of climb his number one priority. The maximum speed of the Dr I was unexceptional but the plane came into its own in close-proximity dogfights in which victory or defeat was decided by a plane's agility.

A rapid turn, for example, could only be executed using the control surfaces, and pilots sometimes had to set the rudder in the opposite direction in order to stop the Dr I from rolling too far and ending up on its back. There was general agreement that no other plane could match the Dr I in executing flat horizontal turns—Allied aircraft would literally fall out of the sky while performing this delicate maneuver.

A deadly weapon in the hands of experienced pilots thanks to its outstanding maneuverability and all-round visibility,

Balancing the control surface forces with control horns

In the early days of flying, the operation of an aircraft's control surfaces required considerable physical effort on the part of the pilot because the greater the control surface deflection, the greater the force with which the airstream acted on it. Control surface balancing, along with other forms of force balancing, was a simple, purely mechanical way of reducing this pressure to manageable levels. The further the control surfaces move away from the direction of the main wing, the further the balance (or "control horn") moves in the opposite direction, reducing the amount of power needed to control the aircraft. For different designs of aerodynamic balance, compare the Fokker Dr I's elevators and ailerons and the ailerons of the Pfalz D III.

The extremely short wingspan of the Fokker Dr I made it supremely agile, but inexperienced pilots found it almost impossible to control.

Von Richthofen's last flight

On April 21, 1918, Manfred Freiherr von Richthofen failed to return from a combat mission. During a battle with a British flight he was pursuing a Canadian pilot, Captain May, at superior altitude. May's flight commander, A. Roy Brown, hurried to May's assistance in his Sopwith Camel and succeeded in diving towards the Red Baron unobserved from behind. Brown later reported that he opened fire at close range. His first salvo destroyed von Richthofen's elevator and tore the rear of his plane to shreds and his second ripped the side of his fuselage away. Brown declared that von Richthofen looked around before slumping down in his cockpit. The other members of von Richthofen's flight watched in horror as his Dr I appeared to make a perfect landing behind enemy lines. It is not known for sure whether it was Brown who was responsible for downing von Richthofen or machine gun fire from an Australian pilot at a lower altitude. The wreckage of the Dr I was largely destroyed by souvenir hunters.

The British paid proper respect to the fallen enemy airman and buried him with full military honors. Royal Flying Corps headquarters sent a wreath bearing the words: "To Captain von Richthofen, a gallant and worthy enemy."

the Dr I nevertheless posed a continual threat to its own men due to its structural deficiencies. It was superior to most of its opponents in dive capability, however.

Another problem area was the approach to landing as the long slender fuselage was vulnerable to gusts of wind that would render the rudder completely ineffectual. Furthermore the middle wing interfered with the flow of air to the elevator when the latter was in landing attitude. The plane and pilot were protected from the worst consequences of this through the fitting of skids under each of the lower wing's tips.

Development

The fuselage of the Dr I consisted of a fabric-covered welded steel framework, while the wings were of fabric-covered wooden construction. The wingspan of the upper wing was considerably greater than that of the bottom wing and had conspicuous, overlapping ailerons. The strong box-frame construction of the three wings—two of which were joined to the fuselage—meant that bracing wires could be almost entirely dispensed with. In combat this meant one less point of vulnerability as the destruction of a bracing wire led almost inevitably to the loss of the plane.

Due to poor workmanship—Fokker neglected to carry out quality controls on its wing supplier—accidents were common. On October 30, 1917, Heinrich Gontermann—commander of Jasta 15 with 38 confirmed victories to his name—was demonstrating the maneuverability of the Dr I when his upper wing broke off and he was killed. After another Dr I came apart the following day, all Dr Is were grounded until their wing spars had been replaced.

P.49 above: the wreckage of von Richthofen's aircraft being evaluated by the Allies after he was shot down.

Anthony Fokker— the Flying Dutchman

Anthony Fokker was born on April 6, 1890, in Kediri, Java—then part of the Dutch East Indies—but returned to the Netherlands with his family at the age of five.

Anthony was a very mediocre schoolboy but one gift that did come to the fore in his early years was his love of technology—the attic of his childhood home was filled with a model railway he had constructed himself.

At a loss to know what career their son should pursue, his parents sent him to Germany. His original destination was a college for auto mechanics where flying lessons were also available. However, neither the only available aircraft nor the instructor appeared to be able to fly.

After the airplane was destroyed during a crash landing, Fokker continued under his own steam—financed by his father—and his first two flying machines took to the skies in 1910: an unnamed experimental plane and Spin I.

As well as an outstanding designer (see p.24), Anthony Fokker proved to be a resolute and resourceful individual with a flair for recognizing the mood of the times. After the war was over, his aircraft and production equipment were in imminent danger of being confiscated by the Allies but he managed to get his plant and planes loaded onto a train and whisked them away to safety in the Netherlands, an enterprise that is hard to imagine being possible without the complicity of the German authorities. On July 21, 1919, Anthony Fokker

founded a new aircraft company, Nederlandse Vliegtuigenfabriek Fokker, and resumed his career as a famous aircraft manufacturer.

Anthony Fokker (middle), Bruno Loerzer, and Hermann Goering.

Airco D.H.2

The unusual design of this single-seat biplane, with its lattice tail and pusher propeller, is immediately striking. As the British and French launched their major push on the Somme on June 24, 1916, the D.H.2 proved a match for the German fighters and achieved considerable success against the "Fokker Scourge."

The Airco D.H.2 was also flown under difficult conditions in the Middle East.

Geoffrey de Havilland

Geoffrey de Havilland created a number of pioneering aircraft for the Aircraft Manufacturing Company (Airco), which he joined in 1914.

The D.H.2, a development of the D.H.1, was the second design for which he was personally responsible. "D.H.," as he was almost universally known, belonged to that early band of pioneers who as well as designing both engines and aircraft, also learned to fly the machines they created. Geoffrey de Havilland used his initials to denote both the model and his intellectual ownership of these types. One fortunate consequence of this was to distinguish him from the mass of designers whose names are only known in specialist circles.

In 1920 he took Airco over and founded a new firm of his own, the De Havilland Aircraft Company. His endeavors produced an exceptional family of aircraft extending all the way to the Comet jet airliner.

Pusher propeller

The D.H.2 prototype first flew in 1915 before the invention of a workable machine gun synchronizer gear. As machine gun fire could not yet be reliably synchronized with a revolving propeller, it was decided to literally

AIRCO D.H.2
Single-seat fighter
Wingspan: 28 ft. 3 in. (8.61 m)
Length: 25 ft. 2 in. (7.68 m)
Height: 9 ft. 7 in. (2.91 m)
Empty weight: 944 lb. (428 kg)
Maximum take-off weight: 1,442 lb. (654 kg)
Power plant: 1 × Gnôme Monosoupape rotary, 100 hp (74 kW), or Le Rhône rotary, 110 hp (81 kW)
Maximum speed: 93 mph (150 km/h)
Operational ceiling: 13,993 ft. (4,265 m)
Range: 224 miles (360 km)
Armament: 1 × forward-firing Lewis .303 in. (7.7 mm) machine gun

Lanoe Hawker

Hawker was one of the creators of modern aerial combat tactics. He had introduced an important innovation at the outset of his career by arming his Bristol biplane with a machine gun and, true to his motto "attack everything," had achieved considerable success with it. He was rewarded with high military honors. In July 1915 he became the first airman to win the Victoria Cross after shooting down three German aircraft. He had already won the Distinguished Service Order just three months before for destroying a Zeppelin with hand grenades. Promoted to major, he was given the command of No. 24 Squadron, Royal Flying Corps (RFC), where he developed the tactic of formation flying that was to remain valid for many years to come. On November 23, 1916, Lanoe Hawker became the Red Baron's eleventh victim after one of the longest documented dogfights of the war. Von Richthofen later called him a "valiant fellow, an English Immelmann."

take the propeller out of the firing line and install it behind the cockpit as a pusher prop. This allowed the gun to be installed in the nose of the aircraft and thus to fire unimpeded in the direction of flight. Unfortunately, this meant the engine had to be positioned in the main line of fire of enemy fighters, and if the power plant were hit the plane was almost certain to crash. Furthermore, debris from a destroyed engine was also likely to damage the plane's lattice tail.

The pusher configuration, with engine and propeller mounted behind the pilot, was a way of getting around the problem of shooting through the propeller arc.

Taking aim

Although the pusher propeller did not stop pilots from shooting in the direction of flight, the idea did not occur to "D.H." to install one or more fixed machine guns in the cockpit. Instead, machine gun mounts were fitted to the right and left of the windshield so that the pilot himself could choose the most effective position from which to take aim at a given target. Not only did he have to heave the gun, which weighed around 27 lb. (12 kg), from one side to the other, he also had to shoot with one hand while controlling his plane with the

FLYING AN AIRCRAFT
Flight controls
The broomsticks to which the control wires were attached during the pioneering days of flying and the joysticks of modern aircraft are worlds apart. Nevertheless, a number of important principles have remained unchanged:

The control column operates the ailerons and elevators and thus determines roll and pitch. It makes no difference whether it is a column as such—the traditional, two-handed control element—or a modern sidestick—a small control lever that sends electronic instructions to the onboard computer.

The rudder—and thus yaw, the movement around the aircraft's vertical axis—is controlled by two foot pedals. Moving from car to plane is not without its perils, therefore—although on some planes the wheel brakes are operated by the pedals.

"Trimming" is the term used to describe the balancing of the forces and moments acting on an aircraft. In order to relieve the strain on the pilot, the holding load on the controls (column and pedals) should be zero. When using muscle power to activate the rudder, for example, trimming is effected by means of rudder trim tabs. Trim tabs can balance out nose or tail heaviness and neutralize the effects of engine failure in the case of multi-engined aircraft.

other. Complaints by pilots eventually led to the machine gun being fixed in position in the middle of the nose, which meant effectively that aim was taken with the whole aircraft.

The D.H.2's armament remained a weak point throughout the aircraft's history. With only one machine gun it was no match for the more modern fighters.

Active service
In February 1916, No. 24 Squadron, the RFC's first dedicated fighter squadron, was newly equipped with a single type of aircraft, the Airco D.H.2.

Once a number of teething problems had been remedied, pilots came to value the plane's all-round visibility and outstanding flying characteristics. In terms of the most important aspects of performance—rate of climb, maneuverability and top speed—the D.H.2 proved itself vastly superior to the Fokker monoplanes.

The Airco D.H.2 highlights the flimsy construction of the early fighters perhaps better than any other aircraft of its day.

During the five-month Battle of the Somme, the D.H.2 managed to win back air superiority and was only outclassed when Germany's new Albatros and Halberstadt fighters appeared at the end of 1916.

Preparing for take-off! A member of the ground crew awaits orders to swing the propeller of an Airco D.H.5.

AERODYNAMICS
Thrust of the propeller

The fourth key aviation variable (see pp.29 and 35) is thrust. Movement, or speed, is necessary for flight because lift is only generated when there is a sufficiently fast flow of air over the wings. In the case of gliders, speed is provided by the aircraft's descent. Even in an upcurrent, the glider is descending relative to the current—despite gaining in height above the ground.

For powered flight, an additional driving force is required and in many cases this is provided by the propeller. The principle at work here is fundamentally the same as that of the wing. In the case of a front-mounted propeller, forward thrust is provided by the movement of the airscrew. The pressure in front of the blade is lower than that behind it and the aircraft is therefore pulled forward.

A pusher propeller is mounted behind the cockpit and, as its name suggests, pushes rather than pulls the aircraft through the air. The blades of a propeller are not flat but twisted—the term used to describe this angling of a propeller blade is pitch. Pitch corresponds to the angle of attack of a wing—greater angle of attack = coarser pitch = more thrust. Variable-pitch propellers were introduced in the 1930s because a low angle of attack—fine pitch—is ideal for take-off and climbing as it allows the engine to turn at a higher speed whereas a coarser pitch is better suited to horizontal flight at cruising speed as it delivers adequate thrust at lower engine speeds.

Another advantage of variable-pitch propellers is that they can be set to a glide position. In the event of engine failure, planes are perfectly capable of landing unpowered. In a normal setting, however, a propeller could be driven by the airstream like a wind turbine, causing further damage to the engine. A glide setting prevents this from happening by presenting the leading edge of the propeller blade to the direction of flight.

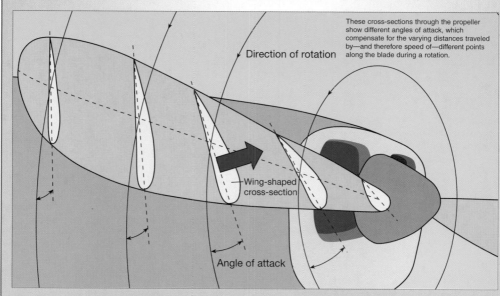

These cross-sections through the propeller show different angles of attack, which compensate for the varying distances traveled by—and therefore speed of—different points along the blade during a rotation.

Direction of rotation

Wing-shaped cross-section

Angle of attack

NIEUPORT 17

During the first two years after the development of the fighter, many different basic designs emerged, some of which even had four and five wings. A number of these designs led down technological blind alleys, while the monoplane and biplane proved their worth and survived, nevertheless providing plenty of controversy along the way. The Nieuport offered a promising alternative to one or two-winged planes. With a significantly shorter lower wing, this sesquiplane—literally one-and-a-half wings—managed to combine the virtues of both types for a time.

NIEUPORT 17
Single-seat fighter
Wingspan: 27 ft. (8.22 m)
Length: 18 ft. 10 in. (5.74 m)
Height: 7 ft. 6 in. (2.33 m)
Empty weight: 904 lb. (410 kg)
Maximum take-off weight: 1,246 lb. (565 kg)
Power plant: Le Rhône 9Ja rotary, 110 hp (80.9 kW) or Le Rhône 9Jb rotary, 120 hp (88.3 kW)
Maximum speed: 106 mph (170 km/h)
Operational ceiling: 17,388 ft. (5,300 m)
Range: 186 miles (300 km)
Armament: first series mostly 1 Vickers .303 in. (7.7 mm) machine gun on the upper wing; then 1 synchronized machine gun (usually Vickers .303 in./7.7 mm) fixed to front of fuselage

Nieuport 17

The primary fighter of the Armée de l'Air until 1917, the Nieuport 17 dominated the skies above the Western Front for a considerable length of time.

Based on the Nieuport 11—nicknamed "Bébé" because of its short wingspan—the new sesquiplane entered service in March 1916. Its characteristic shortened lower wing served primarily as a support for the V-shaped wing struts and only secondarily as an airfoil. Nieuport's designers had worked hard to strengthen the lower wing relative to earlier models in order to avoid the problem of wing twisting to which Types 11 and 16 had been prone. The Nieuport 17 convinced with its maneuverability, rate of climb, and excellent top speed. It combined the advantages of the monoplane—speed—with those of the biplane—agility and strength. Better in every respect than the Fokker and Halberstadt fighters of the day, the Nieuport 17 retained its

The Lafayette Escadrille

The "Escadrille Américaine," a squadron of US volunteers attached to the French Air Service, was formed in 1916, in other words before the USA entered the war. Its members had a variety of reasons for signing up. Some were motivated by a thirst for adventure, others by their belief in the Entente cause. Following German protests against what they saw as a breach of neutrality, the unit was renamed the Lafayette Escadrille after the Marquis de Lafayette, a French general who in 1777 had joined George Washington in the American War of Independence. The squadron was equipped with Nieuports and SFADs. Its significance was less military than political as its active participation in combat a full year before the USA's entry into the war demonstrated clearly where American sympathies lay. The members of the squadron had a penchant for entertaining in style. Their British and French comrades turned up in droves to enjoy the Americans' lavish hospitality including endless boisterous poker games and fine cuisine. The squadron's mascots were a pair of lion cubs called "Whiskey" and "Soda."

Group photograph of the Lafayette Escadrille with a lion cub, one of its exotic mascots

superiority until the Albatros D III and Fokker D VII made their appearance in the skies above the Western Front. The Nieuport was the main fighter of the French until spring 1917 and is closely associated with numerous aces. It won widespread acceptance and was used by six national flying services. The Canadian Billy Bishop achieved 47 aerial victories in it while Albert Ball—44 victories—thought so highly of his Nieuport that he falsified the results of new model trials so that he wouldn't have to switch aircraft.

Société Anonyme des Établissements Nieuport

Brothers Édouard and Charles Nieuport began building aircraft in 1908. Charles played an important role in ensuring that the French military recognized the value of a flying corps at an early stage and the production figures speak for themselves: in 1910 around 1,300 planes were built in France compared to fewer than 100 in Germany and French pilots held all the major world records.

This superiority showed at the beginning of the First World War. In 1911 the Swiss designer Franz Schneider, who had worked for Nieuport between 1909 and 1911, had switched to the newly founded Luftverkehrsgesellschaft (LVG) in Berlin-Johannisthal and under pressure from the events of war developed an illegal Nieuport copy for the firm.

The Nieuports were already technologically obsolete, however, by the time this "pirate" version, a biplane, was ready.

A Nieuport replica bearing the squadron emblem of the Lafayette Escadrille. The US volunteers chose the head of a Sioux warrior as their aircraft marking.

AIRCRAFT WINGS—BASIC TERMS AND CONCEPTS

The first thing to say here is that there is no universal solution for wings any more than for any other part of the aircraft. The right compromise between the advantages and disadvantages of each individual design has to be made in order to suit the intended purpose.

Profile

The profile refers to the shape of the wing cross-section and plays an important part in determining the wing's aerodynamic properties. A thick wing will generate plenty of lift but will also be correspondingly slower. A slender wing will allow greater speed but generate less lift. There are two main types of wing profile. In the case of a laminar profile, the top and bottom surfaces of the wing have an almost equal camber. At the thickest part of the wing, the camber will be the equivalent of around 50–60 percent of the profile depth. The advantage of this design is that the air flows over the wing with little turbulence, following the outline of the airfoil—laminar flow. Due to the relatively small difference in pressure between the top and bottom surfaces of the wing, the lift generated by such a design is lower. Typical of the aircraft of the First World War, on the other hand, was an asymmetrical design with a convex upper surface and a concave or almost flat lower surface.

Chord

Chord refers to the—mean—distance between the leading and trailing edges of the wing. The ratio of profile thickness to chord says a lot about the wing's characteristics. Leaving aside the issue of wing surface area, the Phantom II has a thickness to depth ratio of around 5 percent and can attain Mach 2 with a battle load of 12 tons while the Lockheed Hercules, whose equivalent ratio is 18 percent, can carry a useful load of 45 tons but

is capable of little more than 385 mph (620 km/h).

Wing loading

Wing loading is the total weight of an aircraft divided by the surface area of its wings. As the weight of powered aircraft alters during flight, so too does the wing loading. Airplanes with a higher maximum speed have a higher wing loading. Wing loading is therefore a useful measure of the forces a design of aircraft has to be able to withstand.

Aspect ratio

The ratio of wingspan to wing depth—chord—is known as the aspect ratio. A wing with a high aspect ratio will be long and narrow like those of high-performance gliders. This design reduces leading-edge turbulence and therefore induced drag (see p. 35). But here too there is no *non plus ultra*: wings with a high aspect ratio are structurally more demanding and heavier than short, broad wings.

Sweep angle

The sweep angle is the degree to which a wing deviates from the perpendicular—with the aircraft's longitudinal axis. A strongly swept wing is ideal for high speeds but for take-off and landing—at lower speeds—a moderate sweep offers

significant advantages. This state of affairs gave rise to the modern swing-wing—variable geometry—concept whereby an aircraft's wings are only slightly swept for take-off and very heavily swept for high-speed flight.

Angle of incidence

The angle of incidence is the angle between the fuselage—longitudinal axis—and root chord of the wing. In most aircraft the leading edge of the wing is slightly higher than the trailing edge. The angle of incidence is not to be confused with the angle of attack. The latter always refers to the angle presented to the airflow and is variable whereas the angle of incidence is fixed.

The angle of incidence ensures a stable flight attitude:

1. Wings subject to equal lift

Angle of incidence/
dihedral

2.

Gust

A gust of wind destabilizes the plane.

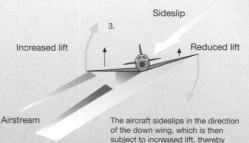

Sideslip

3.

Increased lift

Reduced lift

Airstream

The aircraft sideslips in the direction of the down wing, which is then subject to increased lift, thereby restoring the plane's stable attitude.

BETWEEN THE WARS

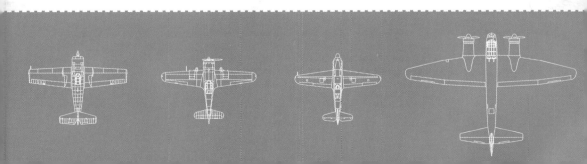

GLOSTER GLADIATOR

On the one hand, the Gladiator was one of the best biplane fighters ever built; on the other, it was an anachronism that marked the end of a 20-year era. That the Gladiator entered service at all highlights the conservative outlook of the RAF's strategists, as it was already hopelessly inferior to the modern monoplane designs by the time it was ordered in 1934.

GLOSTER GLADIATOR II
Single-seat biplane fighter
Wingspan: 32 ft. 3 in. (9.83 m)
Length: 27 ft. 5 in. (8.36 m)
Height: 10 ft. 4 in. (3.15 m)
Empty weight: 3,450 lb. (1,565 kg)
Maximum take-off weight: 4,751 lb. (2,155 kg)
Power plant: 1 × Bristol Mercury VIIIA or VIIIAS 9-cylinder radial, 840 hp (626 kW)
Maximum speed: 257 mph (414 km/h)
Operational ceiling: 33,005 ft. (10,060 m)
Range: 440 miles (708 km)
Armament: 4 × Browning .303 in. (7.7 mm) machine guns

Specification F.7/30

Royal Air Force specification F.7/30, issued in 1931, called for an all-weather fighter with a minimum top speed of 250 mph (402 km/h) and four machine guns. Another aircraft

The Gladiator's basic design—biplane with rigid landing gear—was obsolete by the time it entered service.

developed to meet this specification was the very first Spitfire prototype, which admittedly bore little resemblance to the version that eventually went into mass production.

The requirements of F.7/30 were met by a privately developed aircraft for which the designs had already been completed by the Gloster company. The first prototype of the privately financed Gladiator (factory designation SS.37) was found to be lacking somewhat in performance when it was tested in 1934. The second prototype, which was ready the following year, was therefore fitted with a more powerful Bristol Mercury IXS radial engine (830 hp/619 kW) and went into production the same year under the name Gladiator I. Initially the plane still had a laminated wooden double-bladed propeller but this was replaced in 1937 by a three-bladed metal propeller. In February 1937, No. 72 Squadron (Tangmere) became the first of a total of nine RAF squadrons to re-equip with Gladiator Is.

Variants

The Gladiator's basic design marks it out as a typical product of the early 1930s. It had strut-braced wings, a fabric-covered fuselage, and non-retractable cantilever landing gear. Concessions to modern aircraft design included an enclosed cockpit, hydraulically operated air brakes, and the doubling of the original two Vickers .303 in. (7.7 mm) machine guns to a total of four Browning machine guns of the same caliber located on either side of the fuselage and in a pod under each of the lower wings.

Three main variants were developed over time: the Gladiator I (1938), the Gladiator II, which was upengined to the Bristol VIIIA or VIIIAS radial (840 hp, 626 kW), and the Sea Gladiator for carrier-supported operations. In addition to mountings for catapult and retaining cables and arrestor hooks for deck take-off and landing, the Sea Gladiator was also equipped with marine radio and an inflatable dinghy stowed under the fuselage between the two legs of the landing gear. The Sea Gladiator entered service in 1939. Around 60 planes were specially manufactured as carrier aircraft and a further 38 were former RAF Gladiator IIs re-equipped for the Royal Navy.

Export success

Whether it was due to price or availability, the Gladiator was bought and deployed with considerable success by 16 countries. In spring 1940, a handful of Gladiators succeeded in defending Malta—a base of immense strategic importance to British positions in the Mediterranean and North Africa—against Italian bombers. The Gladiator indeed boasted outstanding handling characteristics. The word among pilots was that the biplane may have been outperformed and outgunned but it was never outmaneuvered. The Gladiator was also successful in North Africa and Greece—providing it managed to steer clear of the Messerschmitt Bf 109.

The RAF withdrew the Gladiator from combat service in 1942 but continued to use it as an all-weather reconnaissance plane and advanced trainer.

The Gladiator's machine guns, which were built into its wings, being reloaded.

The Gladiator's enclosed cockpit was one of its few concessions to modern developments in fighter design

BREWSTER F2A BUFFALO

The Brewster F2A Buffalo, designed as a carrier plane, was the US Navy's first all-metal monoplane fighter. Although technologically state-of-the-art, opinion remains divided today about the Brewster Buffalo—some people regard it as the worst fighter of the Second World War while others consider it to have been a technological leap forward.

BREWSTER F2A-2 BUFFALO
Carrier-borne single-seat fighter
Wingspan: 35 ft. (10.67 m)
Length: 26 ft. 3 in. (8.00 m)
Height: 12 ft. 2 in. (3.70 m)
Empty weight: 4,630 lb. (2,100 kg)
Maximum take-off weight: 7,165 lb. (3,250 kg)
Power plant: 1 × Wright R-1820-40 radial delivering 1,200 hp (895 kW) at take-off and 900 hp (671 kW) at 13,999 ft. (4,267 m)
Maximum speed: 323 mph (520 km/h)
Operational ceiling: 30,512 ft. (9,300 m)
Range: 950 miles (1,530 km)
Armament: 4 machine guns (2 each on fuselage and wings). Each pair .295 in. (7.5 mm), .30 in. (7.62 mm) or (usually) .50 in. (12.7 mm)

The cockpit of the Brewster Buffalo, revealing an extremely sparse instrument panel by today's standards.

XF2A—the prototype

The US Navy wanted to replace its obsolete biplanes with a new type. The contract was awarded to the Brewster Aeronautical Corporation despite the company being a newcomer among the aircraft manufacturers. The prototype, known as the XF2A, first flew in 1937 and delivered only a marginally better performance than the biplanes of the day. The designers tested the whole aircraft—many sources claim for the first time ever in the USA—in a wind tunnel. The insights gained from this and the changes subsequently made eventually gave the Buffalo a top speed of 300 mph (484 km/h) at 17,000 ft. (5,182 m). Flight tests were resumed and, although a prototype was badly damaged while landing on an aircraft carrier, the plane's flying characteristics were so promising that the government placed an initial order for 54 F2A-1s.

The Buffalo's advanced technology included hydraulically operated split flaps that allowed the plane to perform carrier landings at a minimum speed of around 66 mph (107 km/h) without stalling.

The manufacturer's production facilities were not so advanced, however. The first production Buffalo was ready in July 1938 but it took until December for a squadron's complement of planes to be completed.

USS *Saratoga*

The first 11 Buffalos to enter service were delivered to fighter squadron VF-3 on aircraft carrier USS *Saratoga* in June 1939 but the remaining aircraft under this initial order were sold to Finland. At the beginning of 1939, the US Navy had ordered 43 of the improved F2A-2 and these were commissioned in September 1940.

The Buffalo in combat

In the end, most Buffalos were based on dry land. The US Navy pilots in their Buffalos stood little chance against the overwhelming superiority of the Japanese Mitsubishi Zero and its battle-hardened pilots, and the contest between the two resulted in disaster for the Americans.

In Finland, it was quite a different story. There the Brewster achieved a victory ratio of 26:1—26 enemy aircraft destroyed for every Buffalo lost—the record for any Second World War fighter. Not bad for the "world's worst fighter"!

The Brewster's short, stubby body anticipates later US models.

Although designed for carrier-borne operations, the Buffalo flew most of its missions from dry land.

The retractable landing gear of the I-16 was a technical innovation and the plane's overall design was highly advanced.

POLIKARPOV I-16

With this stubby fighter, Nikolai Nikolaevich Polikarpov, one of the founding fathers of the Soviet aeronautical industry, wrote a very special chapter in the history of Soviet aviation. The I-16—the "I" stands for "Istrebitel," fighter—was one of the world's first cantilever monoplanes. Featuring a low-wing design, the I-16 was also the first production fighter with retractable landing gear. Despite its open cockpit and cumbersome engine cowling, the I-16 was the fastest and most maneuverable fighter in the skies in the mid-1930s and served as a model for many later combat aircraft. Virtually unstable around all three axes, the I-16 demanded extreme vigilance on the part of the pilot as it had a tendency to go nose up while banking and then stall.

POLIKARPOV I-16 TYPE 24
Single engined single seat
Wingspan: 29 ft. 2 in. (8.88 m)
Length: 20 ft. (6.10 m)
Height: 7 ft. 11 in. (2.41 m)
Empty weight: 3,285 lb. (1,490 kg)
Maximum take-off weight: 4,546 lb. (2,062 kg)
Power plant: 1 × Shvetsov M-63 9-cylinder radial, 1,100 hp (850 kW)
Maximum speed: 304 mph (489 km/h)
Operational ceiling: 29,199 ft. (8,900 m)
Range: 460 miles (740 km)
Armament: 4 × ShKAS (Shpitalny-Komaritski) machine guns with 650 rounds of ammunition each or 2 × fuselage-mounted ShKAS and 2 × ShVAK (Shpitalny-Vladimirov) .787 in. (20 mm) cannon with 180 rounds each

Prison as a design studio

It is not known for sure why Nikolai N. Polikarpov and his team had fallen out of favor. What is known, however, is that State Aircraft Works No. 39, where the prototype of the I-16 was conceived, was a penal institution.

Under Stalin's watchful eye, the design team produced a fighter that, for a number of years, placed Russia at the forefront of the world aviation industry.

I-16

Prototype TsKB-12 (Central Design Bureau, aircraft no. 12) flew for the first time in December 1933 and mass production began in 1934—a full three years before the Spitfire. It entered service one year later and was presented to the Soviet public in that year's May Day parade.

Mosca

The Polikarpov had its baptism of fire in the Spanish Civil War. The first planes were delivered to the Spanish government troops in October 1936. The Republicans christened it the "Mosca" (fly) while the Nationalists, less flatteringly, named it the "Rata" (rat). The I-16 demonstrated its combat effectiveness and superior maneuverability against the Heinkel He 51B biplane fighters that Germany had supplied to the rebels. Only with the appearance in the Spanish skies of the Messerschmitt Bf 109 did the air superiority of the "Mosca" and its successor the "Super Mosca" come to an end.

A total of 290 I-16s were supplied to Spain and a further 30 manufactured under license remained in service until the end of 1953. The Polikarpov also proved successful on the Soviet–Japanese front in 1939 until the arrival of the Nakajima Ki-27.

Even greater numbers of the I-16 were deployed in the Great Patriotic War, as the Second World War is known in Russia. At the outbreak of war in 1941, around 60 percent of Soviet pilots flew Polikarpovs! While the type had been revolutionary in the 1930s, by this time it was somewhat dated and was unable to hold its own against the faster and more heavily armed modern German fighters.

Technology

The Polikarpov I-16 was a single-seat, low-wing monoplane of composite construction. Its wooden fuselage was a semi-monocoque design clad with aluminum (nose) and plywood (tail). The framework of its partly fabric-covered metal cantilever wings consisted of two tubular

steel spars with aluminum ribs. The rudder was of fabric-covered metal construction and a rigid, non-steerable tail skid was fixed to the underside of the tail.

Landing required the relatively broad ailerons to be dropped by 15 degrees, thereby serving as landing flaps. This was a highly modern design but in other respects the I-16 was rather primitively built and equipped, possessing neither hydraulics nor electrics. A curious detail was the functioning of its landing gear. Although the undercarriage was retractable, the pilot had to perform 44 laborious revolutions of a hand crank in order to bring it in. The landing and radiator flaps were also manually adjusted.

Around 7,000 Polikarpov fighters were built plus a further 1,639 two-seater trainers.

Even in the Russian winter, not every Polikarpov had an enclosed cockpit. The landing skids, on the other hand, were indispensable.

The Polikarpov I-16 was known by many names including "Mosca" (fly) and "Rata" (rat).

MESSER-SCHMITT BF 109

The Luftwaffe's standard fighter struck fear into the heart of its opponents. Its forward-looking design and outstanding performance made it one of the best fighters of its day. The Bf 109 was of enormous tactical value and played an important part in Germany's "Blitzkrieg" victories.

> **MESSERSCHMITT BF 109 G-10**
> Single-seat fighter
> **Wingspan:** 35 ft. 6 in. (9.92 m)
> **Length:** 29 ft. 8 in. (9.04 m)
> **Height:** 8 ft. 6 in. (2.59 m)
> **Empty weight:** 6,173 lb. (2,800 kg)
> **Maximum take-off weight:** 7,496 lb. (3,400 kg)
> **Power plant:** 1 × Daimler-Benz DB 605D inverted V-12, 1,475 hp (1,085 kW); 1,800 hp (1,324 kW) for short periods with MW-50 water-methanol injection
> **Maximum speed:** 426 mph (685 km/h)
> **Operational ceiling:** 38,058 ft. (11,600 m)
> **Range:** 348 miles (560 km)
> **Armament:** 2 × MG 131 .512 in. (13 mm) machine guns mounted above the engine and 1 × MG 151/20 .787 in. (20 mm) machine gun or Rheinmetall Borsig MK 108 1.18 in. (30 mm) cannon, under-fuselage racks for a further 2 MK 108s or bombs

Development

Advanced technology and outstanding performance made the Messerschmitt Bf 109 one of the best fighters of its day.

A competition involving the direct comparison of a number of designs was held in 1935 in order to select a new primary fighter for Germany. Initially, BFW (Bayerische Flugzeugwerke) was not invited to enter due to peacetime hostility between Erhard Milch, Hermann Goering's deputy in the aviation ministry, and Willy Messerschmitt. Fortunately, Rudolf Hess—Deputy Führer and Reichsminister without portfolio—was a private customer of Messerschmitt, who was also supported by Major Wimmer, head of the technical department of the German Air Ministry, and so the company was able to participate in the end. Both Hess and Wimmer knew that Messerschmitt already had a finished design, the BFW Bf 108 four-seater tourer that could easily be converted into a fighter.

The Bf 109's Achilles' heel
The Bf 109's greatest handicap was its limited range of just 348 miles (560 km). During the Battle of Britain, pilots were often unable to provide German bombers with more than 10–20 minutes of protection before running out of fuel and having to make an emergency landing in the English Channel.

This aircraft was not revolutionary but was certainly up to date in terms of aircraft design.

After the competition, Messerschmitt and his competitor Heinkel were each awarded a contract to build ten pre-production examples and the final production contract went to BFW.

The new model was eventually unveiled at the 4th International Flying Meeting in Zurich-Dübendorf in 1937. In addition to one emergency landing—the pilot was the renowned Ernst Udet, who with 62 air victories had been the second most successful fighter ace in the First World War—the Bf 109s achieved four race victories.

On November 11 the same year, the Bf 109 V13 set a new world speed record of 380 mph (611 km/h)—albeit with a Daimler Benz DB 601 injection engine rather than the Rolls-Royce Kestrel that powered the pre-production series. Featuring a higher rotational speed, the DB 601 was capable of 1,700 hp (1,250 kW).

The Bf 109's narrow-track landing gear demanded maximum concentration from pilots when landing.

Bf 109 or Me 109?
The aircraft's correct designation has been the cause of much debate. The facts of the matter are that Willy Messerschmitt did not take over BFW until 1938, having previously been a shareholder and chief designer. The plane's original designation was therefore Bf 109, and so it remained!

AERODYNAMICS
Flaps/high-lift devices

The main purpose of flaps and slats is to improve a wing's lift performance by altering its profile. The diagrams below show cross-sections of different flap/wing systems (wing = blue, flap = black).

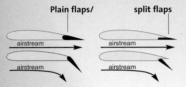

Plain flaps/   split flaps

Plain flaps and split flaps represent the simplest solution. Like ailerons, they are hinged surfaces positioned along the trailing edge of the wing but, unlike ailerons, they only swing downwards. In the case of plain flaps, the whole of the trailing edge drops while in the case of split flaps the upper edge of the wing remains immobile with just the end portion swinging down. Split flaps are rather more effective than plain flaps during landing as they do not adversely affect airflow over the upper surface of the wing. Plain flaps, on the other hand, improve take-off performance. Both systems work the same way. As has been explained elsewhere, a thick wing is better suited to generating lift and each of these flap systems gives the wing profile the effect of greater thickness when hinged down, thereby increasing lift at the expense of drag and facilitating lower landing speeds.

Fowler flaps

Fowler flaps extend backwards as well as downwards in order to give the wing the effect of greater depth in addition to greater thickness, thereby increasing the surface area for lift generation.

Slotted flaps

Slotted flaps also extend downwards and backwards. They also direct air into the airstream over the upper surface of the wing through a gap between the flap and the wing. This shifts the turbulence zone—the point at which no more lift is generated—to a position behind the wing. Stall speed is reduced, enabling the aircraft to fly and land at a slower speed.

Slats

Slats are located on the leading edge of the wing and work by guiding the airstream at the front of the wing in the right direction. With a high angle of attack, the airstream separates from the upper surface of the wing, creating turbulence and destroying lift. Remember, the fast flow of air over the top of the wing creates the low pressure that is necessary for flight. Slats allow significantly higher angles of attack because they ensure that the airflow remains adjacent to the wing. This in turn substantially improves an aircraft's climbing capacity and maneuverability. Slats have at various times been fixed into position but were later automated, deploying independently at faster speeds.

Removable fairings made it easier to maintain, rearm and repair the aircraft.

The Messerschmitt's cockpit reflects the state of technology during the period leading up to the Second World War.

Wilhelm "Willy" Messerschmitt

Willy Messerschmitt's fascination with flying dated from his youth. With the help of his mentor Friederich Harth, the director of planning of the city of Bamberg, he started building aircraft at the age of 15.

He went on to train as a designer at Munich Technical College between 1918 and 1923 and founded his first company, Messerschmitt Flugzeugbau GmbH in Bamberg shortly after qualifying.

In addition to his work as an entrepreneur and aircraft designer, he also found time to teach and was made a professor in 1937. His collaboration with Bayerische Flugzeugwerke had also been developing rapidly and by 1927 he had already sold the company the production rights to his successful passenger plane the M18. He was made Technical Director of BFW and took over the firm in 1938.

Messerschmitt continued to prosper under the Third Reich, rising to the position of *Wirtschaftsführer*—a select group of industrialists of acknowledged importance to the wartime economy—but resigned his various offices in 1942 following differences of opinion with the regime. After the war he was classified during the denazification process as a "fellow traveler." He continued to pass on his abundant knowledge through his work as a consultant and returned to aircraft manufacturing in 1955 as a partner of Messerschmitt-Bölkow-Blohm GmbH.

He died in Munich in 1978.

Active service

From spring 1937, when the Bf 109B first saw combat with the Condor Legion in the Spanish Civil War, to the end of the Second World War, countless variants of the Bf 109 were deployed on every front on which Germany was engaged. The list of pilots who flew the plane reads like a Who's Who of Germany's Second World War aces. The Bf 109 went on to become the most successful fighter of the war. Production continued until 1945 and even beyond. Including the examples manufactured under license, around 33,000 units were built.

Versions

The performance and combat effectiveness of the Bf 109 were continually upgraded in order to ensure that the plane kept pace with the new fighters being deployed by Germany's enemies. It would be impossible to describe all the different variants. By the end of the war

The canopy of the Bf 109 F-2. The solid plate visible on the right was part of the armor plating provided for the pilot's protection.

there had been eleven different models and model "G" alone had 26 sub-variants.

The plane's aerodynamics, which were extremely good to start with, were constantly being refined and its performance improved—from the prototype's 610 hp (448 kW) and top speed of somewhat over 250 mph (400 km/h) to the 1,800 hp (1,320 kW) and 450 mph (720 km/h) of model "K."

The plane's armament was also repeatedly upgraded. In model "B" the original two machine guns were supplemented by a third .312 in. (7.92 mm) MG 17 that fired through the hollow propeller shaft. Model "C" was already equipped with four machine guns, two above the engine and two in the wings, but before long large-caliber machine cannon and additional assembly sets for bombs or other under-fuselage or under-wing weapons were added to this arsenal. Bf 109 model "K," for example, had two .512 in. (13 mm) MG 131 machine guns—mounted above the engine—and a 1.18 in. (30 mm) machine cannon. This configuration gave the pilot concentrated firepower, but the fact that the weapons were grouped in a small area made aiming difficult.

What made the Bf 109 so exceptional?

Design—this cantilever monoplane with aerodynamic lines, a monocoque airframe, and retractable landing gear meant the era of the biplane had indeed come to an end.

Innovative technology—injection engines were introduced for the first time ever in some of the later models. This allowed the Bf 109 to perform maneuvers that would have caused carburetor models to stall by starving their engines of fuel.

Wings—the Bf 109's wing design is still in use today. It was based on a single spar with a torsionally rigid leading edge. Compared to other contemporary aircraft types, the Bf 109's wing loading was very high at over 41 lb/sq ft. (200 kg/sq m)—the Hawker Sea Hurricane's, for example, was just 32 lb/sq ft. (154 kg/sq m). This means the Bf 109's wing surface area was small relative to its weight. While its wings enabled the Bf 109 to achieve a high maximum speed, slow flight, including slow maneuvers and take-off and landing, was more of a problem. For this reason the designers equipped the wings with leading-edge slats and slotted flaps (see panel on p.68).

Performance—the new generation of lengthways-mounted V12 engines enabled the plane to have a narrow front and slender fuselage and thus to achieve higher speeds. Later models were further enhanced by pressurized cockpits that facilitated higher altitudes and the MW-50 (additional water-methanol injection) and GM-1 (oxygen enrichment through injection of liquefied nitrous oxide) systems that improved the plane's performance at take-off and high-altitude, respectively.

Combat effectiveness—the Bf 109 was either a match for or superior to the best Allied fighters.

G for Gustav

Model "G" was built in significant numbers. Its new DB-605A engine had a larger supercharger that necessitated a number of bulges in its cowling, earning the Bf 109 G the nickname "Bulge" (*die Beule* in German). Sub-variant G-10—nicknamed the "Super Bulge"—standardized all the different versions featuring the same equipment.

The Galland or Erla clear-view canopy that improved the visibility from the cockpit was common to all the G-10 models.

The Bf 109's armament was continually improved over the years, yet aiming would always remain difficult.

87

NAKAJIMA KI-27

Japan has often been accused in the West of plagiarism—and sometimes without good reason. The accusation does not apply to the Nakajima Ki-27. The designers of this cantilever monoplane were well ahead in the race to build the best fighter of the day. Claire Chennault, commander of the US volunteer force the "Flying Tigers," said of this type that it climbed like a rocket and was as agile as a squirrel. Its weaknesses were its modest top speed and poor armament. The Allies gave the Ki-27 the code names Abdul (China/Burma) and Nate (southwest Pacific).

NAKAJIMA KI-27B
Single-seat fighter
Wingspan: 37 ft. 1 in. (11.31 m)
Length: 24 ft. 8 in. (7.53 m)
Height: 9 ft. 2 in. (2.8 m)
Empty weight: 2,403 lb. (1,090 kg)
Maximum take-off weight: 3,946 lb. (1,790 kg)
Power plant: Nakajima Ha-1 Otsu air-cooled 9-cylinder radial, best performance at 9,514 ft. (2,900 m): 780 hp (574 kW)
Maximum speed: 286 mph (460 km/h)
Operational ceiling: 34,449 ft. (10,500 m)
Range: 388 miles (625 km)
Armament: 2 × Type 89 .303 in. (7.7 mm) machine guns, racks for 4 × 55 lb (25 kg) bombs

The otherwise excellent handling characteristics of the Nakajima Ki-27 were limited by the typically large frontal area of its radial engine.

Primary fighter of the Japanese Army Air Service 1937–1942 (Type 97)

The Ki-27 was designed for the Japanese Imperial Army fighter competition held in 1935. Its designers gave top priority to the maneuverability and climbing capability of the aircraft and consequently the smallest possible airframe was built around the Nakajima Ha-1b radial engine—which delivered 780 hp (574 kW) at 9,500 feet (2,900 m). In order to reduce weight, it was decided not only not to equip the plane with armor plating but also to dispense with tail wheel, retractable landing gear, and starter motor. The result was a small fighter of outstanding maneuverability and climb capability whose maiden flight took place on October 15, 1936. Following trials, the Ki-27a went into production in 1937 and after being equipped with a canopy, was sent straight into combat. In 1939 it was succeeded by the Ki-27b. In the southwest Pacific and Manchurian theaters the Nakajima was able to hold its own against the Russian I-15s and I-16s, but by the end of 1942 it was definitively outdated and was withdrawn from the front line.

whose mineral resources—mainly hard coal and iron ore—Japan urgently needed for its expansion plans, was created. Disputes concerning the location of the border, which was marked—or not, according to the Soviets—by the Halha (Khalkhin Gol) river, led in 1939 to five months of fighting during which the Soviet Polikarpov I-15s proved vastly inferior to the Ki-27. One of the pilots who took part in the conflict was top ace Hiromichi Shinohara, who scored 58 victories before being killed later the same year.

The fixed landing gear of the Nakajima Ki-27 may have been outdated by 1937 but it reduced the fighter's technical complexity and also its weight.

The Nakajima Ki-27 was an exceptionally agile lightweight fighter but its lack of armor plating increased the risk to its pilots.

Including licensed production, a total of 3,396 Ki-27s were built—a far greater number than any other Japanese pre-war type. It remained the standard fighter of the Japanese army air service until finally being replaced by the Ki-43 Hayabusa and others.

The Nomonhan Incident—the Battle of Khalkhin Gol

Since 1905, Manchuria had been split into Russian and Japanese spheres of influence. In 1932 the Japanese puppet state of Manchukuo,

Wing loading

Wing loading, which offers an insight into a plane's flying characteristics, is the gross weight of an aircraft divided by its wing area. In general it can be said that a low wing loading will allow good handling and maneuverability—albeit at the cost of relatively low speeds. The Nakajima Ki-27 had a wing loading of 18 lb/sq ft. (86 kg/sq m) while the American Curtiss P-40 fighter, which was

developed around the same time, had a wing loading of over 36 lb/sq ft. (180 kg/sq m). The wing loading of modern jet fighters is many times that of the First World War fighters.

The wing loading of the Fokker D VII, for example, was around 9.5 lb/sq ft. (47 kg/sq m), while that of the McDonnell Douglas F-4E Phantom II is around 112 lb/sq ft. (559 kg/sq m).

CURTISS P-40

The Curtiss P-40 was an adaptation of the P-36. Its use of an inline power plant configuration significantly reduced the engine's frontal area and thus drag too.

The P-40 was the US Army Air Corps' (USAAC's) first mass-produced fighter/fighter-bomber and was developed by designer Donovan Berlin from the tried and tested P-36 airframe. The P-40 was loved by pilots for its easy flying characteristics but hated for its inadequate maneuverability and mediocre performance. Although controversial—it was described by some as "the best second choice"—the Curtiss became the workhorse of numerous flying units, and many airmen owed their lives to its robustness.

The doctrine of "bombers before fighters"

In the mid-1930s, the USAAC High Command ranked strategic bombing above the tactical benefits of fighter interception. The role of the fighter was seen as defending the homeland rather than escorting bomber formations. Throughout the development of the P-40, therefore, great emphasis was placed on robustness, close defense, and low-altitude coastal protection. Speed and high-altitude capability were neglected and the USAAC High Command thus lumbered the P-40 with a built-in handicap that significantly reduced its effectiveness in an interceptor role.

CURTISS P-40E-1 WARHAWK
Single-seat fighter/fighter-bomber
Wingspan: 37 ft. 4 in. (11.38 m)
Length: 31 ft. 9 in. (9.68 m)
Height: 12 ft. 4 in. (3.76 m)
Empty weight: 2,880 lb. (6,349 kg)
Maximum take-off weight: 4,131 lb. (9,107 kg)
Power plant: 1 × Allison 1710-39 liquid-cooled V12, 1,150 hp (846 kW)
Maximum speed: 343 mph (552 km/h)
Operational ceiling: 28,871 ft. (8,800 m)
Range: 525 miles (845 km)
Armament: 6 × .50 in. (12.7 mm) machine guns, 3,704 lb. (1,680 kg) bomb load

Hawk—Warhawk—Kittyhawk

The P-40 is regarded as the high point of the famous Hawk series developed by Curtiss Aircraft under Chief Designer Donovan Berlin. Ordered in 1937, the prototype—designated

XP-40)—flew on October 14, 1938. The company name for this aircraft was the Hawk 81A. The first production machines (P-40) flew in April 1940. Robust with light controls—one reason for the type's good handling—the P-40 was underarmed by European standards—just two "fifties," .50 in. (12.7 mm) Colt Browning MG-2 machine guns—and offered the pilot no protective armor-plating, not even a self-sealing fuel tank. These shortcomings were remedied in the improved P-40B but added to the weight and therefore impaired performance. Nevertheless, the RAF bought 1,180 of this model including 230 that had been destined for France's Armée de l'Air but had not yet been shipped when France capitulated. In the UK the P-40 was named the Tomahawk, a

The cockpit of the Curtiss P-40. Some of the instrument labels are in French and some are in English.

A flight of "Flying Tigers." The painted shark's mouth was the emblem of the American Volunteer Group.

Glenn H. Curtiss—pioneer, entrepreneur, and world record holder

Individuals are not always accorded the place in history they deserve. Glenn H. Curtiss is a prime example.

The hundredth anniversary of the first officially witnessed powered flight was celebrated in 2003 and the names Orville and Wilbur Wright are familiar to schoolchildren everywhere. But with official recognition of their accomplishment, the Wright brothers seem to have achieved everything they set out to achieve and from that moment on they spent their energy jealously and litigiously guarding their secret. They apparently had no interest in the further development of powered flight.

Not so Glenn H. Curtiss, who, although known to specialists and enthusiasts, never achieved the fame of Orville and Wilbur Wright. This he nevertheless deserved as he can justifiably be called one of the founding

fathers of the US aviation industry. Curtiss showed an enthusiasm for technical subjects and mathematics at an early age. His contemporaries remember him as a slow thinker, however, and describe him as taking time to think problems through. Initially, Curtiss repaired and made bicycles. He then started to motorize them and, unhappy with the engines that were available at the time, began to build his own power plants. At this he was so successful that in 1903 he set a world speed record of 64 mph (103 km/h) over a mile, and four years later became the fastest man in the world with a speed of 136 mph (219 km/h). Having developed an interest in flying in 1904, Curtiss sold his motorcycle company in 1910. Although an attempt to interest the Wright brothers in Curtiss Motors failed, in 1908 he joined Dr. Alexander Graham Bell's Halifax-based Aerial Experiment Association. As an acknowledged engine expert, Curtiss was made Head of Trials for the aviation research company.

An early result of the company's activities was the famous "June Bug" built by Glenn Curtiss in 1908. Another of Curtiss's aircraft that would prove extremely popular was the Curtiss JN-4, nicknamed the "Jenny," a two-seater trainer of which over 6,000 were built.

later model, the P-40N, became known as the Kittyhawk, and just to add to the confusion, in the USA the P-40 was known from model F onwards—or E according to some sources—as the Warhawk and featured two additional .50 in.-caliber (12.7 mm) machine guns. A number of models were powered by the Rolls-Royce Merlin engine manufactured under license by Packard while the final model, the P-40N, was fitted with the Allison inline engine.

The P-40 also entered service with the air forces of Turkey, South Africa, Canada, Australia, New Zealand, and even the Soviet Union. By the time production ceased in 1944, 13,738 P-40s had been built.

Opponents

In the skies above Europe it became clear only too quickly that the P-40 was no match for the Luftwaffe fighters and it was therefore deployed in North Africa—and elsewhere—as a fighter-bomber instead. Similarly in the Pacific, the Curtiss faced the Mitsubishi A6M Rei-Sen with which it was unable to compete on equal terms.

In China, on the other hand, the P-40 came up against the Nakajima Ki-43 Hayabusa and in the hands of the—initially irregular—American Volunteer Group pilots (the "Flying Tigers") was able to assert itself successfully in that theater of war.

"B" for bomber, "F" for fighter
Military aircraft designations can be confusing—in the USA no less than anywhere else. The US forces designate aircraft according to purpose, which is why modern jet F-15 Eagle was manufactured by McDonnell Douglas but its contemporary the F-16 Fighting Falcon was manufactured by General Dynamics. Common to both—in addition to being named after birds of prey—is the letter "F," which stands for "fighter."

Here are some of the abbreviations used by the US Air Force—those used by the US Navy differed to some extent—in the period before 1960:
A—light bomber
B—medium or heavy bomber
P—fighter ("p" for pursuit).

大公今

The air inlet beneath the aircraft's nose was a characteristic feature of the Curtiss P-40.

HEINKEL HE 51

The Heinkel He 51 is of note not for its performance or innovative construction but for its historical significance. Following the long-term restrictions imposed by the Versailles Treaty, this biplane was the first fighter to be officially built in Germany since the First World War. It was based on a tried and tested design that was neither modern nor forward-looking.

HEINKEL HE 51 C
Single-engined single-seat biplane fighter
Wingspan: 36 ft. 1 in. (11.00 m) upper wing; 28 ft. 3 in. (8.60 m) lower wing
Length: 27 ft. 7 in. (8.40 m)
Height: 10ft. 6 in. (3.2 m)
Empty weight: 3,223 lb. (1,462 kg)
Maximum take-off weight: 4,189 lb. (1,900 kg)
Power plant: 1 × BMW VI 7.3Z water-cooled V12, 750 hp (552 kW)
Maximum speed: 205 mph (330 km/h)
Operational ceiling: 24,606 ft. (7,500 m)
Range: 497 miles (800 km)
Armament: 2 × synchronized MG 17 .312 in. (7.92 mm) machine guns mounted on the nose; under-wing racks for 4 × 110 lb. (50 kg) bombs

After a long gap imposed by the Versailles Treaty, publicly avowed aircraft production resumed for the first time in Germany with the Heinkel He 51.

A short career

The Spanish experience demonstrated that this biplane, which was already obsolete by the time it entered service, was fit at best to fight other biplanes. So inferior was it to its opponents in Spain—Polikarpovs I-15 and I-16—that before long the Heinkel was used only for ground-support operations or for tasks that did not involve direct combat. By 1938 it was decommissioned as a fighter and for the next five years was used for combat training. Including licensed production, 625 He 51s were built.

The round section cut out of the middle of the upper wing was designed to improve visibility above and to the front and was a typical feature of biplanes.

The Luftwaffe's first standard fighter

At the beginning of the 1930s, the aircraft designer Ernst Heinkel believed it was possible for Germany to openly violate the Versailles Treaty without any sanctions—and he was proved right. Not long before, so-called "high-speed airliners" (*Schnellverkehrsflugzeuge*) had been built in Germany that were really fighters in disguise but the He 51 was now unveiled to the public with no attempt to conceal its true nature. Designed in 1932, the first prototypes flew in May 1933 at a time when the new German Air Force was still operating in secret. Deliveries began in July 1934. By the time the creation of the Reichsluftwaffe was officially announced in March 1935, Jagdgeschwader 1 Richthofen was already equipped with He 51s and ready for action.

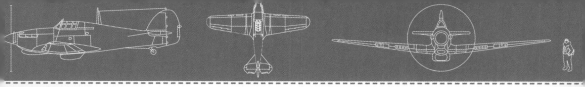

HAWKER—DEMON, FURY, HURRICANE

HAWKER FURY II
Single-seat fighter
Wingspan: 30 ft. (9.15 m)
Length: 26 ft. 3 in. (8.00 m)
Height: 9 ft. 6 in. (2.89 m)
Empty weight: 2,745 lb. (1,245 kg)
Maximum take-off weight: 3,490 lb. (1,583 kg)
Power plant: 1 x Rolls-Royce Kestrel VI inline V12, 640 hp (477 kW)
Maximum speed: 222 mph (357 km/h)
Operational ceiling: 29,528 ft. (9,000 m)
Range: 261 miles (420 km)
Armament: 2 x Vickers Mk.IV .303 in. (7.7 mm) machine guns, under-wing racks for light bombs

Hawker Aircraft Ltd. was responsible for some of the best-known fighters of all time—the Harrier developed during the postwar period, the Hurricane dating from the Second World War and before that the Fury, probably the most elegant biplane fighter of all time.

The Hawker Hurricane became one of the best fighters of the Second World War.

Demon

The Demon was an interim solution pending completion of the Fury. Deliveries of this two-seat fighter-bomber—a development of the Hart—began in March 1931.

Around 200 Demons were built with a range of engines. The Demon was armed with a Lewis .303 in. (7.7 mm) machine gun for the observer as well as two forward-firing Vickers .303 in. (7.7 mm) machine guns. After 1936, all new

HAWKER HURRICANE MK.IIC
Single-seat fighter,
ground-support aircraft and fighter-bomber
Wingspan: 40 ft. (12.19 m)
Length: 32 ft. (9.75 m)
Height: 13 ft. 1 in. (3.99 m)
Empty weight: 5,650 lb. (2,563 kg)
Maximum take-off weight: 8,183 lb. (3,712 kg)
Power plant: 1 × Rolls-Royce Merlin XX
supercharged and liquid cooled piston V12,
1,280 hp (955 kW)
Maximum speed: 334 mph (537 km/h)
Operational ceiling: 35,630 ft. (10,860 m)
Range: 1,079 miles (1,737 km)
Armament: 4 × Hispano-Suiza .787 in. (20 mm)
cannon, under-wing racks for 2 × 500 lb.
(227 kg) bombs or 8 × 60 lb. (27.2 kg) rockets

break through the magic 200 mph (322 km/h) barrier—and with hitherto unknown handling characteristics at that. Although designed as a fighter with good climb and capable of high speeds, the Fury was so stable that it could be flown hands-free and could be recovered from a stall or pull out of a spin with ease. The Fury's rate of climb from ground level was 41 ft. (12.5 m) per second.

The prototype, named the Hornet, was funded by the company and flew for the first time in March 1929. After being purchased by the Air Ministry and entering service with the RAF in 1931, the production model was christened the "Fury."

Many Hawker Hurricanes were built in so-called "shadow factories" disguised as country houses or other civilian buildings.

Neville Duke (left), fighter ace and Hawker Aircraft test pilot, in conversation with Sidney Camm, the Hurricane's designer.

Demons were equipped with a hydraulically operated turret to the rear and many existing examples were fitted with it too. In all, 239 Demons were built.

Fury—the biplane par excellence

The Fury is widely regarded as the most attractive biplane of all time, combining an outstanding, streamlined design with superior technology. It was the RAF's first fighter to

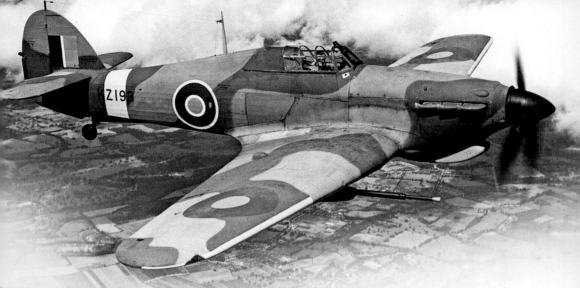

The Hurricane's armament was later increased to as many as twelve wing-mounted machine guns.

Harry Hawker

Harry Hawker was an Australian who was lured to England by his enthusiasm for the adventure of powered flight. Before becoming a mechanic—later Chief Designer—and test pilot with Sopwith Aviation, he made ends meet as a flight instructor. His readiness to take risks is demonstrated by the following anecdote: on April 10, 1919, Harry Hawker and his navigator Mackenzie Grieve took off for the first transatlantic flight in a Sopwith appropriately named the "Atlantic." Having taken off from the same place as the later successful Alcock and Brown (St. John's, Newfoundland), they experienced technical problems off the Norwegian coast, almost within reach of their destination, and had to make a water landing. They were rescued by a Danish freighter without radio, and their obituaries had already been written by the time they arrived back in England a week later. The £10,000 prize money—put up by the *Daily Mail*—had eluded them but the British king rewarded their bravery with a consolation prize of £5,000.

When insolvency loomed for the Sopwith company as the result of a large postwar tax demand, the firm was liquidated and in 1920 Harry Hawker and Thomas Sopwith founded H.G. Hawker Engineering Co. Ltd. with two other partners.

Harry Hawker was not personally involved in the development of the Fury or Hurricane as he had been killed in a flying accident in 1921. Thomas Sopwith perpetuated his memory in the name of the successor company, Hawker Aircraft Limited, securing the pioneer's place in the aviation hall of fame.

In 1936 and 1937 the RAF took delivery of the improved Fury II, whose Rolls-Royce Kestrel VI engine (640 hp/477 kW) delivered 20 percent more power than the previous model, raising the aircraft's top speed to 222 mph (357 km/h). Some of the 262 specimens built were sold to Yugoslavia, while others served in Persia, Portugal, Spain, and South Africa.

By the beginning of the Second World War, the RAF had already decommissioned its Fury fighters and replaced them with Hurricanes and Gloster Gladiators.

Hurricane

The Hurricane was one of the two best British fighters of the Second World War. It was the first to break the 300 mph (483 km/h) barrier and proved to be one of the most versatile and adaptable of all types. Conceived as an interceptor, the Hurricane also served as a ground-support aircraft, carrier-borne Navy fighter, light bomber, and anti-tank aircraft. During the Battle of Britain between July and October 1940, it proved an even better gun platform than the Spitfire and more effective against German bombers.

The design

Chief Designer Sidney Camm had recognized the biplane's limits at an early stage and in 1933 began work on a new design referred to internally as the "interceptor monoplane." The result was a synthesis between experience and innovation: a tried and tested fabric-covered tubular steel fuselage, modern retractable landing gear, and an enclosed cockpit. Prototype K5083 took off for its maiden flight on November 6, 1935, powered by a Rolls-Royce PV-12 engine. The first production Hurricane Mk.I, equipped with a wooden two-blade propeller and the new Merlin II engine, flew for the first time in October 1937.

Production begins

The enormous order for 600 aircraft—originally 1,000 had been envisaged—would have caused other manufacturers problems, but not Hawker Aircraft. Preparations for mass production had been begun months before receipt of the order, thus allowing the largest-ever single peacetime aircraft order to be handled smoothly. Within the first three months, 40 aircraft had been produced. This was largely due to the particular construction method involved. Many of the individual parts could be manufactured by small or medium-sized workshops and were simply assembled at the Hawker works. When the German bombing attacks began, this decentralized production offered the additional benefit that there were no obvious large-scale production facilities to aim for. During the war, individual elements of production were farmed out to so-called "shadow factories" that could not be identified as armaments factories. This system of

Two British squadrons trained the Soviet pilots before the aircraft were handed over.

disguised factories allowed goods essential to the war effort to be produced in secret. The shadow factories included castles and country houses.

The Hurricane's modular construction method also meant that individual structural components could simply be substituted for improved versions, thereby allowing the type to adapt quickly and easily to new challenges.

Operation Sea Lion

As specified in Adolf Hitler's directive of July 16, 1940, a precondition for Germany's planned German invasion of England was the achievement of total air supremacy. However, the Luftwaffe met with fierce resistance from the British Spitfires and Hurricanes. During the Battle of Britain, the Hurricane proved an ideal gun platform and was even more

effective in combating the German bombers than the modern Spitfire. Although the Hurricane was inferior to the Messerschmitt Bf 109 in terms of performance, it was the skill of the pilots that would determine victory or defeat. By the end of the Battle of Britain, Hurricanes had destroyed more German aircraft than all Britain's other air defenses—fighters, anti-aircraft guns, barrage balloons—added together. They had enormous firepower—eight Browning .303 in. (7.7 mm) machine guns coordinated in such a way that

The impressive sight of six Hawker Hurricane Mk.IICs of No. 3 Squadron Fighter Command flying in formation.

the fire from all eight converged at a point 750 ft. (230 m) in front—a single burst of fire was enough to shoot a plane down. The Hurricane Mk.IIB in turn boasted twelve .303 in. (7.7 mm) machine guns while the Mk.II C, of which over 4,700 were built, had four .787 in. (20 mm) Hispano-Suiza cannon plus racks for one or two bombs.

The ground-support version was armed with either two or four 1.57 in. (40 mm) cannon that fired tank-busting ammunition, earning it the nickname "can opener."

Although providing enormous penetrating power, these cannon had one serious disadvantage: because they were mounted beneath the wings and had enormous recoil when fired, the loss of just one gun significantly impaired the aircraft's handling.

Continual refinement

The Hurricane was constantly being modified and improved. The initial Rolls-Royce Merlin II inverted V12 engine was replaced by a succession of others. The Mk.II's Merlin XX with two-stage supercharger had a take-off rating of 1,300 hp (831 kW) and delivered a top speed of 334 mph (537 km/h) at an altitude of 22,000 ft. (6,700 m). Alongside the Rolls-Royce Merlin, some Mk.IIIs were fitted with the Packard Merlin built in the USA under license and the Mk.IIE was developed into the Mk.IV with the new Merlin 24 (1,620 hp/1,192 kW).

Merchant Navy and Fleet Air Arm

A Hurricane variant unofficially known as the "Hurricat" was used by the Merchant Navy. Carried by merchantmen on small flight decks and launched by catapult, these Sea Hurricane IAs provided protection for the convoys. They were only successful to a limited extent however, because once launched, the pilot's only options were to make a water landing, bail out or look for land. Around 50 Hurricats were used. Later, additional fuel tanks were fitted in order to extend the range of planes deployed in this way.

The Hurricane IBs, on the other hand, converted from the Mk.I and Mk.II versions, were "real" carrier aircraft with arrestor hooks and folding wings.

The manufacturers

A total of 12,780 Hurricanes were built in the UK—including over a thousand by Gloster Aircraft and 300 by Austin Motors—plus a further 1,451 in Canada by the Canadian Car and Foundry Works. The Hurricane was deployed by 19 countries, with the largest number—nearly 3,000—going to the Soviet Union. Most of the aircraft delivered to the Soviet Union entered service as two-seat versions for use in a ground-attack role.

The last of well over 12,000 Hurricanes to be built being made ready for a ceremony.

An armorer handling the impressively large ammunition of the Hurricane's .787 in. (20 mm) cannon.

GRUMMAN F4F WILDCAT

At the beginning of the 1940s, this stubby single-seat, mid-wing monoplane was the primary fighter of the US Navy. Its robustness and firepower made it the only serious opponent in the battle with the Japanese Mitsubishi A6M2—known generally as the Rei-Sen or Zero.

Wildcat and Buffalo

The stubby Grumman F4F Wildcat fighter remained in service from 1942 until the end of the war.

The F4F-1 prototype was designed as a biplane and lost out to the Brewster Buffalo in the competition to secure the US government contract for a new Navy fighter. The third, monoplane version, the F4F-3, was equipped with a more powerful Pratt & Whitney Twin Wasp engine with two-stage supercharger that substantially boosted the plane's performance,

---

**GRUMMAN F4F-4
WILDCAT**
Carrier-borne single-seat fighter
Wingspan: 38 ft. (11.58 m)
Length: 28 ft. 9 in. (8.76 m)
Height: 11 ft. 4 in. (3.45 m)
Empty weight: 4,650 lb. (2,109 kg)
Maximum take-off weight: 6,100 lb. (2,767 kg)
Power plant: 1 × Pratt & Whitney R-1830-86 Twin Wasp air-cooled 14-cylinder twin radial, 1,200 hp (895 kW)
Maximum speed: 318 mph (512 km/h)
Operational ceiling: 34,908 ft. (10,640 m)
Range: 1,274 miles (2,050 km)
Armament: 6 × Browning M-2 .50 in. (12.7 mm), under-wing racks for 2 × 249 lb. (113 kg) bombs or 6 × 5 in. (127 mm) rockets

allowing it to secure an order from the US Navy. The F4F-3 was also used in Europe, notably by the British Fleet Air Arm, which renamed it the "Martlet."

Wildcat versus Mitsubishi A6M Zero

The F4F was at that time vastly inferior to the Imperial Japanese forces' best fighter in terms of climbing ability, maneuverability, and speed. The Wildcat's main strengths, meanwhile, were its toughness and firepower. Thanks to the Grumman's ability to withstand fire, Mitsubishi pilots were often unable to fire off enough ammunition to shoot a Wildcat down whereas the Zero would have exploded in a fireball had it sustained the same number of hits. Up to model F4F-3, the Grumman mounted four .50 in. (12.7 mm) machine guns while the Zero was armed with two rifle-caliber machine guns and two .787 in. (20 mm) cannon with just 20 rounds apiece. Model F4F-4, which entered service in 1942, was upgraded to six .50 in. (12.7 mm) machine guns. Not all pilots approved of this development because the same amount of ammunition continued to be provided, reducing the firing time. Many were of the opinion that "if you can't hit the target with four machine guns you won't be able to hit it with six either."

Pilots were also unhappy about having to hand-crank the F4F's landing gear. If the landing gear was not fully cranked and locked into place, the crank could spring back resulting in injury to the pilot. A further complicating factor was that the landing gear had a relatively narrow track. Although a straight line could to some extent be held when landing on a carrier thanks to the arrestor cable, accidents were not uncommon. Far more problematic, however, were landings on fixed airstrips, because without the restraining force of the arrestor cable it was difficult to hold the Wildcat steady, resulting in frequent accidents.

Folding wings

One wonderful engineering achievement was the introduction of folding wings, which halved the amount of space needed to stow a plane either above or below deck. At first the folding mechanism was hydraulic but this increased the aircraft's weight and wing

loading. The second, improved system involved manual folding by the deck crew. The wings folded not only upwards but also backwards, ending up almost perpendicular to the fuselage, in which position they were secured by stays.

The naval battles of Midway and the Coral Sea

The F4F was the most important weapon of the US Navy and US Marine Corps in the battles of Midway and the Coral Sea, which were fought soon after the USA entered the Second World War. But it remained in service even after the introduction of the F6F Hellcat and F4U Corsair. The F4F was particularly useful as it could operate from the short flight decks of small escort carriers. When Grumman adapted its plant to production of the F6F, the F4F continued to be produced by General Motors as the "FM."

The F4F-4 remained in active service until the end of the war. A total of 7,722 were built.

The US Grumman F4F was a typical example of a fighter powered by a radial engine.

In the service of the Fleet Air Arm, the Grumman F4F was renamed the "Martlet."

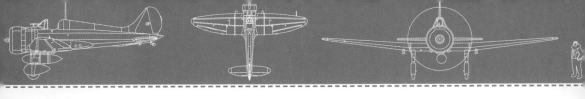

MITSUBISHI A5M

The Japanese navy's first carrier-borne monoplane fighter was designed for uncompromising speed and maneuverability. With its outstanding performance, modern all-metal construction, and clean, aerodynamic lines, the A5M meant that Japan was now one of the world leaders in fighter aircraft design.

MITSUBISHI A5M4
Single-seat fighter
Wingspan: 36 ft. 1 in. (11.00 m)
Length: 24 ft. 9 in. (7.55 m)
Height: 10 ft. 9 in. (3.27 m)
Empty weight: 2,681 lb. (1,216 kg)
Maximum take-off weight: 3,765 lb. (1,708 kg)
Power plant: 1 x Kotobuki 41 air-cooled radial, 710 hp (522 kW)
Maximum speed: 273 mph (440 km/h)
Operational ceiling: 32,808 ft. (10,000 m)
Range: 1,200 miles (746 km)
Armament: 2 x Type 89 .303 in. (7.7 mm) machine guns, under-wing racks for 2 x 66 lb. (30 kg) bombs

Sino-Japanese War

The Mitsubishi A5M was one of the fighters used in the attack on Pearl Harbor.

During its first flight in February 1935, the A5M prototype exceeded by far the stipulated top speed of 217 mph (350 km/h), achieving some 280 mph (450 km/h). During the Sino-Japanese War, the second production model, the A5M2, became the Japanese navy's most important fighter thanks to its superior speed and maneuverability. It was powered by the Kotobuki KAI 3-ko radial engine with a maximum output of 690 hp (471 kW).

Production continued until 1941, by which time a total of 982 had been built. The Mitsubishi was still in front-line service at the time of the attack on Pearl Harbor on December 7, 1941. The following year, it was replaced by the A6M Zero. The type's final deployment was as part of the wave of kamikaze ("divine wind") attacks that took place during the later stages of the war.

Year 2596

The A5M's internal designation was Type 96, derived from the year under the Japanese *Kigen* system—used by the military in Imperial Japan—in which the aircraft was adopted. Under this system, A.D. 1936 is the 2,596th year after the inauguration of Japan's mythical founder Emperor Jimmu.

Divine wind

The original meaning of the word *kamikaze*—literally "divine wind"—was "typhoon," and twice in its history, Japan was saved from defeat at the hands of superior forces by whirlwinds: in 1274 and 1281 Kublai Khan's hordes were overcome by storms as they attempted to conquer the Japanese empire. It seems safe to assume that the Japanese who prayed for a "divine wind" when the country was on the verge of defeat at the end of the Second World War made this connection with a fateful change of fortune in time of war.

Use of the word *kamikaze* to designate suicide attacks arose in the West. In Japan, the combat units that carried out the attacks were called tokkotai. One of the units was called Shimpu. It so happens that the character for Shimpu has two meanings, one of which is kamikaze.

This final desperate campaign cost over 2,000 Japanese and 12,000 Allied lives but the kamikaze pilots could not make history repeat itself.

The A5M was deployed for the last time by Japanese pilots on kamikaze suicide missions.

The Mitsubishi's landing gear was positioned at the lowest point of the plane's gull wings, just before they angled upwards.

FOKKER D XXI

The Fokker D XXI and US Grumman F4F had one thing in common: while they were both unexceptional, they were fully developed and available when needed. The Fokker was designed to be robust, easy to maintain, and good value for money. It was originally intended to serve in the Dutch East Indies but ended up being deployed in very different climate zones. When air forces started to get caught up in an arms race in the mid-1930s, a lot of interest was shown in the D XXI from other European countries due to its ready availability.

A flight of Fokker D XXIs in the camouflage of the Netherlands Air Force.

FOKKER D XXI
Single-seat fighter
Wingspan: 36 ft. 1 in. (11.00 m)
Length: 27 in. (8.22 m) Mercury; 26 ft. 3 in. (8.00 m) R-1535
Height: 9 ft. 8 in. (2.94 m)
Empty weight: 3,179 lb. (1,442 kg) Mercury; 3,382 lb. (1,534 kg) R-1535
Max. take-off weight: 4,519 lb. (2,050 kg) Mercury; 4,819 lb. (2,186 kg) R-1535
Power plant: (Dutch) 1 × Bristol Mercury VIII 9-cylinder radial, 830 hp (620 kW); (Danish) Mercury VI S, 645 hp (482 kW); (Finnish) Pratt & Whitney R-1535-SB4-G Twin Wasp Junior 14-cylinder twin radial, 825 hp (616 kW)
Max. speed: 286 mph (460 km/h) Mercury; 273 mph (439 km/h) R-1535
Operational ceiling: 36,089 ft. (11,000 m) Mercury; 31,988 ft. (9,750 m) R-1535
Range: 590 miles (950 km) Mercury; 559 miles (900 km) R-1535
Armament: (Dutch) 4 × FN-Browning M 36 .312 in. (7.9 mm) machine guns; (Danish) 2 × Madsen .312 in. (7.9 mm) machine guns, 2 × Madsen .782 in. (20 mm) cannon; (Finnish) 4 × .303 in. (7.7 mm) machine guns

The state of technology and the Fokker

Developed originally for the Dutch East Indies Air Force, the Fokker XXI became the primary fighter of three European air forces. The lack of a precise specification resulted in a mediocre final product, however. Although retractable landing gear was no longer new by 1935, the year of the Fokker's design, the D XXI still had a fixed chassis. In other areas, too, Fokker opted for tried and tested solutions. The construction was metal-clad welded steel tubing from the nose to the cockpit with a fabric-covered rear fuselage and tail. The wings consisted of a wooden framework with a Bakelite/plywood covering. The plane did, however, have an enclosed canopy—it is unlikely that Finland would have ordered seven aircraft and built a further 90 under license otherwise.

The prototype first flew in March 1936, powered by a Bristol Mercury VI S. The production versions were equipped with Mercury VIIs or VIIIs.

At the outbreak of war in 1939, Holland had 36 Fokker D XXIs in service, of which 28 were ready for action. The Dutch aircraft proved surprisingly effective in combat. What they lacked in performance, they made up in maneuverability. It should be pointed out, however, that they were not especially easy to fly. The controls were oversensitive in many situations, for example when executing a loop. The landing speed was relatively fast and the plane had a reputation for suddenly dropping a wing when coming in to land. Should this wing then touch the ground, the result would be an abrupt, involuntary swerve. The tail wheel also had to be made more secure in order to prevent the plane from swerving while taxiing.

The Winter War of 1939–40

The D XXI was well suited to conditions in the first Soviet-Finnish War—known too as the Winter War. It was normal for snow-covered auxiliary landing strips to have to be used for maintenance, re-arming, and take-off. The fixed landing gear was easy to equip with skids and the plane's straightforward construction enabled it to be maintained easily. The Fokker performed better against the Soviet I-15s and I-16s, which were already considered obsolete by this time, than against modern fighters in the Western European theater. Most of the Series IV models manufactured under license by Finnish state aircraft factory Valtion Lentokonetehdas ("VL") were fitted with the American 14-cylinder Pratt & Whitney R-1535-SB4-G Twin Wasp Junior twin radial engine. Some of the Finnish Fokkers remained in service until 1948.

The Danish government also adopted the D XXI, albeit purchasing only three aircraft and building a further ten under license.

The third licensee was to have been the Spanish Republic but its new aircraft factory was overrun by the Nationalists shortly before production was due to start.

Robust, reliable, and easy to maintain—the D XXI was very much in the Fokker tradition.

Fokker D XXIs serving in the Soviet-Finnish Winter War

SUPER-MARINE SPITFIRE

This flying legend was the only RAF aircraft to remain in service throughout the entire Second World War—going through 24 main versions. It was the effectiveness of the RAF's Spitfires and Hurricanes that saved the UK during the Battle of Britain. Although the propaganda of the day may have exaggerated the Spitfire's contribution to the frustration of Germany's invasion plans, it is certain that the fighter had enormous development potential and in its different guises was constantly being restored to a leading position among the fighters of the Second World War.

SUPERMARINE SPITFIRE MK IA
Single-seat fighter
Wingspan: 36 ft. 10 in. (11.23 m)
Length: 29 ft. 11 in. (9.12 m)
Height: 12 ft. 8 in. (3.86 m)
Empty weight: 4,810 lb. (2,182 kg)
Maximum take-off weight: 5,844 lb. (2,651 kg)
Power plant: 1 × Rolls-Royce Merlin II liquid-cooled, 7 gal. (26.7 l) V12, 1,015 hp (746 kW); variable pitch three-blade propeller
Maximum speed: 346 mph (557 km/h)
Operational ceiling: 30,499 ft. (9,296 m)
Range: 415 miles (668 km)
Armament: 8 × Browning Mk.II .303 in. (7.7 mm) machine guns; in 1940 some examples of the Spitfire Mk.IB were fitted with Hispano-Suiza .787 in. (20 mm) cannon and 4 × .303 in. (7.7 mm) machine guns

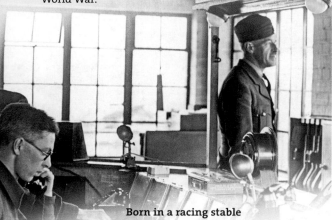

Born in a racing stable

Inside a Fighter Command control tower: a British officer watches aircraft taking off for a night-time mission.

In 1931, Supermarine started to apply its experience of building racing seaplanes to the task of designing a new fighter, initially as a private, internal development. This original prototype had gull wings and bore little resemblance to the later Spitfire. Neither this nor the second design by Chief Designer Reginald J. Mitchell and Supermarine Aviation—a subsidiary of the Vickers Group since 1928—met with the approval of the Air Ministry. Further research was conducted and the third design, the Type 300, was so convincing that before testing had even been completed, 310 aircraft had been ordered. The Spitfire was born.

This first Spitfire was endowed with a retractable undercarriage, enclosed cockpit, and all-metal fuselage.

Prototype K5054 took off from Eastleigh Aerodrome near Southampton on March 5, 1936, for what turned out to be a successful maiden flight. By June 1936, the British Air Ministry had placed an initial order for 310 aircraft. The first of these were delivered on August 4, 1938—to the Royal Air Force at Duxford, where No. 19 Squadron became the first unit to fly the new fighter now named the "Spitfire."

Sadly, R.J. Mitchell did not live to see the Spitfire go into production as he had died at 42 years of age in 1937. His successor as chief designer was Joseph Smith.

Single-seat fighter
Wingspan: 36 ft. 19 in. (11.26 m)
Length: 32 ft. 11 in. (10.04 m)
Height: 13 ft. 6 in. (4.12 m)
Empty weight: 7,158 lb. (3,247 kg)
Maximum take-off weight: 11,290 lb. (2,651 kg)
Power plant: 1 x Rolls-Royce Griffon 64
liquid-cooled V12, 2,375 hp (1,747 kW);
five-blade propeller
Maximum speed: 450 mph (724 km/h)
Operational ceiling: 42,995 ft. (13,105 m)
Range: 580 miles (933 km)
Armament: 4 × British Hispano-Suiza .787 in.
(20 mm) cannon; under-fuselage and under-
wing bomb racks

teething troubles, Supermarine designed the new fighter so carefully around the Rolls-Royce engine that Spitfire prototype K5054 was able to achieve 348 mph (560 km/h) at an altitude of 17,388 ft. (5,300 m) on its first outing.

During the course of 1941, it became apparent to Spitfire Mk.V pilots that the Merlin 45 had been relegated to second place by a completely unknown type of fighter powered by a radial engine. The emergence of the Focke-Wulf Fw 190 created an urgent need for enhancement of the Spitfire's performance, and fortunately Rolls-Royce had a new engine, the Merlin 60, ready to go into production. The Mk.IX, based on the Mk.V, was developed to accommodate the new power plant. Two two-stage superchargers boosted the engine's performance, enabling the Spitfire to compete again. The maximum output from the Merlin 60 was nearly double that of the Rolls-Royce Goshawk engine that powered the very first version of the Spitfire. Over 7,000 of the Mk.V and its derivative the Mk.IX were built.

Joseph "Joe" Smith, who replaced Reginald Mitchell as Supermarine's Chief Designer after the latter's premature death.

The power plant

Developments in aircraft and engine design were always closely intertwined. The most powerful aero engine available in 1931 was the Rolls-Royce PV12, which would achieve fame as the Merlin. Although the PV-12 (1,030 hp/757 kW) was still suffering from

Obstacles
The Spitfire was nearly never built. Mass production was slow starting up, which meant the project was almost cancelled before it had properly begun. One of the reasons for this was the unusual wing design, as a result of which the Spitfire required three times as many man-hours to build as the Messerschmitt Bf 109. Although orders had been placed for over 2,000 Spitfires, by August 1940 only 19 squadrons had been equipped with the new fighter.

The Supermarine Spitfire has often been called the most elegant fighter of all time. It has achieved enormous recognizability.

Spitfires of No. 243 Squadron, equipped with a bubble canopy to give the pilot all-round visibility.

Stall

Lift is generated by the flow of air over the wing. The angle between the wing position and the horizontal is called the angle of attack. If the aircraft raises its nose, giving the wings a steeper angle of attack, increased lift will initially be generated but only up to the critical stall point, where the airflow will suddenly separate from the surface of the wing, causing lift to decrease.

A lack of speed can also cause an aircraft to stall. Airflow will separate from the wing if a plane flies too slowly, falling below its minimum speed ("stalling speed"). At high altitude, stalling can be corrected by simply increasing speed by dipping the aircraft's nose but close to the ground there is a danger of crashing.

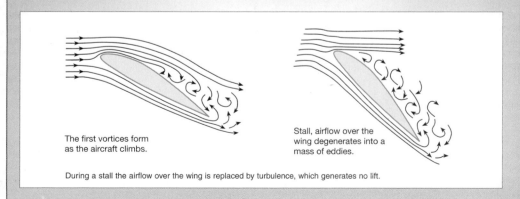

The first vortices form as the aircraft climbs.

Stall, airflow over the wing degenerates into a mass of eddies.

During a stall the airflow over the wing is replaced by turbulence, which generates no lift.

The Merlin's successor, the Rolls-Royce Griffon allowed the Mk.XII to reach speeds of up to 450 mph (724 km/h) while, in a dive, the Mk.XIX photo-reconnaissance version could surpass even this.

The Spitfire wings

The Spitfire's large, elliptical wings had low loading and gave excellent maneuverability at the high speeds made possible by their flat cross-section. Thanks to this design, the wings generated low induced drag, a factor that also contributed to the aircraft's good speed.

The unusual thing about the wing was its profile. It was dihedral in design; in other words, the leading edge was not flat but deviated from an imaginary straight line by -0.5 to +2 degrees.

When banking close to the point of stall, this meant the wing roots would stall first. The control surfaces on the trailing edge of the wing would judder continuously, alerting the pilot and allowing him time to correct the plane's attitude in time to avoid falling into a spin.

The pilot's workplace. The instrument panel is up to date and pared down to the essentials.

A Spitfire after crash-landing on the sea during the invasion of Sicily. The three small swastikas by the cockpit denote the number of enemy aircraft shot down by this plane.

The three basic designs

The A wing carried eight .303 in. (7.7 mm) machine guns. Their caliber was to prove too small, however, and consequently it was common for Messerschmitt fighters to be riddled with bullets but not destroyed. The B wing was therefore equipped with two .787 in. (20 mm) cannon and four .303 in. (7.7 mm) machine guns. The C wing was in turn equipped with either four cannon or a combination of machine guns and cannon. Also known as the Universal wing, this third type was introduced on Mk.VC.

The Spitfire—a beautiful machine but not perfect

For all the euphoria surrounding this successful aircraft, it is worth remembering that nothing is perfect, and a comparison with the Messerschmitt Bf 109 sheds interesting light on the Spitfire's strengths and weaknesses.

The Spitfire was clearly superior in terms of maneuverability and, depending on the model, speed too, but the fitting of the .787 in. (20 mm) cannon made the adversaries roughly equal in terms of firepower.

The Bf 109's rate of climb was better and its fuel injection system gave it a better dive capability whereas the Spitfire's carburetor had a tendency to fail under negative G-forces. This meant that instead of nosing straight into a

Two ground crew preparing a Spitfire for its next mission.

dive, the Supermarine's pilots had to prepare for a dive with a downwards half roll, losing a few decisive seconds in which the opponent could maneuver himself into a superior position.

Where all-round visibility was concerned, the Spitfire was again in front as its clear, non-paneled canopy allowed the pilot literally to see more.

After its conversion into a carrier-borne fighter under the name Seafire, the additional burden of the naval equipment—e.g. arrestor hook—made the plane somewhat tail-heavy. Added to this, the narrow track of its landing gear meant there were many accidents taking off from and landing on the short aircraft carrier decks.

The Spitfire on every front

The Spitfire served on all fronts that lay within the UK's sphere of influence: in Europe, in the deserts of North Africa, on the Indian Subcontinent, in Burma, and on the steppes of the Soviet Union. After the war, Israeli Spitfires even went into combat against Egyptian Spitfires.

Seldom was any plane so loved by its pilots and so feared by its opponents. Production finally ended in March 1948 with the last of 54 Mk.24s. The Spitfire remained in active service with the RAF until 1954, however, and with other air forces well into the 1960s. In total, 20,346 Spitfires and 2,334 Seafires were built.

The Spitfire still possesses an enormous fan base today and is a welcome sight at air shows.

La Coupe d'Aviation Maritime Jacques Schneider—the Schneider Trophy

French flying enthusiast Jacques Schneider was particularly interested in seaplanes. In order to give this branch of aviation a new impetus, he endowed the trophy that bears his name and presented it to the Aéro Club de France in 1913—some sources say 1912. The trophy, and the prize money that went with it, was awarded to the winner of a race, which was eventually extended to 217 miles (350 km), over a triangular course. Not only did the air race attract enormous crowds of onlookers, it also won the interest of the governments of the participating countries as it offered an opportunity to drive aircraft design and construction forward and measure their country's achievements against those of the other nations.

Critics claim the Schneider Trophy and the prestige it conferred—comparable perhaps to the Football World Cup—was the only reason for any interest at all in aircraft development in the UK at the beginning of the 1930s. The main characteristics of racing planes—aerodynamic design and high-performance engines—were equally applicable to fighters and it is no surprise the competing aircraft were generally built with financial support from their respective governments.

Reginald Mitchell, the father of the Spitfire, designed three Schneider Trophy winners. His Supermarine aircraft won three competitions in succession, in 1927, 1929 and 1931. In accordance with the rules of the competition, the trophy returned permanently to the UK and into the safekeeping of the Royal Aero Club.

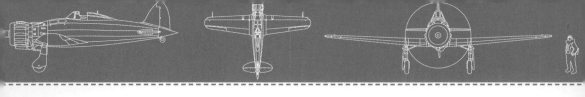

MACCHI C.200 SAETTA

Mario Castoldi designed the C.200 Saetta (Italian for "Lightning") for Macchi in 1936. A wonderful plane in terms of handling and all-round visibility, the C.200 suffered from a weak engine and indifferent firepower of just two .50 in.-caliber (12.7 mm) machine guns. Despite these shortcomings, the Saetta—along with the Fiat CR.42 biplane—formed the backbone of the Italian air force, the Regia Aeronautica, at the time of Italy's entry into the war. The fact that there were only 156 serviceable C.200s available gives an idea of the strike power of the Italian fighter force in 1940.

MACCHI C.200 SAETTA
Single-seat fighter/fighter-bomber
Wingspan: 34 ft. 8 in. (10.58 m)
Length: 26 ft. 10 in. (8.19 m)
Height: 11 ft. 6 in. (3.51 m)
Empty weight: 4,189 lb. (1,900 kg)
Maximum take-off weight: 5,157 lb. (2,339 kg)
Power plant: 1 × Fiat A.74R.C.38 air-cooled 14-cylinder twin radial
Maximum speed: 313 mph (503 km/h)
Operational ceiling: 29,199 ft. (8,900 m)
Range: 354 miles (570 km)
Armament: 2 × .50 in. (12.7 mm) Breda-SAFAT machine guns mounted in the nose; additional under-wing racks for two bombs up to 353 lb. (160 kg) in the C.200 C.B (Caccia Bombardiere) fighter-bomber version

Modern design in conservative hands

Despite its many modern construction details, the Macchi Saetta suffered from a lack of power.

The initial C.200 prototype (MM.336) first flew on December 24, 1937. In 1938 it was selected as the winning design in the state fighter competition and an order was signed that same year for 99 production machines. As an all-metal, low-wing cantilever monoplane with an oval cross-section fuselage, the Macchi C.200 was thoroughly modern from the point of view of technology. Its dual-spar wing was formed of three sections, the middle of which was integrated with the fuselage. The retractable landing gear, enclosed cockpit, and hydraulically activated flaps and ailerons—which could also be operated jointly—were state of the art.

The Saetta's controls were sensitive and well balanced and the aircraft's handling and maneuverability were outstanding. The emphasis Castoldi placed on all-round visibility is reflected in the characteristic humped fuselage design.

Italian fighter pilots were a conservative bunch, however, and in response to their protests, an open cockpit and fixed tail wheel were restored in the main production model. Furthermore, when the first C.200s were delivered to the units, one squadron even rejected the new aircraft in favor of the tried and tested Fiat CR.42 biplane, which was agile but outdated.

A built-in headwind

Radial engines do not necessarily mean poor performance. The Vought Corsair is a case in point. Sheer power can more than compensate for the disadvantages of high drag. However, the C.200's 870 hp (672 kW) 14-cylinder twin radial engine was insufficiently powerful to make up for the handicap of the plane's large frontal area. It was nevertheless the most powerful engine available in Italy at that time. On the instructions of the military, the Italian aircraft industry had prioritized the development of the radial engine, which was deemed to be more reliable, and neglected the development of inline or V engines in the 1,000 hp class. As a result, the C.200's more powerful successor, the C.202 Folgore, was powered not by an Italian engine but by an imported Daimler Benz DB 601A-1 V12. Later production fighters were equipped with a license-built

version of this power plant, the Alfa Romeo RA.1000 RC 41-I Monsone. Production of the new engine was slow to get under way, however, which meant the service life of the C.200 had to be significantly extended. In total, 1,153 Saettas were built.

The aftermath of an attack: destroyed Regia Aeronautica aircraft, and in the foreground a Saetta.

DEWOITINE D.520

This single-engine low-wing monoplane was probably the Armée de l'Air's best French-built fighter of the Second World War. The German occupation forces rated it so highly that the ceasefire treaty of 1940 expressly called for the surrender or laying-up of all aircraft of this type.

By the time Germany launched its invasion of France on May 10, 1940, only one French fighter group had re-equipped with the D.520. Although the few available Dewoitines and their pilots acquitted themselves well, they were unable to affect the outcome.

DEWOITINE D.520
Single-seat fighter, all-metal, low-wing cantilever monoplane
Wingspan: 33 ft. 6 in. (10.20 m)
Length: 28 ft. 3 in. (8.60 m)
Height: 8 ft. 5 in. (2.57 m)
Empty weight: 4,672 lb. (2,119 kg)
Maximum take-off weight: 5,897 lb. (2,675 kg)
Power plant: 1 × Hispano-Suiza 12Y45 liquid-cooled V12, 935 hp (697 kW); the first production aircraft were equipped with the less powerful Hispano-Suiza 12Y31
Maximum speed: 332 mph (535 km/h)
Operational ceiling: 33,629 ft. (10,250 m)
Range: 770 miles (1,240 km)
Armament: 1 × .787 in. (20 mm) Hispano-Suiza HS404 cannon, 4 × MAC 34M39 .295 in. (7.5 mm) machine guns in the wings

Why "D.520"?

The model designation D.520 refers to the minimum top speed of 320 mph (520 km/h) that had been stipulated by the French Air Ministry in its unofficial C 1 specification of 1937. Although the first of three prototypes failed to meet this requirement, an order for over 200 aircraft was placed before the second prototype even left the ground. The third prototype (D.520-03) flew for the first time in March 1939, and on November 2 that year the first production D.520 completed its maiden flight.

Service history

The first French fighter unit to be equipped with the new fighter was the Groupe de Chasse I/3, which was issued with unarmed examples for evaluation purposes in January 1940. In April and May that year it then received its first combat-ready machines. The defeat of France and ensuing ceasefire (June 23, 1940) marked the start of a checkered history for the D.520. The Germans immediately ordered completion of

all semi-finished aircraft and the resumption of production—which eventually ceased with the completion of the 905th plane in summer 1944. Many D.520s were taken over by the air force of Germany's ally Vichy France and distributed to the fighter training schools of the German and Italian air forces. The D.520 did not come back into the hands of the new French Air Force until after July 1944.

The remaining D.520s were eventually converted into two-seat trainers—designated the D.520 DC—before being decommissioned in 1953.

Combat effectiveness

This fast, maneuverable aircraft was one of the leading fighters of the Second World War. While unable to match its high-performance opponent the Bf 109 in terms of top speed and rate of climb, the D.520 scored well on agility and dive capability.

Although production of the D.520 initially got under way relatively quickly, it was held up by a series of teething troubles with the result that crew training could not begin until

January 1940. On May 10, 1940, the day Germany invaded France, only 79 aircraft—some sources even say as few as 36—were in service and only those of Groupe de Chasse I/3 were fully combat-ready. Although these machines proved their worth in the Battle of France with 108 confirmed and 39 unconfirmed victories for 85 losses, there were not enough of them to change the course of history.

One of the D.520s captured by the Germans. The type was deemed so dangerous by the Luftwaffe that the ceasefire treaty expressly stipulated the surrender of all examples.

BOEING F4B/P-12

The Boeing F4B was one of the most successful US fighters of the interwar period and remained the USA's primary fighter for many years. First introduced by the US Navy as the carrier-borne F4B and by the US Army Air Corps (USAAC) as the P-12, it was the last US biplane fighter in active service. The Boeing was also the last type for over 20 years to be flown simultaneously by each of the separate arms of the US forces—the USAAC, US Navy and US Marine Corps (USMC). The F4B/P-12 era extended from 1929—the year of its initial delivery to the units—until the 1940s.

Boeing

A carrier-borne Boeing F4B-4, the last and best-loved version of the Navy fighter.

Most people would no longer associate the Boeing Aircraft Company with fighters. In the 1930s, things were different and it was production of this late biplane fighter that saw the recently founded company through the Great Depression. Boeing had developed two prototypes at its own risk and handed them to the Navy for testing. The aircraft's performance was judged to be so good that not only the

Navy but also the USAAC ordered versions of the plane. The company's entrepreneurial leap of faith had paid off.

The exceptional handling characteristics of the F4B/P-12 were summed up by one pilot as follows: "You could get the plane to bank just by sticking your arm out of the cockpit." These good flying characteristics remained a feature of all the different F4B/P-12 models despite the additional weight of modifications introduced in the later variants.

BOEING F4B-4/P-12E
Carrier-borne, single-seat biplane fighter
Wingspan: 30 ft. (9.14 m)
Length: 20 ft. 5 in. (6.22 m) F4B-4; 22 ft. 6 in. (6.86 m) P-12E
Height: 9 ft. 9 in. (2.97 m) F4B-4; 8 ft. 1 in. (2.47 m) P-12E
Empty weight: 1,997 lb. (906 kg)
Max. take-off weight: 3,128 lb. (1,419 kg) F4B-4; 2,687 lb. (1,219 kg) P-12E
Power plant: 1 x Pratt & Whitney R-1340-17 air-cooled 9-cylinder radial, 532 hp (391 kW)
Max. speed: 189 mph (304 km/h)
Operational ceiling: 26,299 ft. (8,016 m)
Range: 371 miles (597 km) F4B-4; 570 miles (917 km) P-12E
Armament: 2 × synchronized .30 in. (7.62 mm) machine guns or 1 × .30 in. (7.62 mm) and 1 × .50 in. (12.7 mm) machine guns, max 245 lb. (111 kg) bomb load (P-12)

Small, light, and clean-lined, this 1929 F4B represented the pinnacle of US biplane fighter construction.

The cockpit of the sparsely instrumented Boeing photographed in the assembly shop.

Variants

After entering production, the F4B was continuously updated. From model F4B-3 onwards, the riveted, fabric-covered aluminum framework was replaced with a metal semi-monocoque fuselage, and the fabric covering of the dual-spar wings was replaced by metal sheeting. Delivery of the F4B-3, which was powered by a Pratt & Whitney R-1340-16 engine, began in December 1931. Orders from the US Navy and the USAAC—for a total of 135 of this type—represented the largest contract Boeing had received for nearly ten years and helped the company secure its market position as a major aircraft manufacturer.

The last 25 aircraft under this contract were supplied to the USAAC under the designation P-12F and powered by a Pratt & Whitney R-1340-19 engine rated at 610 hp (447 kW), which delivered better performance at altitude.

The final variants, the F4B-4 and P-12F, were fully distributed by March 1933. In total, 586 of all models were produced. More than half went to the USAAC and the rest were split between the US Navy and the USMC.

The Pratt & Whitney Wasp

Pratt & Whitney (P&W) is one of the world's major manufacturers of aero engines. Thanks largely to its Wasp engine, it has occupied a leading position since the early days of aviation.

P&W was originally founded as a manufacturer of industrial machine tools. In 1925, 65 years into its history, Frederick B. Rentschler joined the firm, setting up the Pratt & Whitney Aircraft Co. P&W provided Rentschler with capital and premises and thus began the triumphal march of its aeronautical engines. The firm's very first model, an air-cooled 9-cylinder radial engine named the Wasp, was a resounding success. The family of engines bearing this name remained in production from 1925 to the 1960s—a total of 34,966 units.

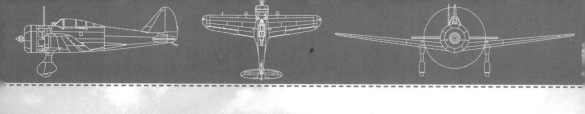

Developed and built in great secrecy, the Nakajima Ki-43 surprised Allied fighter pilots with its outstanding performance.

NAKAJIMA KI-43 HAYABUSA

The Nakajima Ki-43 was built in greater numbers than any other fighter of the Imperial Japanese forces (5,919 built). By European standards it was virtually obsolete by the time it entered service but during the initial phase of the war it became a feared fighter and even forced the Americans onto the defensive. It remained in service until 1945.

Oscar and Jim

Oscar and Jim were the names given to the Hayabusa ("peregrine falcon") by the Allied forces in the southwest Pacific and

---

NAKAJIMA KI-43-IA
Single-seat fighter/fighter-bomber
Wingspan: 37 ft. 6 in. (11.44 m)
Length: 29 ft. (8.83 m)
Height: 10 ft. 9 in. (3.27 m)
Empty weight: 4,345 lb. (1,975 kg)
Maximum take-off weight: 5,825 lb. (2,642 kg)
Power plant: 1 × Nakajima Ha-25 air-cooled 14-cylinder radial with 990 hp (728 kW) take-off rating
Maximum speed: 306 mph (492 km/h)
Operational ceiling: 38,550 ft. (11,750 m)
Range: 808 miles (1,300 km)
Armament: 2 × .303 in. (7.7 mm) machine guns or 1 × .303 in. (7.7 mm) and 1 × .50 in. (12.7 mm) machine guns built into top of engine cowling, under-wing brackets for two additional, discardable 53 gal. (200 l) fuel tanks

---

China/Burma when they became aware of its existence. The Japanese had developed the Ki-43 in conditions of utmost secrecy—the contract had been awarded straight to Dr. Hideo Itokawa and his team without a competition being held—and so the US intelligence service knew nothing about it in advance. When the first Hayabusas were deployed in combat in 1941, they were mistaken for Ki-27s. This was entirely understandable as the Ki-43 was obviously a development of its predecessor the Ki-27, which was also a low-wing cantilever monoplane constructed entirely of metal right down to its flaps. The Ki-43's fuselage was extremely slender and streamlined. Innovations included an enclosed cockpit and retractable landing gear.

Although the Ki-43 met its development specification in full, its fate was initially uncertain. Test pilots complained about the prototype's poor visibility and the additional weight of its retractable undercarriage. In response, Japan's high command decided to build ten pre-production aircraft in different configurations for thorough testing. During the course of in-service testing, pilots were impressed above all with the plane's greatly improved dogfight capability. The first fully-fledged model, the Ki-43-Ia, went into production in April 1941 and units began switching to the new fighter in September.

The peregrine falcon takes off

In Japan, maneuverability and handling were still the main priorities in fighter development and the Hayabusa more than fulfilled this particular requirement—thanks in part to high-lift devices positioned on the trailing edges of the wings next to the fuselage. These so-called "combat" or "butterfly" flaps had the effect of increasing lift and improved the maneuverability of the Ki-43 when banking tightly and at extremely low speeds. Should the plane stall despite these precautions, it would be easy to bring under control again. In short, the Ki-43 was free of aerodynamic deficiencies and was not prone to "moodiness."

In 1943 the Allies were able to evaluate a Ki-43 in a series of mock battles. By this stage they found the Japanese fighter inferior to most modern US types in terms of performance but recognized the considerable danger it posed in dogfights. Not only was the Hayabusa outstandingly maneuverable, it could also accelerate extremely quickly from low speeds, which enabled it to adopt superior attacking positions.

Unfortunately the engine output, armament, and armor of the Ki-43 were no match for those of its foes. Even superficial damage could be disastrous, and so the Ki-43 Hayabusa remained no more than an interim solution between the light, maneuverable fighters of the early 1930s and the better-performing machines of the 1940s.

Although the Hayabusa had forfeited its initial superiority by the end of the war, it remained a formidable opponent in dogfights.

Its lightweight construction made the Ki-43 highly maneuverable but it was unable to withstand the level of battle damage the US types could take.

JUNKERS
JU 88

Originally designed to meet a specification for a high-speed, medium-range bomber, the Junkers Ju 88 developed during the course of the war into the Luftwaffe's most versatile aircraft. It was one of the class of fast dive-bombers called for by Hitler but also proved its worth as a heavy fighter/bomber destroyer. It was particularly successful as a night-fighter against the waves of RAF and USAAF bombers pounding German cities. The Allies regarded the Ju 88 as fast and dangerous and capable of taking a lot of punishment.

The three-seat version of the Junkers Ju 88 with glazed nose for the front gunner.

From bomber to fighter

The firm of Junkers and its engineers W.H. Evers and A. Gassner designed the prototype Ju 88 V1, which first flew on December 21, 1936, as a medium horizontal bomber and dive-bomber in accordance with the Luftwaffe requirement. By the time mass production of the bomber version, the Ju 88 A-1, was getting under way, however, the aircraft's wider potential had been recognized and work was proceeding apace on the development of a heavy fighter version based on the Ju 88 V7 prototype. These fighter and later night-fighter versions eventually accounted for most of the C-series and proved superior in these roles even to the Messerschmitt Bf 110.

The long road to production

As a result of continual refinements to the prototype, mostly in response to new requirements imposed by the Luftwaffe, it was almost three years before the first Ju 88s entered service in 1939.

In addition to horizontal bombers and dive-bombers, torpedo bombers, heavy fighters, and ground-attack aircraft were also developed from the basic type. As a tank destroyer, the Ju 88 was equipped with a 2.95 in. (75 mm) Pak anti-tank gun and 1.97 in. (50 mm) cannon. In the final stages of the war (from May 1944), Ju 88s that were no longer fit for action served as remote-controlled "flying superbombs" in piggyback/Mistel configurations.

The Ju 88 as night-fighter

In 1940, night-time fighter operations were literally a shot in the dark. Furthermore, there was always a danger of being hit by "friendly" anti-aircraft fire. The turning point for the Ju 88 came with Telefunken's development of the Lichtenstein night-fighter radar system. This enabled crews to fix the positions of enemy aircraft in the dead of night and even fire at them without the need for visual contact. Later night-fighter systems also solved the problem of a 20–25 mph (30–40 km/h) loss of speed

JUNKERS JU 88 G-7B
Two or three-seat heavy
fighter/bomber destroyer,
medium bomber, torpedo
bomber, ground-attack aircraft, and
reconnaissance aircraft
Wingspan: 66 ft. 5 in. (20.13 m)
Length: 54 ft. 4 in. (16.55 m)
Height: 15 ft. 11 in. (4.85 m)
Empty weight: 20,062 lb. (9,100 kg)
Maximum take-off weight: 32,386 lb. (14,690 kg)
Power plant: 2 × Junkers Jumo 213 E 12-cylinder
radial with two-stage supercharger, take-off
rating 1,750 hp (1,285 kW)
Maximum speed: 402 mph (647 km/h)
Operational ceiling: 28,871 ft. (8,800 m)
Range: 1,429 miles (2,300 km)
Armament: 4 × MG 151/20 .787 in. (20 mm)
cannon under fuselage, 2 × MG 151/20 cannon in
schräge Musik configuration, 1 × MG 131 .512 in.
(13 mm) machine gun in rear cockpit window

caused by the forest of antennae attached to
the aircraft's nose. Signals were received via
internal antennae instead.

In the night-fighter version, the glazed nose
of the Ju 88 was replaced by a metal cone
containing fixed, forward-firing machine guns

and cannon. The rear gunner became the radar
operator, directing the pilot to enemy bombers.
A substantial upgrading of the aircraft's
firepower included the installation of two
.787 in. (20 mm) MG-FF cannon in the upper
fuselage, which fired obliquely upwards. This
configuration—which the Germans called the
schräge Musik system—allowed the night-
fighters to exploit the defensive blind spot of
enemy bombers and attack from below.

The Ju 88s developed another form of attack
whereby they would follow the British
bombers back to their home airfields, insinuate
themselves into the line of bombers, and shoot
down helpless aircraft as they approached
for landing.

One of Germany's most successful night-
fighter pilots was Captain Heinrich Prinz zu
Sayn-Wittgenstein, who achieved 83 kills—
mostly in Ju 88s—assisted by his radar and
radio operator Sergeant Ostheimer. After
destroying five British bombers using the
schräge Musik system during the night of
January 21–22, 1944, his Messerschmitt Bf 110
was set ablaze by a Mosquito. Having allowed
his crew to bale out, the prince died trying to
save his aircraft.

*The night-fighter
version of the Ju 88
displaying the
forest of antennae
characteristic of
the "Lichtenstein"
night-fighter device.*

*A group of British
experts evaluate the
versatile Ju 88.*

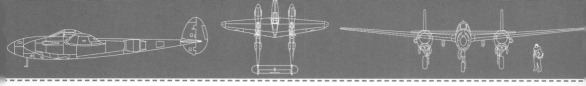

LOCKHEED P-38 LIGHTNING

Although opinion is divided on this twin-engined, long-range fighter with its characteristic twin booms, it cannot be denied that it had a greater range than any plane to date, was extremely fast, and in the hands of pilots with a good aim was an enormously effective gun platform. Many of the technical difficulties that arose during the development of the P-38 had never previously been encountered and gave designers new insights into the construction of high-speed aircraft.

LOCKHEED P-38L LIGHTNING
Single-seat fighter/fighter-bomber
Wingspan: 52 ft. (15.85 m)
Length: 37 ft. 10 in. (11.53 m)
Height: 12 ft. 10 in. (3.91 m)
Empty weight: 12,800 lb. (5,806 kg)
Maximum take-off weight: 21,600 lb. (9,798 kg)
Power plant: 2 × Allison V-1710-111/113 liquid-cooled V12 with fully automatic turbocharger, 1,496 hp (1,100 kW) each
Maximum speed: 414 mph (666 km/h)
Operational ceiling: 43,996 ft. (13,410 m)
Range: 2,600 miles (4,185 km)
Armament: 1 × Hispano M2(C) .787 in. (20 mm) cannon with 150 rounds and 4 × Colt-Browning 53-2 .50 in. (12.7 mm) machine guns with 500 rounds each plus one or two 2,000 lb (907 kg) or 1,600 lb (726 kg) bombs and 10 × 5 in. (127 mm) rockets carried under the wings

The so-called "Christmas tree" rocket launchers, and the machine guns and cannon in its nose, provided the P-38 with unrivalled firepower.

Tactical requirements

There were two main reasons for the development of the Lightning. Firstly, North America's geographical location. A long-range fighter made sense because of the enormous geographical distribution of US interests, and it was in the wide expanses of the Pacific that the Lockheed would achieve its greatest success. Secondly, there were tactical considerations. A similar concept, dating originally from the First World War, was simultaneously being revived in Europe in the 1930s. This was the twin-engined strategic fighter, also known as the heavy fighter and in Germany as the *Zerstörer* ("destroyer"). Typical examples of this type are the Messerschmitt Bf 110 and the Bristol Beaufighter.

In the USA, the USAAC (US Army Air Corps) issued a requirement in 1936 for a twin-engined, long-range, high-altitude interceptor that could attain a speed of 360 mph (580 km/h) at 20,000 ft. (6,100 m) and fly for up to an hour at full throttle.

A number of aircraft manufacturers considered the specification as unrealizable. Not so Lockheed. Hall L. Hibbard and Clarence "Kelly" Johnson boldly took up the challenge and entered into competition with Boeing, Consolidated, Curtiss, Douglas, and Vultee. Before long the twin-engined Lockheed 22, a revolutionary fighter of unusual design with a tricycle undercarriage, was developed at Skunk Works. The most striking external feature of the Lockheed 22 and later P-38 was its twin tail booms, which earned it the nickname the "flying barn door."

The P-38's turbochargers are visible in the top of the engine cowlings. Initially this technology was a US monopoly and was not used in export aircraft.

Clarence "Kelly" Johnson, Hall L. Hibbard, and "Skunk Works"

In 1939, Hall L. Hibbard was Lockheed's chief designer while "Kelly" Johnson, the company's brilliant technician and project manager, was head of the development department. Under Johnson's leadership, this secret technology unit adopted the code name "Skonk Works"—changed in the 1960s to "Skunk Works"—and would eventually acquire a legendary reputation. Among its many pioneering designs was the U-2 high-altitude reconnaissance aircraft (the "Dragon Lady"), which came to the attention of the general public when one was shot down over the USSR on May 1, 1960.

Today the "Skunk workers" continue to handle secret projects but now enjoy official status as the Advanced Development Program of the enormous Lockheed Martin Corporation. They have proudly adopted a skunk as their trademark.

Having been declared the winner of competition X-608 on June 23, 1937, it took Lockheed around a year and a half to develop prototype XP-38. The prototype eventually flew on January 27, 1939, but that is when the real problems started. The XP-38 attained dive speeds at which air compressibility, which had previously played hardly any role in aircraft design, created major difficulties. Gifted designer and aerodynamicist "Kelly" Johnson regarded compressibility as such an insuperable obstacle that he compared it to a brick wall.

The Lightning in Europe

The Lightning had one thing to thank the Old World for: its name, thought up by the British, who found the original one, Atalanta, insufficiently martial. Moreover, the P-38 was not highly rated in the UK. One of the reasons for this was its engine. In the early 1940s the fully automatic turbocharger was still a well-kept US secret and its export was prohibited. The British Lightning therefore had to make do with Allison V-1710-C15R engines minus turbocharger. These were equipped with clockwise-rotating propellers while those of

Compressibility and aircraft design

Compressibility refers to the behavior of matter under pressure. In aircraft design, the particular way in which air behaves under pressure results in aerodynamic resistance in front of the leading edge of the wing—even in the case of the most aerodynamically efficient airfoil. Beginning at a certain speed, the air in front of the wing is so heavily compressed that the pressure balance in the wing's eddy zone becomes uneven and takes the form of shock waves, in other words rhythmically alternating high and low pressure zones. Not only are these overlapping shock waves responsible for the sonic boom when the speed of sound is exceeded, in the case of the later Lockheed Lightnings they also caused the aircraft's structural stability limit to be exceeded with the effect that the tail booms and tail were literally shaken apart by the vibrations.

Another extremely dangerous consequence of compressibility was that in a steep dive the plane would cease to respond properly to the controls. Until high-lift devices were fitted to the Lockheed 22 in the form of Fowler flaps (see p.68), pilots had only a slender chance of pulling their aircraft out of a dive.

the "American" P-38 both rotated outwards—at the top of their arc. Three P-38s (British designation "Lightning Mk I") were shipped to the UK in January 1942 and performed so poorly, attaining a mere 354 mph (570 km/h) at 21,000 ft. (6,400 m) without turbocharger, that the RAF rejected the aircraft.

Another reason was the P-38's handling. Although the plane was not exactly treacherous, highly experienced pilots were nevertheless needed to fly it. In the case of the British Lightning Mk.I, a further complicating factor was that its two clockwise-rotating propellers produced a similar effect to the torque generated by rotary engines, which had an additional adverse influence on the aircraft's flying characteristics. The Lightnings rejected by the British were converted by the US Army Air Force (USAAF) into trainers or thoroughly modified. The USAAF adopted the name "Lightning" at the end of 1941.

In the USA the P-38 enjoys such a good reputation that on July 7, 2006 the Lockheed F-35 (Joint Strike Fighter) was christened "Lightning II."

Operation Vengeance
More combat victories were notched up over the Pacific in P-38s than in any other US type. Operation Vengeance was one of the most spectacular operations in the history of aerial warfare. US radio observers had decrypted a Japanese radio signal that gave them the precise flight schedule of Japan's highest-ranking navy officer Admiral Isoruku Yamamoto, thought to be the architect of Pearl Harbor. It was known that Yamamoto was a stickler for punctuality, and so on April 18, 1943, 16 P-38Gs took off from their base on Guadalcanal for Bougainville. Specially fitted with 310 gal. (1,175 l) supplementary tanks, the aircraft covered nearly 1,120 miles (1,800 km)—an incredible achievement in itself. The Lightnings appeared over Buin airfield at the same time as Yamamoto's contingent of two Mitsubishi G4M bombers and six Mitsubishi A6M Rei-Sens. In the ensuing battle, both bombers were shot down and Yamamoto was killed—Pearl Harbor was thus avenged.

The P-38 as a gun platform
The Lightning's heavy guns were clustered in its nose. The effect of this concentrated firepower has been compared to that of an enormous circular saw. Another advantage of this weapons configuration was that it significantly improved the guns' accuracy and destructive power. A good marksman could hit a target almost two-thirds of a mile (1 km) away.

For long-distance operations, supplementary fuel tanks extended the Lockheed Lightning's range to 2,270 miles (3,650 km).

A captured Mitsubishi A6M. The Japanese roundel was painted over the US emblem for the purposes of a photo shoot. The American star is still visible on the fuselage.

MITSUBISHI A6M REI-SEN

The Mitsubishi A6M is probably the best-known Japanese single-engined fighter of the Second World War and represents the pinnacle of Japanese fighter design. Later types conferred no decisive advantages and so the A6M remained in service throughout the war—from its initial deployment in China in 1940 to the final, desperate kamikaze campaign of the closing stages.

Rei-Sen, Reisen or Zero?

Literature about this air superiority fighter refers to it by a number of different names—even "Zero-Sen," a mixture of the Japanese and American versions. The official Japanese designation was Rei-Sen or Reisen, meaning "first fighter" or "Fighter O," which at least explains the English translation Zero. The official Allied code name for the A6M was "Zeke."

MITSUBISHI A6M
REI-SEN C 53C

Single-seat fighter
Wingspan: 36 ft. 1 in. (11.00 m)
Length: 29 ft. 9 in. (9.07 m)
Height: 9 ft. 9 in. (2.98 m)
Empty weight: 4,175 lb. (1,894 kg)
Maximum take-off weight: 6,508 lb. (2,952 kg)
Power plant: 1 × Sakae 31 radial with water-methanol injection, 1,210 hp (890 kW)
Maximum speed: 354 mph (570 km/h)
Operational ceiling: 37,730 ft. (11,510 m)
Range: 1,118 miles (1,800 km)
Armament: 2 × wing-mounted .520 in. (13 mm) machine guns and 2 × .787 in. (20 mm) Type 99 cannon in the engine cowling, under-wing racks for 2 × 132 lb. (60 kg) bombs

Development

The Mitsubishi A6M was designed by chief designer Jori Horikoshi in response to a requirement of the Imperial Japanese Navy. It first flew on April 1, 1940, and by the end of July 1940 production had already begun of what was officially known as the "Navy Type 0 Carrier-borne Fighter." For ease of storage in the narrow confines of a carrier flight deck and parking deck, the wingtips of the A6M could be manually folded.

That same year, the first A6M pre-production aircraft were tested in the Sino-Japanese War. They proved so successful—destroying 99 Chinese aircraft for only two A6M losses—that US General Claire Chennault, advisor to the Chinese air force and commander of the Flying Tigers, sent an alarming report to USAAC headquarters warning of the prototype's outstanding performance.

At the outbreak of war in the Pacific, the US air force—the USAAC had become the USAAF, the US Army Air Force, in June 1941—was nevertheless taken completely by surprise by the speed and maneuverability of the A6M, having apparently continued to underestimate the quality of Japanese aircraft design.

Pearl Harbor

By the time of the attack on Pearl Harbor, more than 400 A6Ms had been delivered to the Japanese Navy as carrier-borne fighters. During the initial phase of the war, the A6M was superior to any other fighter in terms of final velocity and rate of climb.

A Mitsubishi A6M on patrol over the Japanese islands. A supplementary fuel tank is being carried under the fuselage.

The Mitsubishi Rei-Sen was the Japanese air force's most potent weapon during the Second World War. Those shown here are being made ready for a mission.

The Mitsubishi A6M played a decisive role in the attack on Pearl Harbor. It was superior to any US fighter at that time.

Furthermore, thanks to its extreme agility, it was able to outmaneuver the Brewster Buffalo, Curtiss P-40, and Grumman Wildcat, the main US fighters of the day. The Mitsubishi A6M maintained its air superiority in the Pacific theater as a fighter and bomber escort up to the Battle of Midway.

In 1942 the Americans managed to get their hands on an A6M that had made an emergency landing on the Aleutian Islands, sustaining only minor damage. Its evaluation in the USA resulted in improvements to the newly developed Grumman F4F and F6F Hellcat fighters.

Midway—the tide turns

The A6M's weaknesses were exposed for the first time by the new US fighters. Although the aircraft's lightweight construction made it fast and maneuverable, it also made it more vulnerable to attack. The US fighters were considerably more robust thanks to their self-sealing tanks and superior armor. By this stage,

US industrial production had swung into gear and was supplying the US Navy with large numbers of aircraft carriers and suitable aircraft. This allowed the USA to take the initiative in the Pacific following the Battle of Midway. Japan, on the other hand, was only able to crank up its armaments production to a limited extent and the level of training given to its new Zero pilots was gradually deteriorating. The USA won back the Solomon Islands and drove the Japanese out of New Guinea, the Aleutian Islands, and the Marianas.

In the absence of a suitable successor, the decision was taken to improve the Zero. Variant A6M5 was provided with a bulletproof cockpit canopy and A6M6 was equipped with self-sealing fuel tanks and its performance boosted with water-methanol injection. These developments were not enough to counteract the numerical superiority of the US Navy pilots, however. On June 19, 1944, during the Battle of the Philippine Sea—also known in the USA as the Great Marianas Turkey Shoot—the Imperial Japanese Navy lost between 300 and 400 aircraft and three carriers as a result of which most A6Ms now became land-based fighters and fighter-bombers.

Thanks to superior US fighter defenses, conventional attacks on US aircraft carriers now seemed pointless. The Japanese therefore resorted to the final, desperate strategy of suicide attacks known in the West as "kamikaze" attacks (see p.89).

Isolated suicide attacks by Japanese pilots had been occurring since the beginning of the war. It is thought that the first planned, tactical deployment of a kamikaze unit was that organized by Vice Admiral Arima against a US

Inside the cockpit of ar. A6M Rei-Sen.

carrier group off the Philippine island of Luzcn on October 15, 1944.

The first "official" kamikaze unit was established by Vice Admiral Takijiro Onishi cn October 19, 1944, during the Japanese defense of the Philippines. Special suicide commandos were formed to combat the imminent US invasion. The pilots' task was to crash their planes into enemy aircraft carriers with the aim of causing severe damage to, or ideally sinking, the vessel.

The very next day, 24 pilots volunteered. They constituted four special attack units equipped with Mitsubishi A6M5s. Each aircraft carried a 550 lb. (250 kg) bomb.

On October 29, a number of US ships were hit by six kamikaze attacks in the vicinity of the Philippines. The escort carrier St. Lo was sunk and six other escort carriers damaged. Kamikaze pilots sank 18 major US ships ard damaged many others, some of them seriously, during the retaking of the Philippines alone.

Even heavier than the physical to.l, however, were the psychological consequences of the attacks—the knowledge that one was facing an enemy to whom survival meant nothing and victory everything.

The kamikaze attacks reached their peak during the US invasion of Okinawa in 1945.

THE SECOND
WORLD WAR

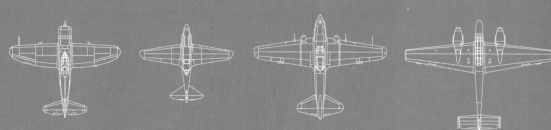

BELL P-39 AIRACOBRA

The P-39 was an unusual aircraft. It was designed not around an engine, as is so often the case, but around a gun. The basic concept was for a high-altitude interceptor that could get within firing distance while remaining out of range of bombers' guns. The 1.5 in. (37 mm) American Armament Corporation T-9 cannon left no room in the nose for the engine, which was therefore positioned behind the cockpit. The propeller driveshaft ran under the pilot's seat to the front of the plane.

BELL P-39N AIRACOBRA
Single-seat fighter/fighter-bomber
Wingspan: 34 ft. (10.37 m)
Length: 30 ft. 2 in. (9.20 m)
Height: 11 ft. 11 in. (3.63 m)
Empty weight: 5,463 lb (2,478 kg)
Maximum take-off weight: 8,201 lb (3,720 kg)
Power plant: 1 × Allison V-1710-85 liquid-cooled V12, 1,217 hp (895 kW)
Maximum speed: 399 mph (642 km/h)
Operational ceiling: 35,006 ft. (10,670 m)
Range: 746 miles (1,200 km)
Armament: 1 × American Armament Corporation T-9 1.5 in. (37 mm) cannon firing through propeller hub, 2 × .50 in. (12.7 mm) machine guns in the nose cowling, 2 × wing-mounted .30 in. (7.62 mm) machine guns, under-wing rack for a 500 lb. (227 kg) bomb

The Airacobra's poor performance at high altitude led the RAF to cancel the remainder of its order.

Management and the turbocharger

Prototype XP-39 was ordered in 1937, and flight testing began in April 1939. That same month the US government signed an order for 13 pre-production aircraft. Delivery of the actual P-39 production model did not begin until January 1941.

After testing by the armed forces, numerous modifications were made to the Airacobra, the most incomprehensible of which was a decision to dispense with a turbocharger. This impaired performance at altitude to such an extent that the P-39 was no longer able to fulfill its originally intended role (interception of high-altitude bombers). Initially the US Army Air Corps (USAAC) refused to introduce the aircraft without a turbocharger.

The response in the UK was similar. Although an order was placed for more than 650 planes, this was cancelled after the P-39 proved disappointing in combat. The best results were obtained with the Airacobra in a ground-support role. Whenever combat took place at higher altitudes, the aircraft's performance diminished markedly. The lion's share of production—more than 4,700 of the 9,558 Airacobras built—was supplied to the Soviet Union under the Lend-Lease program.

From the Pacific to the taiga

The USA soon withdrew the P-39 from the Pacific theater. While it had proven its worth as a strike fighter, it stood no chance against the Mitsubishi A6M and was therefore replaced by the P-38 Lightning and P-40 Warhawk.

The situation in the USSR was quite different. The improved N and Q variants used by the Soviets were free of the teething troubles that had afflicted the earlier models (most importantly problems with the cannon, which had previously been prone to jamming),

and functioned reliably in Russia. By this time the Airacobra's performance had been improved by the removal of its wing-mounted machine guns. This reduced weight while still conforming to Soviet standard armament requirements. In the Soviet Union, aerial battles frequently took place at low altitude, where the Airacobra could be deployed to good effect.

In order to overcome supply bottlenecks, a number of P-39s were also delivered to Italy as the Italian aircraft factories were located mainly in the north, which remained under the control of the Fascists.

Unusual features of the P-39 included its 1.5 in. (37 mm) cannon, which fired through the propeller hub, and access to the cockpit via an automobile-like door.

Tricycle undercarriage

The Airacobra was one of the first fighters to adopt a tricycle undercarriage system and pilots experienced some difficulty switching to the new configuration. When taking off in a plane with a tail wheel or tail skid, airmen were accustomed to accelerating, easing the column forward to raise the tail, and then accelerating further in order to facilitate take-off. With a nose wheel, this method had to be avoided at all costs. If pilots were to move the stick forward out of habit before taking off, this could break the front wheel or even cause the plane to nose over.

This was one of the first times a tricycle system—with fragile nose wheel—had been used on a fighter.

BRISTOL BEAUFIGHTER

This heavy, twin-engined fighter was actually intended as an interim solution but proved its worth on every front, making an important contribution to Germany's defeat in the Battle of Britain. The design department at Bristol Aeroplane Company was evidently more far-sighted than the RAF command and in the interwar years turned its attention to the development of a heavy long-range fighter concept before any equivalent specification had been issued.

BRISTOL BEAUFIGHTER MK IF

Two-seat fighter/night-fighter/torpedo bomber
Wingspan: 57 ft. 10 in. (17.63 m)
Length: 41 ft. 8 in. (12.70 m)
Height: 15 ft. 10 in. (4.82 m)
Empty weight: 15,591 lb. (7,072 kg)
Maximum take-off weight: 21,098 lb. (9,570 kg)
Power plant: 2 × Bristol Hercules III air-cooled 14-cylinder double-row radial, 1,550 hp (1,140 kW)
Maximum speed: 309 mph (497 km/h)
Operational ceiling: 26,476 ft. (8,070 m)
Range: 1,168 miles (1,880 km)
Armament: 4 × nose-mounted .787 in. (20 mm) cannon and 6 × wing-mounted Browning .303 in. (7.7 mm) machine guns

Leslie G. Frise

The night-fighter version of the Mk.VIF, showing the flame baffles on its exhaust manifolds and the pointed antennae of its Arrowhead air interception radar.

Bristol's chief designer Leslie G. Frise and his colleague Roy Fedden, the firm's engine designer, had discussed the possibility of developing a single-seat fighter based on a Bristol bomber—either the Beaufort or the Blenheim—and presented their proposals to the Air Ministry in 1938.

This resulted in official specification F.11/37 for a heavily armed fighter with a gun turret for a second crew member. Frise and Fedden designed a twin-engined, two-seater fighter with devastating firepower: four fixed .787 in. (20 mm) cannon located underneath the nose and a further six .303 in. (7.7 mm) machine guns mounted in the wings.

In line with the specification, a dorsal observer's turret was added to the middle of the fuselage. An initial order for 300 Beaufighters was issued and the first prototypes took to the air in July 1939.

The airframe

The name "Beaufighter" was an amalgamation of "Beaufort"—an existing Bristol bomber—and "fighter," and the airframe was in turn an amalgamation of tried and tested—and most importantly available—components. This explains the short development time of less than a year from receipt of order to maiden flight. The wings, tail unit and landing gear were all taken from the Beaufort and the front of the fuselage somewhat shortened, giving the Beaufighter its characteristic snub-nose appearance. The prototypes were powered by one of the company's own engines, the Bristol Hercules.

One unpleasant characteristic of the Bristol was its longitudinal instability, which could be critical during take-off and landing. An attempt was made to solve this problem by fitting later versions with a dihedral tailplane but was not entirely successful.

Operational service

The Beaufighter began its service career with night-fighter unit No. 29 Squadron in October 1940 and achieved its first confirmed night-time victory that same month. Production continued until 1945 in the UK and 1946 in Australia and ran to 5,928 units. The last specimens to remain in service were retired by the RAAF, the Australian Air Force, in 1960.

The Beaufighter also served in a host of other air forces including those of Canada,

A Royal Observer Corps center, where information about aircraft movements was collated.

New Zealand, South Africa, and the USA. Others ended up after the Second World War in Portugal and Turkey. Beaufighters fought in all

A truncated version of the Beaufort fuselage served as the basis for the Beaufighter.

Israel

In 1948, a number of Beaufighters even found their way—via a circuitous route—into the hands of the Israeli army. They were bought by a film company and took off in the UK for what initially appeared to be a perfectly normal film shoot—only the pilots apparently forgot their way home! Hours later, the British aviation authorities learned that the aircraft had disappeared. They were next spotted over the Mediterranean on their way to Israel...

The Beaufighter's unguided rockets could be fired in pairs or all eight at once in a salvo.

the theaters of war as well as over the North Atlantic, the Mediterranean, and the Pacific.

Distribution of duties

During the development phase, it had been assumed at Bristol that the new aircraft would have a top speed of 335 mph (540 km/h) but in reality the Beaufighter Mk.I, powered by twin Bristol Hercules III double-row radials, fell about 25 mph (40 km/h) short of these expectations. Slower than the Hawker Hurricane with, moreover, a higher fuel consumption, the Beaufighter was clearly not suitable as an interceptor for daytime use.

The Beaufighter came into its own at night, however. In 1940 the Luftwaffe had stepped up its night-time bombing raids on England and remained more or less unchecked until the Beaufighter entered service.

Two British Coastal Command Beaufighters attack a German convoy off Norway, inflicting heavy damage on the enemy.

The Beaufighter had all the properties of a good night-fighter: it was fast enough to gain an upper hand over the German bombers and possessed outstanding firepower—one salvo on target was enough to guarantee heavy damage—yet the positioning and arrangement of its guns left enough room for the installation of the newly developed AI Mk.IV radar system. The space taken up in the Beaufort by the bomb aimer was converted into a covered nose, the bottom of which accommodated the plane's cannon.

The Bristol Blenheim Mk.IF, which was equipped with radar, had previously been used as a night-fighter but was slow, with a top speed of 267 mph (430 km/h). The Beaufighter delivered the performance this temporary solution had lacked. Before long, however, different engines had to be used because the bomber fleet—and the Short Stirling in particular—had priority. This resulted at the end of 1941 in the Mk.II, powered by Rolls-Royce Merlin XX engines. The more powerful Rolls-Royce Griffon was also used in some specimens.

The Beaufighter protected the night skies above Britain until the appearance of a much faster aircraft, the De Havilland Mosquito, but its time was by no means over. Mk.X, one of the major variants, with production running to some 2,205 units, entered service in 1943. Powered by two Bristol Hercules XIV engines, the Mk.X was capable of a top speed of 320 mph (515 km/h). In addition to its standard armament, it was also equipped with an 18 in. (457 mm) torpedo and was deployed successfully against shipping. This Coastal Command variant was also known as the "Torbeau."

The Mk.Xs deployed by Fighter Command were identical in design except that they were fitted with wing racks for eight 90 lb. (41 kg) rockets, allowing the Beaufighter to be used successfully in a ground-attack role.

Variants C and F

Letters C and F were derived from the air force arms deploying that particular version. C stood for Coastal Command, an arm of the RAF created primarily for coastal protection duties. An F was appended to the model numbers of those aircraft used by Fighter Command.

In addition to their different engines—Bristol Hercules, Rolls-Royce Merlin and others— the Beaufighter variants also differed in terms of armament. Common to both were the four nose-mounted cannon. The Fighter Command aircraft were also fitted with six wing-mounted machine guns and subsequently racks under the fuselage and wings for eight RP-3 rockets and two bombs. Coastal Command, meanwhile, had its Beaufighters fitted with one or two machine guns in the observer's turret and a torpedo.

The cockpit of a Beaufighter. The layout of the numerous instruments seems confusing but was typical of the day.

DE HAVILLAND D.H. 98 MOSQUITO

The Mosquito's smooth wooden fuselage was an important factor in its speed. The example shown here is an RAAF (Royal Australian Air Force) D.H. 98.

The De Havilland Mosquito was a quirk of aviation history that owed its fame to its ability to master tasks for which it was not originally intended. It was conceived as a light, fast bomber, but developed during its service history into the most versatile Allied warplane of the Second World War. It was a fighter, night-fighter, reconnaissance plane, bomber, torpedo bomber, submarine hunter, and more besides. Its technology was simultaneously pioneering and outmoded. Its wooden fuselage made it invisible to radar, light, and fast—so fast, in fact, that it could simply outpace pursuing German fighters at altitude.

DE HAVILLAND D.H. 98 NF XIX MOSQUITO

Two-seat night-fighter
Wingspan: 54 ft. 2 in. (16.50 m)
Length: 41 ft. 11 in. (12.77 m)
Height: 15 ft. 9 in. (4.79 m)
Empty weight: 15,968 lb. (7,243 kg)
Maximum take-off weight: 19,621 lb. (8,900 kg)
Power plant: 2 × Rolls-Royce Merlin 25, 1,635 hp (1,200 kW) each
Maximum speed: 375 mph (604 km/h)
Operational ceiling: 27,887 ft. (8,500 m)
Range: 1,905 miles (3,065 km)
Armament: 4 × British Hispano .787 in. (20 mm) cannon

Pursuing an individual path

With the Mosquito, the design team around Geoffrey de Havilland was pursuing a highly unconventional path that seemed completely out of sync with the ideas of the day. The RAF command was therefore highly skeptical of the design. It was only the outstanding performance of the prototype that convinced them of the value of this private initiative.

Initially it was decided to dispense with defensive guns and armor because the Mosquito was so fast it could easily outpace most Luftwaffe fighters. Some variants were even able to gain an upper hand over the Spitfire in combat training. In one sense the

Mosquito was old-fashioned: it was a warplane constructed entirely of wood at a time when all-metal construction had become the norm. At the same time, however, it was extremely modern. Composite materials—such as plywood, out of which it was made—are materials of first choice today when a combination of lightness and strength is called for.

The Mosquito lived up to its name: it could attack in small groups and administer a painful sting to the enemy before escaping unscathed. With its elegant lines it was also a beautiful aircraft although without the temperament of a diva.

Geoffrey "D.H." de Havilland, the Mosquito's designer, in a photograph dating from the First World War.

The lead plane ("A-Apple") attacks a supply ship in the Norwegian harbor of Sandefjord.

No. 143 Squadron—another successful attack against shipping off the coast of Norway.

In terms of its effect, a salvo of unguided rockets can be compared to a broadside from a battleship.

Geoffrey de Havilland

The British aviation pioneer and designer Geoffrey de Havilland had founded his own company, De Havilland Aircraft Co. Ltd., in 1920. This new company was highly successful. One of its many successes was the Tiger Moth, adopted by the RAF as its main trainer. A total of 8,500 Tiger Moths were built and the plane remained in service until 1951.

In August 1936 the British Air Ministry invited de Havilland to submit proposals for a medium bomber (specification P.13/36) that could also perform a reconnaissance role. In order to minimize the time it spent over enemy territory, the new aircraft was to be capable of reaching a cruise speed of 280 mph (450 km/h) at 16,400 ft. (5,000 m).

De Havilland was not interested. At this time his company was focusing on the construction of civil aircraft. By July 1938, however, the threat posed by the Third Reich had become so real that his thoughts turned back to the idea of a light bomber.

De Havilland and his designers R.E. Bishop, R.M. Clarkson, and C.T. Wilkins pursued new-old methods, favoring wood as a construction material. Their main argument was the ratio of weight to strength. Other than in terms of torsional rigidity (ability to withstand twisting), wood compares well with duralumin and steel in this respect. Another convincing argument was the availability of wood. Whereas metals were classed as scarce and vital to the war effort, wood was not. The labor shortage during times of war was another factor in favor of wood: the concept being considered by de Havilland could be realized by carpenters and piano-makers. The decision not to equip the plane with defensive weapons reduced weight further and boosted the aircraft's maximum speed.

The Royal Air Force and the prototypes

The RAF was unsure about the Mosquito. The commander in chief, Sir Arthur "Bomber" Harris, favored carpet bombing by large, four-engined bombers such as the Avro Lancaster or Handley Page Halifax. Nevertheless, at De Havilland they continued to believe in the eventual success of their concept, and work progressed on the prototype as the Battle of Britain raged in the sky above. A bomb would fall in the immediate vicinity of the plant at least once every five days and the De Havilland workers spent 25 percent of their working day in the air-raid shelter. Despite the difficulties work continued, and on November 25, 1940 after ten months and 26 days, the maiden flight took place with Geoffrey de Havilland Jr at the controls. Bomber prototype W4050 needed to be revised, however, as the Air Ministry had postponed the concept of a fast, unarmed bomber in favor of a heavily armed fighter and amended the supply contracts accordingly. The new prototype (W4052) flew on May 15, 1941, piloted by the head of the company, and entered active service four months later.

The cockpit of a night-fighter Mosquito. The observer's radar screen can be seen in the top right of the picture.

Radio detection and ranging-radar

The precision of night-time operations was significantly improved by the development of radar guidance systems. Practical systems "for the detection of remote metal objects using electronic waves"—as the procedure was first described in Christian Hülsmeyer's 1904 patent specification for a *telemobiloscope*—were developed in both the UK and Germany during the 1930s. In 1934 the Scot Robert Watson-Watt was asked by the British military to investigate the tactical possibilities of

so-called "death rays." Watson-Watt proved that no such source of energy existed but came up with a radio wave detection system almost as a by-product of his research. His work led to the development of the Chain Home early warning system, an almost invisible defensive wall along the south coast of England. Along with the results of research conducted by Alan Reeves and Frank Jones, this was subsequently developed into the OBOE (Observer Bombing Over Enemy) bomber guidance system.

A Mosquito launches a rocket attack off the Norwegian coast during the final winter of the war.

NF (night-fighter) and FB (fighter-bomber)

The NF II night-fighter, of which 465 were built, entered service in 1942. Armed with four .787 in. (20 mm) cannon and four Browning .303 in. (7.7 mm) machine guns, the NF II was intended for a home defense role. Although camouflage paint reduced its top speed, it nevertheless posed a serious threat to enemy intruders. Among its successes was the destruction of more than 600 German V1 rockets.

One problem experienced by the early Mosquito night-fighters related to the radiators built into the leading edges of the wings. During night-time operations, Mosquitoes had to get very close to their opponents in order to stand a good chance of success and, as a result, enemy aircraft would often shatter into many pieces. The Mosquito's radiators would often be damaged by wreckage and it was not uncommon for aircraft to limp back to base on one engine.

Initially the nose-mounted Arrowhead airborne radar system A.I. Mk.IV or V was used, which took its name from the shape of its antennae.

Production

Taking into account licensed production, a total of 7,781 Mosquitoes were built. The type produced in the largest numbers (2,718) was the FB (fighter-bomber), one particular variant of which (the FB XVIII) was armed with a Molins 2.24 in. (57 mm) 6-pounder gun for use against ships. This armor-busting gun—which weighed almost a ton!—had a powerful recoil, necessitating a head-on approach during which the Mosquito was vulnerable. Before long the 6-pounder was therefore replaced by eight unguided rockets.

Construction method

The Mosquito construction method was way ahead of its day. The fuselage was manufactured in two halves, greatly facilitating the installation of the electronics and control mechanisms. The material—Canadian birch plywood with an intermediate layer of balsawood—was developed specially for De Havilland. In order to increase rigidity the wings were constructed as a single unit and positioned afterwards. The fuselage was fitted with bulkheads and ribs in order to increase its structural strength. Particular care was paid to the aerodynamics: streamlined forms and an extremely smooth external skin reduced drag to a minimum. The D.H. 98 proved extremely rugged, capable of taking hits and flying on one engine. It had numerous nicknames—including "Mossie," "Wooden Wonder," and "Termite's Dream"—and was extremely well loved by its crews. The Mosquito also suffered the fewest losses—just 193—of any British Second World War bomber.

Designations

The letters incorporated in the names of the different variants refer to the intended role of that particular model.

These were:

B for bomber

F for fighter

NF for night-fighter

FB for fighter-bomber

PR for photo-reconnaissance

T for trainer

TT for target tug, a role in which Mosquitoes were used by the RAF until 1961.

Armorers reloading a D.H. 98. Up to eight 1.07 in. (27.2 mm) rockets could be carried on under-wing launch rails.

MESSER-SCHMITT ME 163 KOMET

The Messerschmitt Me 163 united two revolutionary concepts: it was the first tailless swept-wing and rocket-powered aircraft to go into production. Its climbing ability was sensational for the day, yet rocket engines soon turned out to be a technological blind alley as a means of aircraft propulsion.

MESSERSCHMITT ME 163 B-1A KOMET
Single-seat rocket-powered interceptor
Wingspan: 30 ft. 8 in. (9.35 m)
Length: 19 ft. 2 in. (5.85 m)
Height: 9 ft. (2.74 m)
Empty weight: 4,211 lb. (1,910 kg)
Maximum take-off weight: 9,504 lb. (4,310 kg)
Power plant: 1 × Walter HWK 109-509-A 1 liquid-fuel rocket producing 3,305 lbf (14.70 kN) thrust
Maximum speed: 597 mph (960 km/h)
Operational ceiling: 39,501 ft. (12,040 m)
Endurance: 7.5 minutes
Range: 50 miles (80 km)
Armament: 2 × Rheinmetall-Borsig MK 108 1.18 in. (30 mm) cannon with 60 rounds each

The Me 163 was the first example of a rocket engine being used to power a mass-produced aircraft.

The Walter HWK rocket engine

The basic concept developed by Dr. Alexander Lippisch was an experimental aircraft designed for research into breaking the sound barrier. The Me 163's sensational rate of climb made it an appealing prospect as a fighter.

The description "rocket-powered interceptor" indicates that the Walter HWK 109-509-A 1 was an actual liquid-fuelled rocket engine with combustion chamber and blast pipe rather than simply a solid-fuel rocket. From engine variant 509D onwards, two extremely volatile fuels, the oxidizer (or *T-Stoff*) hydrogen peroxide (H_2O_2) and the fuel itself (the *C-Stoff*),

hydrazine hydrate, were brought into contact
with each other in the combustion chamber,
producing thrust via a jet nozzle. This allowed
previously unthinkable speeds to be achieved.

Compressibility and climb rate

The Me 163 could travel at speeds approaching
those at which air compressibility was a
problem and aircraft could become difficult to
control. Although the plane's design would
probably have allowed it to cope with the
speed of sound, this was never put to the test.

The plane's rate of climb was also
sensational. It could reach 39,370 ft. (12,000 m)
in just three minutes but, unlike conventional
engines, its rocket engine did not rely on
oxygen and was therefore capable of powering
the plane even higher, to some 52,500 ft.
(16,000 m), an altitude beyond the reach not
only of propeller aircraft but also of the best jet
of the day, the Me 262.

Development of the Me 163

The Me 163 was the result of aerodynamic
research conducted by Dr. Alexander Lippisch
with two gliders developed by the German
institute for glider research (*Deutsches
Forschungsinstitut für Segelflug*), the DFS 39
and 194. Dr. Lippisch's gliders were tailless,
swept-wing aircraft that served as the original
test bed for experiments with rocket
propulsion and its effect on the flying
characteristics of tailless aircraft.

As a rocket-powered aircraft, the Heinkel-
built experimental He 176, had already flown,
it was only natural that Dr. Lippisch should
want to use a similar Walter rocket engine.
From early 1939, Dr. Lippisch conducted his
research at Messerschmitt AG in Augsburg.
This resulted in the Me 163 A. Following

successful glide tests by Heini Dittmar, rocket
engines were fitted and powered flight tests
were carried out at Peenemünde in summer
1941. Deliveries of the first production models
began in early 1944. Due to delays with the
supply of engines and the time required for
testing and the training of pilots and ground
crew, it was May 1944 before the Me 163 B-1a
was ready to be deployed as a day-fighter
against the B-17s of the US Eighth Air Force.
Data concerning the number of bombers shot
down by the rocket fighter varies considerably
as aerial victories all but ceased to be recorded
during the later stages of the war. The figure is
thought to be around 20–60.

The Me 163 Komet could achieve a rate of
climb of 13,125 ft. (4,000 m) per minute but only
for periods of 180 seconds.

*The Me 163 Komet
could achieve a rate
of climb of 13,125 ft.
(4,000 m) per
minute but only
for periods of
180 seconds.*

Seven minutes of maximum performance

The Komet's clear advantage lay in its rate of climb and maximum speed, which were astonishing for the day. The initial rate of climb of the Me 163 B-1 was 252 ft. (80 m) per second! With its engine running, it was virtually unstoppable. This enormous speed presented problems when attacking bombers, however. In order to avoid ramming a foe, the Me 163 had to veer away at a distance of 650 ft. (200 m) from its target. Due to the relatively short range of the MK 108 (rate of fire 600 rounds per minute), however, the furthest firing distance was around 2,130 ft. (650 m). This left the pilot with a window of just 1,480 ft. (450 m) in which to fire, a distance covered by the Me 163 in one or two seconds. The huge difference in speed between the fighter and its prey made it almost impossible for the pilot to successfully take aim and it is hardly surprising that so many Me 163 pilots missed when attacking US bombers.

Brandis airfield

The small propeller on the Komet's nose was not a form of emergency propulsion but was for the generation of electricity.

Because of the rocket fighter's extremely short operational range, it had to be based either in the direct flight path of the enemy bomber streams or else in the immediate vicinity of the object to be protected. The first fighter unit to receive the Komet was I. Gruppe Jagdgeschwader 400, which was equipped with the Me 163 B-1a in May 1944 and transferred to Brandis airfield outside Leipzig to protect the Leuna chemical plant. A second JG 400 squadron was formed and equipped with Me 163s and stationed in Venlo in the Netherlands, but when it was discovered that no enemy bombers were flying to Germany via that route, this second unit was also moved to Brandis. This meant around 40 Komets and a corresponding number of pilots were based at Brandis. This effective combat unit was also given responsibility for defending the Buna plant near Halle, which meant the entire force of Me 163s was deployed in protecting the manufacture of synthetic fuels vital to Germany's war effort.

The chase

After take-off, the Me 163s would climb to an interception altitude of 32,800 ft. (10,000 m) and would then have a maximum of four minutes in which to attack. Walter subsequently developed a power plant with an additional cruise combustion chamber, which extended the combat time to nine minutes. Operations were extremely dangerous due to the high volatility of the fuels and their unpredictable response to vibration. The landing gear consisted of a double-wheeled dolly jettisoned after take-off. The Komet landed on an extensible, sprung skid located forward of the center of gravity.

The Me 163's accident statistics were almost as impressive as its performance data. Numerous aircraft came to grief when landing, and many fatal injuries were caused by the corrosive fuel—one of the tanks was located behind the pilot. The pilots' protective suits offered only limited protection against this danger. It was therefore essential that pilots used up all their fuel during the sortie and began their landing approach with empty tanks. During this glide back to base, the Me 163 was extremely vulnerable to attack by Allied escort fighters.

Another problem occurred when pilots jettisoned their landing gear too early during take-off: the wheels sometimes bounced back and damaged the plane or even caused it to crash.

Refueling had to be carried out by special highly trained staff under the safest possible conditions. If even the smallest quantities of the two different fuels accidentally came into contact with each other, the inevitable outcome would be an uncontrolled explosion in which neither pilot nor crew would stand a chance.

As a result partly of the considerable technical difficulties involved and partly because the anticipated military success never materialized, the Me 163 was withdrawn from service before the end of the war.

The volatile nature of the fuel made taking off extremely hazardous for Komet pilots.

The Focke-Wulf Fw 190 may not have been as popular as a number of other models but for a period it was the best fighter on the Western Front.

FOCKE-WULF Fw 190

The Fw 190 "Würger" ("shrike") represents the pinnacle of German fighter design during the Second World War and ranks among the very best of its type. Its appearance over the English Channel early in 1941 relegated the best British fighter of the day—the Spitfire Mk.V—to a distant second.

FOCKE-WULF FW 190A-8
Single-seat fighter/fighter-bomber
Wingspan: 34 ft. 5 in. (10.50 m)
Length: 29 ft. 10 in. (9.10 m)
Height: 13 ft. 11 in. (3.95 m)
Empty weight: 6,989 lb. (3,170 kg)
Maximum take-off weight: 10,803 lb. (4,900 kg)
Power plant: 1 × BMW 801D2 14-cylinder double-row radial, 1,730 hp (1,272 kW)
Maximum speed: 395 mph (635 km/h) for short periods with the GM-1 nitrous oxide injection unit
Operational ceiling: 37,434 ft. (11,410 m)
Range: 559 miles (900 km)
Armament: 2 × Rheinmetall-Borsig .512 in. (13 mm) machine guns and 4 × Mauser 151/20 .787 in. (20 mm) cannon or 2 × .787 in. (20 mm) and 2 × 1.18 in. (30 mm) cannon

Kurt Tank (in overalls), the FW 190's chief designer, was a pilot as well as an engineer.

Kurt Tank and his team

When Professor Henrich Focke left Focke-Wulf Flugzeugbau in 1932, engineer Kurt Tank became head of flight testing and the design department and was made technical director the following year. Among the better-known aircraft developed under his supervision were the FW 56 "Stösser," FW 200 "Condor," and FW 44 "Stieglitz." Kurt Tank was not simply a theoretician but a pilot through and through. He bore the title *Flugkapitän* and tested numerous models personally.

Operation Donnerkeil

Following operations in the Atlantic, three of Germany's biggest warships (heavy cruiser *Prinz Eugen* and battleships *Scharnhorst* and *Gneisenau*) lay at anchor in the French naval port of Brest. Attacks by a total of 299 British bombers had left them unscathed. After the sinking of the *Bismarck*, the prospects for further German campaigns on the open seas looked bleak and it seemed advisable to withdraw the three capital ships through the English Channel to German harbors. The Luftwaffe operation to protect the vast convoy that set out on February 11,

1942 bore the graphic name "Donnerkeil" ("thunderbolt"). Over 200 British fighters, bombers, and torpedo bombers tried in vain to prevent the break-out. The German convoy passed through the Channel in daylight practically under the noses of the British on February 12 and arrived almost unharmed in Kiel (*Gneisenau* and *Prinz Eugen*) and Wilhelmshaven (*Scharnhorst*) the following day. Tactical command of the German fighters and night-fighters used in the operation was held by Oberstleutnant Adolf Galland, commander of fighter wing Jagdgeschwader 26.

A successor to the Bf 109

The Fw 190 was intended as a successor to the Messerschmitt Bf 109, and a development contract to this effect was awarded by Ernst Udet, head of the technical department of the Reich Air Ministry, in 1938. The first prototype (V 1) took off for its maiden flight on June 1, 1939. The second prototype (V 2) flew in October and was powered to over 375 mph (600 km/h) by its 14-cylinder BMW 139 radial

The "Black 12" of Captain Bruno Stolle (8. Gruppe Jagdgeschwader 2) being made ready in Brest, France, for a combat mission.

engine. Unfortunately the engine proved unreliable, making the cockpit unbearably hot, among other problems. Even after the BMW 139 had been replaced by the higher-performance BMW 801, which had an improved cooling system, excessive temperatures in the cabin remained a major cause of complaint until

The extremely "tidy" and clearly laid out cockpit of the FW 190.

When used as a fighter-bomber, the FW 190 carried a 550 lb. (250 kg) bomb.

mid-1942. Attempts to remedy the problem by moving the pilot's seat further back, reducing the engine's frontal area, and fitting a more powerful radiator fan with a more efficient fan wheel were only partially successful.

Pre-production aircraft, designated Fw 190 A-0, were tested at the Luftwaffe's central test center in Rechlin. As it was intended that the Bf 109 should remain the Luftwaffe's standard fighter, there was initially no great urgency to develop the Fw 190 to production readiness. This was just as well. Although the aircraft displayed exceptionally good flying characteristics—its speed, roll rate maneuverability, and handling met with unanimous enthusiasm from the pilots—its BMW engines gave rise to constant complaints. Most of the teething problems were remedied through close collaboration between members of Jagdgeschwader 26 "Schlageter"—under the leadership of Oberleutnant Otto Behrens and Fliegerstabsingenieur Battmer—on the one hand and Kurt Tank and his assistant Willi Kaether on the other.

II Gruppe Jagdgeschwader 26 "Schlageter"

In summer 1941, Jagdgeschwader 26 became the first unit to be equipped with the Fw 190. Its task was to secure the skies over the English Channel. It soon became clear that the Focke-Wulf was superior to the Bf 109 in almost every respect. Only in terms of speed at higher altitudes—over around 16,400–19,700 ft. (5,000–6,000 m)—and rate of climb did the Messerschmitt have the advantage. In addition to better overall performance and handling, the Fw 190 also possessed a better (wider track) undercarriage and was considerably more bulletproof thanks to its air-cooled radial engine. The Fw 190 was highly unusual as a powerful gun platform that was also an extremely agile dogfighter.

One of the Fw 190's first major combat operations was to secure air superiority for the break-out of a fleet of major German warships from Brest through the English Channel to Kiel and Wilhelmshaven (Operation Donnerkeil).

GM-1 injection

Piston engines suck in air from the surrounding environment and have an optimum operating environment with relation to ambient pressure: the so-called "full pressure zone." With increasing altitude the ambient pressure (air pressure) drops, and as an aircraft climbs its engine performance diminishes. One way to increase high-altitude performance is to boost the induction air pressure. Another is to inject oxygen into the engine. The GM-1 system injected N_2O (nitrous oxide), as this releases more oxygen in the combustion chamber than ambient air would, boosting engine output for limited periods of time. Another advantage of nitrous oxide is that cold air absorbs more oxygen and the N_2O cooled the charge air in the BMW-801 engine as it condensed.

Operational service

The unusual thing about the Fw 190 when it first saw action in 1941 was without doubt its bulletproof air-cooled BMW radial engine combined with excellent handling, high speeds, and powerful armament comprising both cannon and machine guns. Probably the most decisive aspect of its development, however, was its versatility, which made it an efficient multi-purpose weapon and munitions carrier. Unlike the Bf 109, it could be used not only as a fighter but in a wide range of other tactical roles too. On the minus side was the

An alternative weapons configuration: a Focke-Wulf carrying eight 110 lb. (50 kg) SC50 bombs.

relatively poor performance of the early models at altitude. This shortcoming was remedied in model Fw 190D, which was equipped with a liquid-cooled inline engine.

The appearance of the Fw 190 above the English Channel gave the RAF an unpleasant shock as the German fighter was clearly superior to the Spitfire Mk.V. Because it was so unusual for a German fighter to have a radial engine, the British initially assumed the new fighters to be captured US Curtisses. They then had a stroke of luck when a German pilot became confused and landed at an airfield in the south of England (some sources claim he deserted). This gave the RAF an opportunity to evaluate an Fw 190 in detail and compare it to the Spitfire.

The insights gained from this experience resulted in British specification F.2/43, which eventually gave rise to the Spitfire Mk.IX. This new version of the Spitfire, recognizable from its slightly longer nose, was equipped with a new Rolls-Royce Merlin 60 engine. This gave it an edge over the Bf 109 and put it on a par with

the Fw 190. This provides a clear illustration of the arms race at work. A new and better fighter from one side provokes the development of an improved model by the other and so on.

It could also be claimed that the decisive factor in this arms spiral was the level of training received by those in whose hands the weapons were placed. Although national pride played an important part, the best fighter planes on either side were only as good as the pilots who flew them.

Model Fw 190D ("Langnase")

The most unusual Fw 190 variant was model D (1944–1945), nicknamed "Langnase" ("long-nose"). The shape of the Fw 190D's fuselage differed radically from that of its predecessors. Instead of the air-cooled BMW radial, the "Langnase" was equipped with a liquid-cooled 12-cylinder inline Junkers Jumo 213. This new power plant meant the Focke-Wulf was now effective at high altitude too. Many German and Allied pilots considered this model to be the best German fighter of the Second World War. Nevertheless, the BMW radial was returned to for versions F and G.

Auxiliary equipment sets

Like all German fighters, Fw 190s were adapted to their intended uses with auxiliary equipment sets. These sets of standard equipment for different roles were designated by the letter "R" (for *Rüstsatz*) followed by a

Fw 190s of 7. Jagdgeschwader 2 "Richthofen." The undercarriage retracted inwardly into the undersides of the wings. This gave it a wide track and good taxiing characteristics.

number and could consist of drop tanks, bombs, torpedoes, rockets, rocket launchers, additional under-wing cannon, or radar systems. The fighter-bomber version, for example, used equipment set R1, comprising two under-wing bomb racks for 110 lb. (50 kg) bombs or alternatively sets R2 or R3 (two MK 108 or 103 cannon mounted in or under the wing) for ground attack. In an interceptor role against US four-engined bombers, the Fw 190 achieved considerable success with set R6, comprising two 8.27 in. (210 mm) WGr 42 rocket grenades fired from tubes under the wings or R4M comprising .827 in. (21 mm) rockets carried beneath the wings.

One special version of the Fw 190 was equipped with reinforced armor plating and took part in ram attacks against US bombers. The Focke-Wulf was used in a fighter-bomber role in support of ground forces primarily during the Russian campaign but also during the Ardennes offensive. Due to their additional weight, the auxiliary equipment sets impaired the fighter's performance to varying degrees, rendering it vulnerable to attacks by Allied fighters.

The Fw 190 as a night-fighter

In 1943, incoming Allied bombers started to use strips of tin foil—called "window" or "chaff" by the English and *Düppel* by the Germans—to interfere with German radar. For a short while, use of two-seater night-fighters equipped with radar was interrupted and single-engined day-fighters were instead deployed at night above those cities at risk of being bombed.

Enemy bombers lit up by searchlights or recognizable as silhouettes on moonlit nights were visually identified and attacked on sight by fighters. The pilots would simply fly into the middle of the bomber streams unprotected. This disordered style of fighting was referred to by the Germans as the *Wilde Sau* ("wild pig") system.

YAKOVLEV YAK-3

As an air superiority fighter, escort fighter for heavy ground-attack aircraft, or as a ground-attack aircraft itself, the Yak-3 posed a serious threat to its opponents. Thanks to its outstanding maneuverability and speed, it was a good match for the German Bf 109 and Fw 190.

Design emphasis—aerodynamics and weight

Soviet aircraft production under wartime conditions was extremely difficult. Not only did factories have to be shifted ever deeper into Russian territory as German troops started to advance in summer 1941, they also had to work flat out over the following years to replace lost aircraft.

For this reason the Yakovlev Yak-3 was not a brand new design but a development of its predecessor, the Yak-1.

The air intakes in the wing roots were an important feature that differentiated the Yak-3 from other Yakovlev fighters.

Chief designer Alexander Sergeyevich Yakovlev and his team at the state design bureau OKB-115 were under pressure to come up with an effective fighter for altitudes of up to 16,400 ft. (5,000 m) as quickly as possible.

Their solution was to rework the tried and tested airframe of the Yak-1. The same wing design was adopted but on a significantly smaller scale, with shorter span, reduced depth, and a surface area of 156 sq ft. (14.50 sq m).

To save weight the wooden spar was exchanged for a duralumin one—as with model Yak-9, which, incredibly, was ready to enter service before the Yak-3. The oil cooler was fitted into the wing roots and insides of the wings, and the canopy was reduced in size and aerodynamically shaped (without supports) at the front.

The end product was one of the lightest fighters of the Second World War, weighing in at under three tons.

Testing

It became evident in spring 1943 that the Yak-3 was an extremely successful design. Its maneuverability is generally described in superlatives. A full 360-degree turn, for example, could be performed by the Yak-3 in under 20 seconds—and it could climb at the same time! In other words, it could reappear swiftly in a superior attacking position on the tail of the opponent that had previously been following it. The technical sophistication and combat effectiveness of the Yakovlev is illustrated by the fact that German fighter units on the Eastern Front were instructed "to avoid engaging the Yakovlev fighters lacking the under-nose oil cooler below 16,400 ft (5,000 m)." For German fighter pilots, the missing oil cooler was the feature that distinguished the Yak-3 from the more ponderous Yak-1, Yak-7, and Yak-9 fighters.

Its control surfaces were wonderfully responsive, although it was claimed the Yak-3 had a tendency to suddenly drop a wing when coming in to land if the pilot failed to hold a relatively high speed. Another shortcoming was that a high minimum speed was required in order to prevent stalling as the smaller wings did not generate enough lift during slow flight.

The second engine

The second engine to be used in the continually upgraded Yakovlev was the Klimov VK-107, which was first fitted in late fall 1943. Developing 1,620 hp, the VK-107 powered the fighter to a speed of 447 mph (720 km/h) in tests. The first production model to receive the

Waiting for the order to take off. In Germany the Yakovlev was considered an extremely dangerous fighter.

new engine was the Yak-3U, the wings of which were of all-metal construction whereas earlier wings had been part-wood, part-metal.

Production

Production of Yak-3s continued until the beginning of 1946, by which time a total of 4,848 had been delivered to the Soviet forces. But the fighter's history did not end there. Since 1991, the Yakovlev company has been building brand new examples from the original designs for wealthy Second World War aircraft enthusiasts.

The Yak-3's efficient aerodynamic design and low weight made an important contribution to its outstanding performance.

The P-61 Black Widow, a heavy, twin-boom night-fighter, was more maneuverable than its dimensions would suggest.

NORTHROP P-61 BLACK WIDOW

The P-61 was one of the most efficient heavy night-fighters of the Second World War. Also known as the "Black Widow," it was the first-ever purpose-built night-fighter. It was guided by the SCR-520 airborne radar system, had a very good range, and boasted an unrivalled arsenal of weapons. Entering service towards the end of the war, its greatest enemy was time as it was ultimately rendered superfluous by changing tactical requirements.

NORTHROP P-61B
BLACK WIDOW
Night-fighter
Wingspan: 66 ft. (20.12 m)
Length: 49 ft. 7 in. (15.11 m)
Height: 14 ft. 8 in. (4.46 m)
Empty weight: 27,000 lb. (12,247 kg)
Maximum take-off weight: 38,001 lb. (17,237 kg)
Power plant: 2 × Pratt & Whitney R-2800-65 Double Wasp 18-cylinder double-row radials, 2,082 hp (1,492 kW) each
Maximum speed: 363 mph (585 km/h)
Operational ceiling: 34,908 ft. (10,640 m)
Range: 2,995 miles (4,820 km)
Armament: 4 × fixed, forward-firing Hispano .787 in. (20 mm) cannon (with 200 rounds each) mounted in the lower fuselage, 4 × Browning M2 .50 in. (12.7 mm) machine guns (with 560 rounds each) in a remote-controlled rotating turret on top of the fuselage, under-wing racks for 4 × 1,600 lb. (726 kg) bombs

An American for Europe

In 1940 the RAF had a far more pressing need for a night-bomber than the USAAC—the USA was, after all, spared the terror of nightly bombing raids. Nevertheless, senior commanders in the US Army Air Corps were sensitive to the tactical needs of their Allies and shortly after a plea for help was received from the UK to the effect that it had reached production capacity and required help from Big Brother, a specification was issued in the USA in October 1940.

Northrop's tender was accepted and it was awarded a contract to build two prototypes (designated XP-61) followed by an order for 13 pre-production models (YP-61). Although the maiden flight of the prototypes did not take place until mid-1942, 150 production aircraft had already been ordered and the first deliveries were made in October 1943. The production start-up proved so problematic, however, that only 34 aircraft were built during the first year. The dorsal gun turret caused the tail booms to vibrate, while supply bottlenecks and moving the cannon from the wings to the fuselage accounted for further delays.

Flight trials

Although the Northrop was a heavyweight—at considerably over 13 tons empty, it weighed as much as a medium bomber—it handled impeccably and was able to perform all the maneuvers expected of a fighter. It also had an outstanding low-speed flying capability thanks to innovative wing-mounted high-lift

devices—spoilers and special "Zap flaps"—a cross between split flap and slotted flap—that ran almost the entire length of the wings. The speed range in which the P-61 remained fully maneuverable lay between 367 mph (590 km/h) and 90 mph (145 km/h). This meant it could close in on an opponent at high speed and then brake hard in order to get into a commanding position.

Theater of operations

By the time the P-61 entered operational service in Europe in May 1944, the tactical situation had fundamentally changed. The German invasion of Britain had failed and with it the RAF's overriding commitment and significance to national defense—now Nazi Germany became the target of nightly bombing raids. At the time of the Normandy landings (D-Day, June 6, 1944), only a hundred P-61s were stationed in Europe. This relatively small number performed an intruder role, penetrating deep into enemy territory in order to attack strategic targets. In addition to its four 1,600 lb. (726 kg) bombs, the Black Widow's four .787 in. (20 mm) cannon and four .50 in. (12.7 mm) machine guns meant it was more than capable of defending itself.

Although the Black Widow was an extremely successful design, changing tactical requirements rendered it ultimately superfluous.

A fighter the size of a medium bomber. The P-61's maximum take-off weight was some 19 tons.

CHANCE VOUGHT F4U CORSAIR

The Corsair was the first single-engined fighter with a power output of over 2,000 hp (1,492 kW) and the first US plane to exceed 400 mph (650 km/h). This carrier-borne and land-based single-seat fighter remained in service with the US forces from 1943 until the Korean War. The last F4U was supplied in 1952 and withdrawn from active service in December 1954. It remained in service with smaller air forces, however, until the end of the 1960s.

CHANCE VOUGHT F4U-1 CORSAIR
Single-seat fighter/fighter-bomber
Wingspan: 41 ft. (12.49 m)
Length: 33 ft. 4 in. (10.17 m)
Height: 15 ft. (4.58 m)
Empty weight: 8,968 lb. (4,068 kg)
Maximum take-off weight: 13,120 lb. (5,951 kg)
Power plant: 1 × Pratt & Whitney R-2800-8(W) Double Wasp 18-cylinder double-row radial, 2,000 hp (1,492 kW) take-off rating
Maximum speed: 414 mph (667 km/h)
Operational ceiling: 37,073 ft. (11,300 m)
Range: 1,009 miles (1,624 km)
Armament: 6 × wing-mounted Colt/Browning .50 in. (12.7 mm) M2 machine guns with 390 rounds each, maximum bomb load (F4U-1D) 3,968 lb. (1,800 kg)

The Corsair's 18-cylinder Double Wasp radial produced 2,000 hp (1,492 kW) at take-off—a first for the USA.

Gull wing design

In 1938 the Bureau of Aeronautics invited tenders for a new high-performance single-seat fighter for the US Navy's carrier fleet. Rex B. Beisel, chief designer of the Texan Chance Vought Corporation, explored the idea of achieving maximum speed via minimum drag. His basic approach was to combine the

most powerful engine available with an extremely slender fuselage and the largest possible propeller. In order to prevent the Hamilton Standard triple-blade propeller from striking the ground or carrier deck when taking off or landing, an inverted gull wing design was selected. The landing gear was positioned directly beneath the kink in the wings and retracted backwards 90 degrees into the wing. The new Pratt & Whitney R-2800-8 Double Wasp double-row radial engine was chosen, not least because Chance Vought and Pratt & Whitney were both owned by United Aircraft Corporation.

Initial difficulties and later history

The Corsair's service and production life are unrivaled, except perhaps by the F-4 Phantom, but this disguises the fact that it did not have an easy start.

Prototype XF4U-1 first flew on May 29, 1940 and the first production aircraft left the assembly line on June 25, 1942. The US Navy initially rejected the aircraft because it was (and would remain) an unforgiving plane to fly. The aft positioning of the cockpit considerably impaired visibility during landing, which was uncomfortable at the best of times. The gull wing design and torque of the large engine gave the F4U a tendency to get into a curve that was difficult to control as it left the flight deck. Landing accidents mounted and the Corsair proved a nightmare for inexperienced pilots. In order to improve the aircraft's flying characteristics, the two ailerons were eventually increased in size. The type eventually entered service with the US Navy in February 1943 and it quickly won air superiority above the Pacific. The Corsair's

distinctive noise led the Japanese to give it the nickname "Whistling Death."

A sixth of the entire F4U production went to the Royal Navy, which also deployed its Corsairs on carriers in the Pacific. The type was seldom used in Europe.

The Corsair was so successful that it continued to be used in the Korean War, predominantly—and successfully—in a ground-attack role. It was able to carry bomb loads that would have been unthinkable for the first US jets. But it was also effective against jets. On November 8, 1950, navy pilot W.T. Amen shot down a MiG-15 in his F4U.

The fighter-bomber version of the Vought F4U—a US Marines machine in this case—could carry eight unguided rockets.

Foldable wings: essential for a carrier-borne fighter because of the limited space.

The F6F Hellcat's squat shape is deceptive; it was actually the second-largest single-seat fighter of the Second World War.

GRUMMAN F6F HELLCAT

The F6F was intended as an answer to the hitherto superior Mitsubishi A6M Rei-Sen "Zero" and lived up to expectations. The Hellcat was the main reason the US was able to acquire air superiority in the South Pacific. With a kill ratio of 19:1, it was the US Navy's most successful fighter of the Second World War. Responsible for a total of 5,100 kills, the F6F acquired the nickname "Ace Maker," and 305 pilots achieved ace status in the type.

GRUMMAN F6F-3 HELLCAT
Single-seat fighter/fighter-bomber
Wingspan: 42 ft. 10 in. (13.05 m)
Length: 33 ft. 6 in. (10.20 m)
Height: 13 ft. 1 in. (3.99 m)
Empty weight: 9,039 lb. (4,100 kg)
Maximum take-off weight: 13,228 lb. (6,000 kg)
Power plant: 1 × Pratt & Whitney R-2800-19 Double Wasp air-cooled 18-cylinder double-row radial, 2,029 hp (1,492 kW)
Maximum speed: 380 mph (612 km/h)
Operational ceiling: 38,451 ft. (11,720 m)
Range: 1,084 miles (1,745 km)
Armament: 6 × wing-mounted Colt/Browning .50 in. (12.7 mm) machine guns with 400 rounds each; later models could also carry a bomb load of up to 2,000 lb. (907 kg) or 6 × high-velocity aircraft rockets (HVAR), or a combination of 2 × machine guns and 2 × Hispano .787 in. (20 mm) cannon

Grumman Aircraft Engineering Corporation—the "Grumman Iron Works"

After just two years of production, the Grumman F4F Wildcat was obsolete and had trouble holding its own against the Mitsubishi "Zero." Thanks to its considerable experience in building carrier-borne aircraft, on June 30, 1941 Grumman was awarded the contract to build two prototypes.

Prototype XFGF-1, developed by Leroy R. Grumman (President), Leon A. Swirbul (Vice President), and W.T. "Bill" Schwendler (Technical Vice President), bore a certain resemblance to the F4F Wildcat but was significantly larger. To improve aerodynamic efficiency, the fuselage cross-section was changed from round to oval. The F4F's intelligent system of folding and swiveling wings was scaled up and retained. In order to keep wing loading low despite the increased weight and to make sure the take-off distance remained an appropriate length for a carrier, the size of the wings was increased. This gave the Hellcat the largest wings of any single-seat Second World War

fighter. In terms of overall size, it came second behind the Republic P-47 Thunderbolt. One specific improvement met with the unanimous approval of pilots: the replacement of the F4F's hand-cranked landing gear with a hydraulic system.

The F6F's basic concept was very different from that of its direct opponents. It was three-and-a-half times heavier than the A6M and designed not for maximum maneuverability but as an effective gun platform with strong armor and good engine performance. Its six "fifties"—its .50 in. (12.7 mm) machine guns—posed a serious threat to the fragile Mitsubishi. The Hellcat could withstand hits like no other fighter. It was quite common for pilots to return to their carrier with "more holes than aircraft," and many airmen owed their lives to this ruggedness. It was for this reason that the F6F's manufacturer was affectionately nicknamed the "Grumman Iron Works."

Development

Originally Grumman had wanted to make the Hellcat simply an improved version of the F4F that could be produced quickly and which would be powered by the Wright R-2600 or Cyclone 14 engines, both of which were already produced by Grumman for the TBF Avenger torpedo bomber. Requests by the Royal Navy and US Navy for better performance and the lessons learned during the Battle of Midway forced Grumman to replace the Wright engine

There was also a variant of the Grumman Hellcat that, like the Corsair, could carry eight unguided rockets.

Akutan—a lucky break

As in a number of similar cases, fortune smiled on the development of the F6F. At the time prototype XF6F-1 completed its first maiden flight (June 26, 1942), little technical information was known about the Mitsubishi A6M. Then, out of the blue, a US Navy patrol spotted an aircraft lying on its back on the Aleutian island of Akutan. A rescue team was summoned and discovered a near-airworthy Mitsubishi Zero. This was handed over to Grumman for evaluation and the resulting intelligence contributed to the development of the F6F.

with the more powerful Pratt & Whitney R-2800 Double Wasp. The R-2800 (2,029 hp; 1,492 kW) may have proved its worth in the F4U Corsair, but there was no way it could fit into the Hellcat. As a consequence, the airframe of the Hellcat prototypes had to be made a lot bigger. The second prototype (XF6F-3) was almost identical to the first production model, the F6F-3.

Teamwork requiring a high level of concentration: the deck crew of an aircraft carrier during take-off preparations.

A show of manufacturing strength

Grumman quickly built a brand new factory, Plant No. 3. Even before it was finished, the first production machines were rolling off the assembly line—in record time like the whole of the Hellcat's development. It had taken just a year between receiving the order for the prototypes and their maiden flights. Production began three months later. Just 14 aircraft were built in the first month, but by the end of the year 2,555 Hellcats had been completed. Within three years, Grumman had built 12,275 units of this highly successful fighter—without the rapid pace of production causing any obvious weaknesses.

The F6F in operation

The first Hellcats were delivered to the US Navy on January 16, 1943, and planned large-scale carrier operations began in October. On October 5, planes from four US aircraft carriers attacked the Japanese-occupied island of Wake and the F6Fs from the Essex held their own against the Mitsubishi A6M—the first US type to be able to do so. The Hellcat was over 45 mph (70 km/h) faster than the Zero at 16,400 ft. (5,000 m), had a similar climb rate, and thanks to its greater weight and superior power, could always get away from the Mitsubishi in a dive. During the course of this battle, the Hellcats destroyed 22 enemy aircraft for 12 US losses. This had been the Hellcat's baptism of fire; the ultimate test of its effectiveness came during the Marianas landings.

A misunderstanding between pilot and deck crew caused this Hellcat to land at too fast a speed, resulting in a spectacular accident. The aircraft split in two and the front part was only stopped by the last of three barriers.

Aerial combat tactics: the Thach Weave

John S. Thach was the inventor of an aerial combat tactic, based on formation flying introduced in the First World War, which is still used today.

The smallest and most agile of aerial combat units consists of two pilots, a "leader" and a "wingman," flying alongside each other and "watching each other's backs."

On this basis, naval pilot Lieutenant Commander John S. Thach developed his "weave" in order to give the F4F Wildcat a fighting chance against the Zero. It was also used in order to increase the effectiveness of the F6F against the Japanese fighter. Thach was one of the first US Navy squadron commanders to introduce formations of four aircraft fighting in pairs.

His strategy was for two aircraft to fly side by side at a distance of 1,000–1,300 ft. (300–400 m) in order to protect each other. As soon as one member of the pair became aware of an attack on the other, he would immediately bank sharply in the other's direction. The aircraft being pursued would do the same with the result that the two would perform a scissors maneuver. When a Zero positioned itself behind a US aircraft flying as one of a pair and pursued it as it executed this evasive maneuver, it would soon find itself face to face with the guns of its target's wingman. Even if the Zero were to abandon its pursuit, the second aircraft could change direction and still stand a chance of getting the aggressor in its sights. This tactic was an extremely effective response to aerial attack and required no radio warning. Thach initially named his idea the "Beam Defense Maneuver" but once it had been widely adopted by US Navy pilots it became known as the "Thach Weave." Japanese fighter pilots were powerless against it. Close-fought dogfights—previously their forte—became a thing of the past and their only options were to fly off or perish in battle in the Samurai tradition. The Hellcat's final tally speaks for itself. It destroyed over 5,000 enemy aircraft, 4,947 of which were shot down by carrier-borne units.

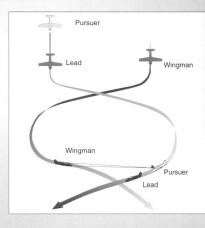

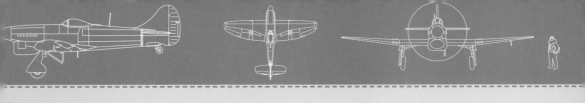

HAWKER TEMPEST

The achievements for which the Tempest is best remembered are probably the destruction of around 800 Fieseler Fi 103 flying bombs (the V1) and the shooting down of 20 Me 262 jet fighters. It was also one of the fastest aircraft of the Second World War and deserves a place in history for that alone.

HAWKER TEMPEST MK V
Single-seat fighter/fighter-bomber
Wingspan: 41 ft. (12.50 m)
Length: 33 ft. 8 in. (10.27 m)
Height: 16 ft. 1 in. (4.90 m)
Empty weight: 9,251 lb. (4,196 kg)
Maximum take-off weight: 13,622 lb. (6,179 kg)
Power plant: 1 × liquid-cooled Napier Sabre IIB, 2,180 hp (1,626 kW) take-off rating
Maximum speed: 435 mph (700 km/h)
Operational ceiling: 35,925 ft. (10,950 m)
Range: 1,541 miles (2,480 km)
Armament: 4 × Hispano Mk.II or Mk.V .787 in. (20 mm) cannon, up to 8 × 3 in. (75 mm) rockets, or 2 × 2,000 lb. (907 kg) bombs

The Hawker Tempest was developed from the Typhoon by Sidney Camm, the progenitor of the Hurricane. It was originally going to be called the Typhoon II.

The development of the Typhoon II, alias the Tempest

The Tempest's predecessor, the Hawker Typhoon, was in fact an extremely potent low-level ground-attack aircraft and low-altitude fighter. It could not fulfill its intended role as an interceptor, however, as it had an extremely modest high-altitude performance. Moreover its tailplane tended to flutter at 300 mph (500 km/h) and could even break off in a dive. A further shortcoming was that at just 90 minutes, its endurance was unacceptable.

In August 1941, therefore, Hawker chief designer Sidney Camm submitted proposals for an improved model to the British Air Ministry. The changes included a thinner wing of semi-elliptical planform, a four-blade propeller, and a more powerful Centaurus engine. The tail assembly and cockpit were also modified. The new model's internal designation during the planning stage was Hawker P.1012.

Two prototypes—still at this stage called the Typhoon II—were initially built in response to specification F.10/41. The first, Mk.I, never went into production even though it was the fastest of all the versions—powered by a Napier Sabre IV engine to over 435 mph (700 km/h). The Air Ministry anticipated bottlenecks in the supply of this engine and ordered a further five prototypes with five different power plants: the Centaurus IV for the Mk.II (two versions), the Rolls-Royce Griffon IIB for the Mk.III, the Griffon 61 for model Mk.IV, and finally the Sabre II for the eventual Mk.V production model.

So many design changes were made to the new model—still at this time referred to as the Typhoon II—that the end result was effectively a completely new aircraft that was given its own name: the Tempest.

The first prototype to bear this name was the Mk.V, which first flew on September 2, 1942. Despite being christened the Tempest, it was still clearly recognizable as a member of the Typhoon family, retaining its predecessor's characteristic radiator, which hung like a beard below the aircraft's nose.

A new feature was the thinner, semi-elliptical wing. Sidney Camm is supposed to have said that the Air Ministry would buy anything that looked like a Spitfire, and this was certainly true of the Tempest's wings.

The tail assembly was also redesigned. Its horizontal surfaces were almost twice as large as those of the Typhoon.

The "beard" radiator beneath the nose was a distinguishing feature of both the Tempest and the Typhoon.

Visible beneath the wing of this Tempest are four of the eight launch rails for its unguided 3 in. (75 mm) rockets.

Tempest II

At the same time that production went ahead with the Tempest Mk.V, the decision was made to proceed with another model as insurance. This was the Hawker Tempest II, equipped with a different engine, the Bristol Centaurus IV. Although the Centaurus did not deliver the same performance as the Sabre, it was fully developed, reliable and extremely maintenance-friendly. A total of 500 Tempest IIs were ordered as early as 1942 but none of the firms awarded contracts had sufficient spare capacity, and so the first aircraft—built by Bristol Airplane Corporation—were not delivered until October 1944—too late to see combat.

Orders and start of operational service

The RAF's initial order for 400 Tempest Is was cancelled before any were built. As anticipated, there were supply problems with the Sabre IV engine and thus the Mk.I never went into production.

The first Tempests to be delivered to the operational units were Mk.Vs. Although powered by the Sabre II instead of the more powerful Sabre IV, the Tempest was still, for a brief period, the fastest fighter in the world and the perfect interceptor.

No. 486 Squadron

In January 1944, 486 Squadron became the first unit to be equipped with the Tempest. Although this squadron was part of the Royal New Zealand Air Force (RNZAF), it was under the command of the RAF.

The RAF command assumed that those pilots who had previously flown the Typhoon would be quickest to get to grips with the new aircraft. This assumption was clearly correct as No. 486 Squadron and the second squadron to be equipped with Tempests, No. 3, declared themselves fully operational the following April.

The Normandy landings

During the Normandy landings, Nos. 3 and 486 Squadrons were tasked to protect the airspace above the UK in case the Germans decided to launch a retaliatory attack against the British mainland. Such an attack failed to materialize and instead the Tempest first saw combat above French territory two days after the landings. A squadron of Tempests encountered six Focke-Wulf Fw 190s and shot three of them down for no British losses.

The Me 262, the V1, and the Allies

Thanks to its exceptional performance, the Hawker Tempest was able to challenge the Luftwaffe's two new high-speed weapons: the Messerschmitt Me 262 and the unmanned V1 flying bomb, the world's first cruise missile.

The Fieseler Fi 103 or V1—the "V" standing propagandistically for *Vergeltungswaffe* ("reprisal weapon")—flew at speeds of around 400 mph (650 km/h), mostly at altitudes of under 10,000 ft. (3,000 m). Shooting them down was not without its perils. In order to avoid being hit by debris, attacking pilots had to ensure they were at least 800 ft. (250 m) away when the flying bombs exploded.

The Tempest had sufficient reserves of speed to be able to retreat swiftly from the danger zone after destroying its target. As a gun platform, the aircraft was so stable that pilots would later succeed in shooting V1s down at night as well. It was simply a question of holding the same altitude and speed, fixing the target's exhaust trail in the sights, and firing. By the time the V1 attacks ended, Tempest pilots had shot down over 800 Fi 103s. The most successful pilot was J. Berry with 61 kills.

Against the Me 262 flying at full speed, the Tempest stood no chance. Nevertheless, it did succeed in destroying a certain number of Messerschmitt jets in the air. One extremely risky tactic was to attack the plane as it came down to land. With flaps extended, the Me 262 had no means of defending itself. The airfields however, were protected by large numbers of quadruple anti-aircraft guns and this method of attack was soon abandoned due to excessively heavy losses. In spite of this, Me 262 pilots regarded the Tempest as their most dangerous opponent.

One other danger should be mentioned. After its operational debut, it was some time before knowledge of the new Hawker fighter

The Tempest's large split flaps gave it outstanding low-flying characteristics.

spread, and not a few aircraft of this type became the victims of US anti-aircraft fire.

Ground attack

In addition to its role as an interceptor, another important role performed by the Tempest was ground attack, particularly after D-Day. During the winter of 1944/45, the Tempest became the scourge of the German supply routes. In February 1945 alone, Tempests destroyed 1,500 road and rail vehicles in addition to the aircraft they shot down.

The fighter-bomber version of the Tempest carried two 2,000 lb. (907 kg) bombs below its wings.

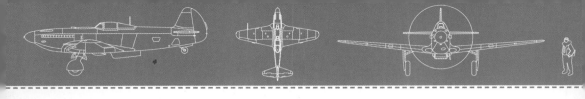

YAKOVLEV YAK-9

The Yakovlev Yak-9 was produced in greater numbers than any other Soviet fighter of the Second World War. Together with the MiG-3 and the Lavochkin LaGG-3, the Yak helped to achieved air superiority over Russia. Late variants remained in service with the Soviet Union's satellite states until the Korean War.

YAKOVLEV YAK-9D
Single-seat fighter
Wingspan: 31 ft. 11 in. (9.74 m)
Length: 27 ft. 11 in. (8.50 m)
Height: 9 ft. 10 in. (3.00 m)
Empty weight: 5,269 lb. (2,390 kg)
Maximum take-off weight: 6,872 lb. (3,117 kg)
Power plant: 1 × Klimov M-105PF-3 liquid-cooled Napier piston engine, 1,360 hp (1,001 kW)
Maximum speed: 374 mph (602 km/h)
Operational ceiling: 34,449 ft. (10,500 m)
Range: 870 miles (1,400 km)
Armament: 1 × ShVAK .787 in. (20 mm) cannon with 120 rounds and 2 × wing-mounted UBS .50 in. (12.7 mm) machine guns with 220 rounds each

Beyond the Urals

The German invasion of the USSR forced the design bureau and assembly shop of Alexander Yakovlev's aircraft factory to a location beyond the Urals, from where deliveries of the factory's first all-metal model, the Yak-9, began in 1942. Having reached the Front in November of that year, the Yak-9 received its baptism of fire in the Battle of Stalingrad (November 1942–end January 1943). According to the reports of German fighter pilots, the first Yak-9Ps were extremely maneuverable—like all Yakovlev fighters—but significantly outclassed by the Messerschmitt Bf 109 in terms of performance. What made it dangerous was its numerical superiority.

Just like the Yak-3 that was being developed at the same time, the Yak-9 was based on Yakovlev's first major success, the Yak-1—and the Yak-7 derived from it—but took a different direction all its own. Yakovlev's aircraft could be described as

constituting modular systems. In the case of the Yak-9, this basic concept may not have produced any truly outstanding flying characteristics but the multitude of equipment sets, variants, and conversions gave rise to one of the most "transformable" fighters of the war. The production statistics speak for themselves: around two-thirds of all Soviet fighters were Yakovlevs—some 36,000 aircraft!

After its emergency landing, this damaged Yak-9 fell into the hands of the Wehrmacht.

The main variants

A total of 22 different versions of the Yak-9 were developed in the Yakovlev-OKB design bureau, of which 15 went into mass production. Here are some of the main variants:

- Yak-9DD long-range fighter, whose drop tank and auxiliary 230 gal. (880 l) fuel tanks in its fuselage extended its range to nearly 1,370 miles (2,200 km), enabling it to escort heavy US bombers.
- Yak-9B fighter-bomber with internal tube bomb bays holding four type FAB-100 220 lb. (100 kg) bombs or 128 type PTAB fragmentation bombs weighing 3.3 lb. (1.5 kg) or 5.5 lb. (2.5 kg).
- Yak-9K, developed from the 9T and armed with a 1.77 in. (45 mm) armor-piercing Nudelmann-Suranov NS-45 cannon.
- Yak-9T37 and Yak-9T45 with a 1.5 in. or 1.77

> **Record production**
> By the time production ceased in 1947, a total of 16,769 Yak-9s plus 6,399 Yak-7s, 4,848 Yak-3s, and 8,723 Yak-1s had been built, making the Yak the most produced series of fighters in the history of aviation!

in. (37 mm or 45 mm) anti-tank/ship cannon; the best-performing variants.
- Yak-9R photographic reconnaissance version.
- Yak-9U with Klimov VK 107-A engine delivering 1,650 hp (1,214 kW). Capable of 435 mph (700 km/h), the prototype was one of the fastest fighters in the world.
- Yak-9V and Yak-9UV two-seater trainers.

Yakovlev aircraft were also used by the Soviet Union's sister states. The aircraft shown here belongs to the Polish air force.

FAIREY FIREFLY

It has not been uncommon in the history of the warplane for types originally planned as fighters to be converted to a reconnaissance role during their operational service. Not so the Fairey Firefly. The Firefly was planned as an armed reconnaissance plane (reconnaissance fighter) from the outset, serving at the same time as a carrier-borne Navy fighter. Its tactical value as an anti-submarine fighter and provider of close air support is reflected in its extremely long service life of 13 years.

FAIREY FIREFLY F I
Navy fighter/anti-sub fighter/reconnaissance aircraft
Wingspan: 44 ft. 6 in. (13.56 m)
Length: 37 ft. 7 in. (11.46 m)
Height: 13 ft. 7 in. (4.14 m)
Empty weight: 9,758 lb. (4,425 kg)
Maximum take-off weight: 14,019 lb. (6,359 kg)
Power plant: 1 × Rolls-Royce Griffon IIB liquid-cooled V12, 1,735 hp (1,276 kW) or Griffon XII, 1,990 hp (1,464 kW)
Maximum speed: 319 mph (513 km/h)
Operational ceiling: 28,018 ft. (8,540 m)
Range: 1,364 miles (2,195 km) at a cruising speed of 204 mph (328 km/h)
Armament: 4 × Hispano-BMK .787 (20 mm) wing-mounted cannon, 2 × 1,000 lb. (454 kg) bombs, or up to 16 × 60 lb. (27 kg) rockets

The Fairey Aviation Company

The Fairey Firefly performed a wide range of roles, mostly for the Royal Navy.

Fairey Aviation had been an important presence in the British aviation market since the First World War. Charles R. Fairey founded the company in 1915 after designing seaplanes for Short Brothers. This may explain why his company's most successful products—notably the Swordfish torpedo bomber and the Firefly, which was intended as a successor to the Fulmar it resembled so much—were all naval aircraft. One of the peculiarities of the Firefly was its second, separate cockpit behind the pilot's, in which the observer sat. This second cockpit was fully integrated into the shape of the fuselage.

Z 1826, the first of four prototypes, had its maiden flight on December 22, 1941. A total of 297 of the first model, the Mk.I, were built by Fairey itself, and a further 132 by General Aircraft Limited.

Deliveries of the first day-fighter Mk.I began in spring 1943 and the type flew its first operation in fall that year.

The Firefly was a successful design. The various changes made during the course of development had resulted in a fighter of improved performance well adapted to carrier use.

The second variant to be produced in large numbers (376) was the FR I reconnaissance fighter. In total, 702 Fairey Fireflies were built.

Carrier suitability

Speed is not the most important attribute for a carrier aircraft. Just as important when it comes to landing successfully on a short flight deck is a plane's low-speed flying capability. The Firefly was equipped with patented Youngman flaps for low-speed flying and patrol flights. Youngman flaps resemble one-piece Fowler flaps and extend from the trailing edge of the wing on two supports. They increased the surface area of the Firefly's already large wings and provided it with greater lift. Not only did the Firefly have superb take-off and landing characteristics, it was also an excellent dogfighter. With its flaps extended—in landing position—it could stand comparison with the best fighters of the day. It was particularly adept at controlled, tight banking at speeds close to its stall speed.

Also to assist with carrier operations, the track width of its landing gear was widened relative to that of its predecessor the Fulmar.

North Atlantic and Korea

The Firefly was capable of performing many different roles—from photographic reconnaissance in preparation for the final successful attack on the German battleship *Tirpitz* and submarine hunting in the North Atlantic, to the bombing of Japanese refineries in the Pacific and low-level attack during the Korean War, not to mention the NF I and NF II Firefly night-fighter versions.

Although the Firefly squadrons began to be disbanded as early as 1946, the last Fleet Air Arm aircraft were not retired until 1956.

The Firefly's ingenious swivel-fold wing mechanism took account of the limited space available on British carriers.

Under its wings and fuselage, the Firefly carried bombs or rockets designed for use against maritime targets.

REPUBLIC P-47 THUNDERBOLT

The Republic Thunderbolt was the heaviest single-seat fighter of the Second World War, with an external load capacity of 1.25 tons (1,134 kg).

The Republic P-47 Thunderbolt, the heaviest single-seat fighter of the Second World War, is a prime example of one of two principal approaches to fighter design. Either aerodynamics and low weight are given priority and the aircraft is powered accordingly or else the most powerful available engine is taken as a starting point and the fighter designed around it. If this work is performed by talented designers, the outcome might be a heavyweight champion like the P-47 Thunderbolt.

Seversky and Kartveli

After the takeover of his firm and its change of name to Republic Aviation, Alexander Procofieff de Seversky was no longer personally involved in the development of the P-47 but the

REPUBLIC P-47D THUNDERBOLT
Single-seat fighter/fighter-bomber
Wingspan: 40 ft. 9 in. (12.42 m)
Length: 36 ft. 2 in. (11.02 m)
Height: 14 ft. 2 in. (4.32 m)
Empty weight: 9,987 lb. (4,530 kg)
Maximum take-off weight: 17,474 lb. (7,926 kg)
Power plant: 1 × Pratt & Whitney R-2800-21, R-2800-59, or R-2800-63, 2,000 hp (1,471 kW) or 2,100 hp (1,545 kW) take-off rating
Maximum speed: 420 mph (676 km/h)
Operational ceiling: 42,028 ft. (12,810 m)
Range: 994 miles (1,600 km)
Armament: 8 × Colt/Browning .50 in. (12.7 mm) M-2 machine guns, 3 or 5 × under-wing racks for tanks, bombs, or rockets up to a maximum weight of 2,500 lb. (1,134 kg)

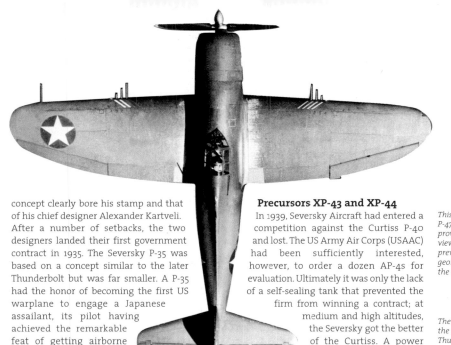

concept clearly bore his stamp and that of his chief designer Alexander Kartveli. After a number of setbacks, the two designers landed their first government contract in 1935. The Seversky P-35 was based on a concept similar to the later Thunderbolt but was far smaller. A P-35 had the honor of becoming the first US warplane to engage a Japanese assailant, its pilot having achieved the remarkable feat of getting airborne during the bombardment of Pearl Harbor.

Precursors XP-43 and XP-44

In 1939, Seversky Aircraft had entered a competition against the Curtiss P-40 and lost. The US Army Air Corps (USAAC) had been sufficiently interested, however, to order a dozen AP-4s for evaluation. Ultimately it was only the lack of a self-sealing tank that prevented the firm from winning a contract; at medium and high altitudes, the Seversky got the better of the Curtiss. A power plant became available in 1940.

This shot of a P-47 Thunderbolt provides a good view of the prevailing wing geometry of the day.

The cartoon wolf on the nose of this Thunderbolt indicates that it was in service with the "Wolf Pack" (56th Fighter Group, 8th Air Force). The marking UN-O shows that it was flown by Lt. Wayne.

When intercepting, the P-47 climbed so high that pilots had to wear oxygen masks.

Turbocharger

In principle, piston engines suck in the gases they need for combustion themselves. As an aircraft gains altitude, air pressure and consequently induction pressure fall and engines are literally starved of the air they need to breathe. This leads to a sharp drop in engine output. During the First World War, altitudes of over 16,400 ft. (5,000 m) were unthinkable for this reason. A solution was found in the form of the turbocharger, a small turbine driven by the engine's exhaust, which compresses the intake air and forces it into the combustion chamber under pressure. This boosts the engine's output. Another possibility is a supercharger, which also forces compressed air into the combustion chamber but is driven by the engine. The disadvantage is that the supercharger itself consumes power. A third means of boosting performance at altitude is with an intercooler as cold air absorbs more oxygen than hot air and as a result combustion occurs at a higher pressure and more evenly.

The turbocharger as a key element in the design concept

During summer 1940, while the P-47 was in the planning stage, chief designer Kartveli tried to marry the projected new aircraft with the various official requirements: as much armor protection as possible for the pilot, significant improvement in operational range relative to that of the Curtiss, and eight wing-mounted .50 in. (12.7 mm) machine guns. These three key requirements meant an enormous increase in weight over the plane's predecessor. The guns alone, without ammunition, weighed over half a ton or 8 × 128 lb. (8 × 58 kg). Only one engine fitted the bill: the R-2800 Double Wasp. In order to improve its performance at altitudes above the full pressure zone, this engine needed to be

RAF Thunderbolts at an airfield in Arakan, Burma, from where P-47s flew missions deep behind enemy lines.

fitted with a turbocharger and it was around this exhaust-driven turbocharger that the airframe was built.

The new fuselage

Exhaust gas and intake air were piped from a lip-shaped inlet in the engine cowling underneath the cockpit to the turbocharger located in the rear of the fuselage. Charge air was in turn fed back to the engine—making a detour via the intercooler. The exhaust gases were then expelled from the underside of the fuselage behind the cockpit. This system of air and exhaust gas piping proved far more robust than the cooling systems used by liquid-cooled engines and was one of the reasons the Thunderbolt was loved by its pilots as an extremely rugged and reliable aircraft. This arrangement of engine and turbocharger produced the characteristic oval "horse-collar" profile of the P-47's front. Openings in the lower part of the engine cowling served as air inlets for the oil cooler and turbocharger-intercooler. The drag created by the aircraft's frontal area was enormous but this arrangement also provided the pilot with outstanding protection, as a head-on hit would initially be absorbed by the engine.

Pratt & Whitney R-2800 Double Wasp
This engine was literally a powerhouse. Depending on the version, the air-cooled 18-cylinder double-row radial engines in the long-lived Wasp series developed between 1,800 and 2,800 hp from a displacement of 12.68 gal. (48 l)! Unfortunately the engine's weight was in proportion to its capacity—it registered over a ton.
    The R-2800 powered numerous renowned aircraft such as the F4U Corsair, the F8F Bearcat, the B-26 Marauder, and the C-118, the military version of the DC-6.
    It was with a modified engine of this R-2800 Double Wasp series that the American Darryl Greenamyer broke the world speed record for horizontal flight in a propeller aircraft with a speed of 482.46 mph (776.44 km/h), wrestling the record from Germany, which had held it for 30 years.

Arrival in Europe—comparisons

Prototype XP-47B completed its maiden flight on May 6, 1941. The first batch of mass-produced P-47Bs was delivered to the US Army Air Force (USAAF) barely 18 months later, in November 1942, and by April 1943 the 56th Fighter Group, 8th Air Force, was fully operational with the P-47D. On the airfields, which were shared with the RAF, the P-47's size seemed even more impressive: the Spitfire's cockpit only came up to its wingtip.

    During the early days of its operational service, the new aircraft suffered to some extent from a lack of range, meaning that

A Thunderbolt fitted with long-distance fuel tanks.

Alexander Procofieff de Seversky

Alexander Seversky was a man with a past. Born into an aristocratic family in Tbilisi, Georgia, he entered the Imperial Russian Naval Academy at the age of 14. By this time he could already fly, as his father was one of the earliest Russian aviators. After training to be an engineer, he joined the Imperial Russian Navy, transferring shortly afterwards to the naval air service. Following a serious accident (in which he lost a leg) in the First World War, Seversky was given personal leave by the Czar to carry on flying. During the course of his 57 combat missions, he scored six—some sources claim 13—confirmed victories, which made him the most successful of all Russian naval pilots.

In March 1918, the new Bolshevik government sent Seversky to the USA as Deputy Naval Attaché and he chose to stay rather than return to a Russia shattered by the revolution. He became an American citizen in 1927.

In 1931 he founded the Seversky Aircraft Corporation on Long Island (New York) with Alexander Kartveli as chief designer. Eight years later he was ousted from the (by this time highly indebted) firm and the corporation changed its name to Republic Aviation.

The multitude of different aircraft types used in the Normandy landings meant clear identification was essential. Shown here is a P-47 in its striking D-Day markings.

bomber escort missions deep into enemy territory had to be postponed. The aircraft's first duties were high-altitude intercepting and the provision of escort protection. Thunderbolts of the first B-series were also frequently deployed as fighter-bombers.

The P-47 proved superior to the Bf 109 and Fw 190 at altitude and in terms of dive capability (at least after dive brakes were fitted from model D onwards), although it was unable to compete with its smaller opponents in agility, climb rate, and turning speed at lower altitudes. US pilots had a way of dealing with this, however: ever since their experiences in the Pacific, diving out of an engagement had become a standard tactic when the odds were against them.

The enormous variety of aircraft types flown by the Allies and the level of training of air defense units in Europe had an influence on the P-47's appearance. As the Thunderbolt and the more slender Fw 190 were easily confused, for safety's sake the P-47 was given conspicuous colored markings—e.g. white stripes or a checkerboard design on the engine cowling—in order to differentiate it from enemy aircraft.

P-47C, D, and others

The P-47C, the second model to be produced in substantial numbers, was equipped with auxiliary tanks in order to extend its range.

The next model—D, the most produced at 12,602 aircraft—could deliver 2,500 hp at 26,250 ft. (8,000 m) for short periods of time

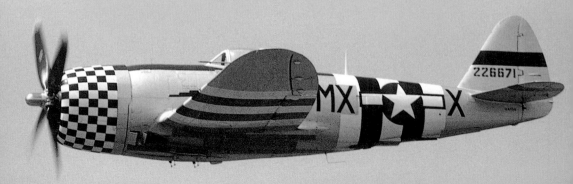

thanks to its water–methanol injection. During the course of its production, the Plexiglas bubble canopy was introduced, which significantly improved visibility to the rear. Another refinement was the strengthening of the under-wing racks for bombs, rockets, or additional drop tanks.

Variant N was the last model to be produced in large numbers. It had an increased wingspan and fuel capacity for long-distance deployment primarily in the Pacific. The later Thunderbolt models were not only effective fighters but also made ideal fighter-bombers thanks to their ability to carry extremely heavy loads. The Royal Air Force received 830 P-47Cs, which, among other uses, were deployed against the German V1 flying bombs.

Retirement

Production of the P-47 Thunderbolt ended in December 1945. A total of 15,660 were built, more than half of which survived the war. Retired by the USAAF in 1945, the Thunderbolt continued to serve with a number of South American air forces in small numbers until the 1960s.

Ferry flight. These Thunderbolts are still lacking their squadron markings and the second aircraft its wing-mounted machine guns.

BELL P-63 KINGCOBRA

The P-63 was a fast, rugged fighter but arrived so late it hardly saw any combat on the US side. The requirements in response to which it was built were out of date by the time of the plane's delivery. In the Soviet Union, the destination of the bulk of production (2,421 aircraft), it was deployed successfully as an interceptor and tank destroyer. A further 114 Kingcobras were also delivered to France under the Lend-Lease program. In the US the aircraft ended its days as a flying target for the training of new pilots—flown by a pilot in an armored cockpit.

BELL P-63A KINGCOBRA
Single-seat fighter/fighter-bomber
Wingspan: 38 ft. 4 in. (11.68 m)
Length: 32 ft. 8 in. (9.96 m)
Height: 12 ft. 7 in. (3.84 m)
Empty weight: 6,376 lb. (2,892 kg)
Maximum take-off weight: 10,500 lb. (4,763 kg)
Power plant: 1 × Allison V-1710-93 inline, 1,344 hp (988 kW); the later model P-63C was equipped with the Allison V-1710-117, whose water injection developed up to 1,821 hp (1,342 kW) for short periods
Maximum speed: 410 mph (660 km/h)
Operational ceiling: 42,979 ft. (13,100 m)
Range: 450 miles (724 km)
Armament: 1 × M4 1.5 in. (37 mm) cannon in propeller hub, 2 × fixed .50 in. (12.7 mm) machine guns firing through the propeller arc, under-wing positions for 2 × .50 in. (12.7 mm) machine guns and up to three 523 lb. (237 kg) bombs

Genesis

It is difficult to put a precise date to the start of work on the Kingcobra because there was an extremely smooth transition from the Airacobra to its successor.

Originally, attempts to improve the Bell P-39 Airacobra led to a number of different prototypes, all of which flew as XP-39 (X = experimental). The improved Airacobra was to have better performance at altitude

and a higher top speed. Following the loss of two prototypes in accidents, the engine originally intended for the new version, a Continental Aviation & Engineering Corporation IV-1430 (an inverted V12), was replaced by the Allison V-1710-47, whose output was barely more than half. The alleged reason was the unreliability of the Continental engine, of which fewer than a hundred had been built. Two prototypes ordered in

The Bell-63 Kingcobra, a development of the P-39 Airacobra, bore a strong resemblance to its predecessor.

"Pinball"—the Bell RP-63

After the war, 300 or so Kingcobras were converted into target aircraft for the training of young pilots. The weapons were removed and the entire aircraft covered with a protective duralumin casing. The front of the canopy was also further reinforced and the oil cooler and intake air apertures covered over.

A fighter version of the Bell P-63 Kingcobra without any racks for additional external loads.

June 1941 were the first aircraft to be given the designation XP-63.

These prototypes had their maiden flights on December 7, 1942—the anniversary of the Japanese attack on Pearl Harbor—and February 5, 1943. A third prototype, XP-63A, was built after the initial two were lost during testing. After a successful maiden flight (April 26, 1943) and satisfactory testing, XP-63A formed the basis for the P-63 Kingcobra production version, the first mass-produced examples of which were delivered in October 1943.

The resemblance between the Kingcobra and its predecessor is unmistakable. Although the fuselage and tail assembly were completely new designs, Bell had continued to rely on a tried and tested basic concept. The positioning of the engine in the middle of the fuselage behind the cockpit was retained, as was the armor-piercing 1.5 in.-caliber (37 mm) M4 cannon that fired through the hollow propeller hub and predestined the Kingcobra for a ground-attack role. While the wing was a new shape similar to that of the P-51 Mustang, the P-63's automobile-style door was another feature borrowed from the Airacobra. As with modern civil aircraft or road vehicles, the pilot entered through this door rather than through the open canopy.

Using comparatively harmless ammunition, the new pilots attempted to score hits on the target plane with their guns. When they succeeded, a red lamp would light up, reminding some airmen of a game of pinball, which became the RP-63's nickname.

The aircraft in the foreground is a P-59A-1, the first production Bell Airacomet. The Airacomet was the first US production jet. In the background is a P-63 Kingcobra.

MIKOYAN-GUREVICH MIG-3

Mikoyan and Gurevich , who would later exert an enormous influence over the Soviet aircraft industry, had just designed their first fighter, the MiG-1, together. This aircraft displayed so many shortcomings that it was replaced by the MiG-3 after just one hundred specimens had been built. The MiG-3 belongs to the generation of fast single-seat interceptors designed and built in the immediate prewar period. It was designed as a high-altitude interceptor—so uncompromisingly, in fact, that all the other requirements fighters are normally expected to fulfill were pushed into the background. The foundations for later problems were thus laid on the drawing board.

MIKOYAN-GUREVICH MIG-3
Single-seat fighter
Wingspan: 33 ft. 6 in. (10.20 m)
Length: 27 ft. 1 in. (8.26 m)
Height: 11 ft. 6 in. (3.50 m)
Empty weight: 5,952 lb. (2,700 kg)
Maximum take-off weight: 7,330 lb. (3,325 kg)
Power plant: 1 × Mikulin AM-35A liquid-cooled V12, 1,350 hp (994 kW) take-off rating, 1,196 hp (880 kW) normal rating; M-100 two-stage high-altitude supercharger; capacity 12.28 gal. (46.5 l)
Maximum speed: 398 mph (640 km/h)
Operational ceiling: 39,370 ft. (12,000 m)
Range: 743 miles (1,195 km)
Armament: 1 × BS .50 in. (12.7 mm) machine gun and 2 × ShKAS .30 in. (7.62 mm) machine guns in nose, two further unsynchronized BS guns added later in under-wing pods, under-wing racks for 6 × RS-82 "Katyusha" rockets or 2 × 220 lb. (100 kg) bombs or 2 × containers for warfare agents

The MiG-3 began to be delivered to units in March 1941.

High-altitude performance

The concept of the high-altitude interceptor was applied to the MiG-3 so rigorously that the fighter ended up with a virtually unique operational ceiling of almost 40,000 ft. (12,000 m). At altitudes of over 16,400 ft. (5,000 m) the MiG performed significantly better than the Messerschmitt Bf 109 and attained its top speed at altitudes at which the performance of Bf models of the same era dropped away sharply. The MiG-3 could fly a full circle in just 23.5 seconds—no record but impressively fast all the same.

Instability and visibility

Speed and agility at altitude came at a price. This relatively small Russian fighter was not an easy plane to fly as it was prone to instability around its longitudinal axis. Wing and tail assembly were close together and constant adjustments were needed to hold a course. The MiG-3 could not be described as inherently stable. This was a problem that had also afflicted the MiG-1. Modification of the wing—the dihedral angle of the outer wing panels was increased—had reduced this aerodynamic weakness but not eliminated it completely.

The positioning of the cockpit well back in the fuselage was responsible for another problem: restricted visibility during take-off and landing. Increasing the length of the MiG-1's fuselage by 4 in. (100 mm) in order to shift the engine and center of gravity forward only exacerbated the problem.

Model change

The transition from the production of MiG-1s to the production of MiG-3s was smooth: the 101st production aircraft left the factory in February 1941 with a number of modifications including a larger fuel tank, the changes to the wing described above, and a new name: the MiG-3. Deliveries to the units of aircraft manufactured on the same assembly line as the MiG-1 commenced in March 1941.

By the time the Wehrmacht invaded the Soviet Union on June 22, 1941 (Operation Barbarossa), 1,269 aircraft had been supplied.

MiG-3 in action

While the MiG-3 was problematic from the pilots' point of view, it was popular with the ground crew. Jittery as it was in the air, it was considered easy to maintain. There were many standard parts, and repairs were generally straightforward—even in the difficult conditions that prevailed at improvised airfields. This quality may explain why, despite all its deficiencies, the MiG-3 remained in service almost until the end of the war. The tactical realities of the Great Patriotic War—as the Second World War was called in the Soviet Union—did not actually

This MiG-3 had to make an emergency landing during the first few weeks of the German invasion of the USSR and fell into the hands of the Wehrmacht in a badly damaged condition.

favor the MiG-3. It was unable to fulfill its intended role as a high-altitude interceptor because aerial combat over the Soviet Union took place at lower altitudes, and attempts to use the MiG as a ground-attack aircraft soon had to be abandoned because of the fighter's inferior performance at low altitude. Its front-line career was therefore relatively short. At the end of 1941, it was pulled back into a homeland defense role and from that point forward was used to protect the airspace above the Soviet capital.

Production ceases

After barely half a year and a total run of 3,322 units, production of the MiG-3 was terminated. There were two main reasons for this: a new competitor in the form of the Lavochkin La-5, which was far better suited to the war with Germany, and an enforced change of engine supplier. The power plant used in the MiG, the Mikulin AM-35A, was no longer being manufactured. Instead, the engine works that previously made it had started producing the AM-38F—for the

---

CONTROL SURFACES

Steering and stability

Essentially, the purpose of flight control surfaces is to generate the forces required to steer and stabilize an aircraft. These control surfaces include the ailerons (**a**) on the wing, which control roll, and the (vertical) rudder (**c**) and (horizontal) elevators (**b**) on the tail assembly.

There are a variety of possible tail assembly configurations, including the conventional arrangement with the horizontal surface positioned below the vertical one, the opposite, T-shaped structure, and a V-shaped arrangement. There are also a number of special configurations, such as canard wings positioned on the aircraft nose.

In addition to controlling the direction of flight around all three axes, the rudder and elevators, which usually form part of the tail assembly, also have another important function: stabilization. Without stabilization of this kind, controlled flight is impossible and, as the MiG-3 illustrates, it can be very difficult to keep an aircraft on course with inadequate technology.

Inherent stability

An inherently stable system is one that restores itself to its normal position following an enforced change of direction. In aeronautics, this means that if an inherently stable aircraft is forced off its path by a gust of wind or an unintentional steering gesture it will restore itself to its normal attitude without any intervention from the pilot. If an aircraft is not inherently stable, the pilot has to continually trim the plane in order to maintain the same course, a process that requires a substantial amount of valuable concentration.

Weathercock stability

This term is more or less self-explanatory. Because the vertical stabilizer behind the wing is positioned in the main airflow direction, in the event of asymmetrical airflow it has a tendency to turn into the main wind direction—just like a windsock—and orient the aircraft around the vertical axis.

Dihedral wing

The final factor that needs to be considered in this examination of aircraft stability is the wing angle—not to be confused with the angle of attack. A positive dihedral—wing design whereby an aircraft's wingtips are higher than its wing roots in level flight—has a beneficial effect on stability. When a disturbance forces an aircraft out of its normal position, this design will produce asymmetrical lift, returning the plane to its normal position. The opposite (anhedral wing), increases maneuverability but reduces inherent stability.

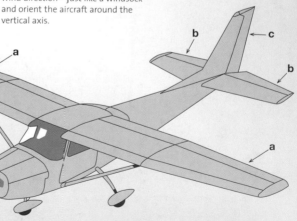

Ilyushin Il-2 Shturmovik. Attempts by Mikoyan-Gurevich to initiate another major production model with a different power plant came to nothing and it was not until after the war, with the MiG-9 (the Soviet Union's second jet), that they were able to pick up where they left off with the MiG-3.

Artem Ivanovich Mikoyan and Mikhail Iosifovich Gurevich

Artem Mikoyan and Mikhail Gurevich first met when they were working for Aircraft Works No. 1 and it was here that the foundations were laid for a collaboration that gave the Soviet aircraft industry a crucial new impetus.

Mikhail Gurevich, who had been associated with aviation since his early youth, was expelled from university under the imperial regime for his proximity to revolutionary ideas and had to complete his studies at the *École Nationale Supérieure de l'Aéronautique et de l'Espace* in France. After the Russian Revolution, he returned to his native country to take up a post as designer and mathematician at the legendary Moscow-based Aircraft Works No. 1 (OKB-1), under director Nikolai Nikolaevich Polikarpov.

Artem Mikoyan had followed a different path, starting his career as a machine-tool operator before becoming a soldier and then studying engineering at a military academy. In 1939, just two years after graduating, he was an assistant to Polikarpov at OKB-1.

At the end of 1939, Mikoyan and Gurevich were directed by the state to set up their own design bureau OKB Mikoyan-Gurevich, the nucleus of an organization that remains a byword for the Soviet aircraft industry today. The new design bureau had extensive powers of its own, was not subject to Polikarpov's orders, and could turn directly to the government if it needed assistance. Moreover, a large contingent of technical personnel and designers was assigned to OKB Mikoyan-Gurevich from among Polikarpov's staff.

The models produced by this new wellspring of aircraft design have become extremely well known and the Soviet state rewarded the bureau's successes with high honors. Both designers were awarded the Order of Lenin in recognition of their achievements, Mikoyan several times over.

The positioning of the MiG-3's cockpit towards the rear of the fuselage substantially obstructed the pilot's view of the ground during take-off and landing.

ILYUSHIN IL-2 SHTUR-MOVIK

With this heavily armored ground-attack aircraft (Russian: TShB = Tiazholyi Shturmovik Bronirovanyi), designer Sergey Vladimirovich Ilyushin created a ground-support aircraft without equal. The production figures alone are breathtaking: it is thought that around 36,000 of the type were built. It would be impossible to overstate its tactical value and, according to the official Soviet line, the victory over Germany was due in no small part to the Il-2. The leaders of the Soviet Union were well aware of the importance of this weapon. Josef Stalin described it as being as important to the Red Army as bread and air and intervened personally on several occasions to secure production.

> **ILYUSHIN IL-2M3 SHTURMOVIK**
> Ground-attack aircraft
> **Wingspan:** 47 ft. 11 in. (14.60 m)
> **Length:** 38 ft. 3 in. (11.65 m)
> **Height:** 11 ft. 2 in. (3.40 m)
> **Empty weight:** 7,165 lb. (3,250 kg)
> **Maximum take-off weight:** 12,946 lb. (5,872 kg)
> **Power plant:** 1 × Mikulin AM-38F liquid-cooled inline V12, 1,750 hp (1,288 kW)
> **Maximum speed:** 281 mph (452 km/h)
> **Operational ceiling:** 21,325 ft. (6,500 m)
> **Range:** 373 miles (600 km)
> **Armament:** 2 × .90 in. (23 mm) cannon, 2 × .30 in. (7.62 mm) ShKAS, 1 × .50 in. (12.7 mm) UBT machine gun in rear cockpit, 882–1,323 lb. (400–600 kg) bomb load either 6 × 110 lb. (50 kg), 6 × 220 lb (100 kg), or 2 × 550 lb. (250 kg). 8 or 4 rockets, either 8 × RS-82 or 4 × RS-132, all with hollow-charge warhead

Photographs like this of the Shturmovik production center were subject to the strictest secrecy in the Soviet Union.

The requirement

As early as the mid-1930s, the Soviet high command had clearly attached a higher priority than other nations to the provision of air support for its troops. Sergey V. Ilyushin submitted his designs for a ground-attack aircraft in 1939. His concept was accepted because his competitor Sukhoi, which had also been invited to submit designs, did not have the necessary spare capacity.

While the Luftwaffe suffered greatly as a result of not maintaining sufficient reserves of personnel and equipment at home for the defense of Germany, the Soviet leadership had at an early stage called for designers to create a ground-attack aircraft primarily in order to defend Soviet territory against potential invaders.

Ilyushin's basic approach was to create a balance between firepower, weight, armor, and speed. The actual specification for the Il-2 was not drawn up until the beginning of 1939. As Ilyushin had already started designing the plane, the first prototype was ready less than a year later, in October 1939.

TsKB-55—the prototype

Whereas the first prototype had been merely a life-size mock-up, the second was a flying version that took off for its maiden flight as TsKB-55 on December 30, 1939. At the controls was Vladimir K. Kokkinaki, "test pilot of outstanding merit," holder of numerous world records, and "Hero of the Soviet Union" twice over. The prototype was powered by a large, liquid-cooled Mikulin AM-35.

After internal tests had been completed, TsKB-55 was handed over for testing by the state and at the end of April 1940 the Soviet air force research institute licensed the plane as a ground-attack aircraft. The aircraft developed by Ilyushin were initially given the designation "TsKB" because Ilyushin was to all intents and purposes head of the Central Design Bureau for which this abbreviation stood. The main problem with the prototype was its lack of speed. Due to its enormous weight, the AM-35 engine could only power the aircraft to 224 mph (360 km/h).

As TsKB-55 also proved deficient in terms of general performance, Ilyushin launched an "emergency program" to create a new version, the TsKB-57. In order to provide the necessary power, engine manufacturer Mikulin developed a new power plant, the AM-38, which enabled the TsKB-57 to reach speeds of up to 261 mph (420 km/h) at low altitude. The TsKB-57 first flew on October 12, 1940. In addition to the new engine, another change was that the rear gunner requested by the military was axed—a bad decision, as time would tell.

The rear gunner covered the Il-2's back with his .50 in. (12.7 mm) UBT machine gun—an extremely dangerous job as the rear cockpit was largely unarmored.

The Il-2's heavy armor could not be penetrated by rifle-caliber ammunition although it did have one weak point: the oil cooler below the fuselage.

The Battle of Kursk

In one of the biggest tank battles in history, over 6,000 tanks and more than two million soldiers confronted each other at the Battle of Kursk, which began on July 5, 1943. The Germans had 2,000 aircraft and the Soviets 3,000. The aim of the Wehrmacht was to cut off the Soviets' westerly salient near Kursk in a pincer movement, thereby weakening the Soviet attack capability to such an extent that the German Army would win back the initiative on the Eastern Front and increase their chances of victory against the Soviet Union.

The Soviets were extremely well informed about the German plans, however. They had concentrated their best units in the area which Germany was planning to attack and had established a well-supported defensive system. Although Hitler had in turn been warned about the Soviet preparations, he decided to press ahead with "Operation Citadel" and attack. Immediately before the start of the German attack, the Soviet artillery opened fire and aircraft bombarded the German tank assembly points. After only partial success in the opening exchanges, the Soviets' luck changed. The German attack unfolded slowly and, from July 7, the Shturmoviks were finally able to pick off tank after tank.

As a result of the British and American landings in Sicily, Germany finally ran out of strength to pursue its offensive in the East and had to break off its offensive at Kursk. Many historians regard the Battle of Kursk as the real turning point in Germany's Russian campaign because from this point on its Eastern Armies staggered from defeat to defeat, and by the end of 1943 almost the whole of USSR territory was back in Russian hands.

Something else was lacking too: a major order for the new plane. Initially the Soviet Air Force saw no need for a heavy armored ground-attack aircraft and production only started when Stalin personally commanded it to.

One of the most produced aircraft of all time

The Il-2 went into production in April 1941. By the outbreak of war on June 22, 1941, only 249 aircraft had been delivered and just two aviation regiments equipped. Although official figures vary considerably, it is thought that by the end of production in 1945 around 36,000 aircraft (Polish sources put the figure at 41,000) had been built, making the Shturmovik one of the most produced aircraft ever.

First experiences

The Il-2 was tested in combat for the first time at the Battle of Berezina, just a few days after the launch of the German invasion. During its

The Shturmovik inflicted heavy losses on the Germans during the tank battle of Kursk.

early combat missions the Il-2 sustained heavy losses, not least because without the rear gunner envisaged in the initial designs, the plane had no effective means of protecting itself against German fighters attacking from behind, their preferred method. Sergey Ilyushin's original designs were pulled out of the drawer and formed the basis for a new version, the Il-2M. The two-seater was delivered to the Front in mid-1942.

The Il-2M was powered by the first of a new generation of uprated Mikulin engines, the AM-38F, and the rear gunner was equipped with a Berezin UBT .50 in. (12.7 mm) machine gun.

The Ilyushin with the best performance, and also the version produced in the largest numbers, was the Il-2M3, which entered service at the end of October 1942 and took part in force in the Battle of Stalingrad.

A multitude of nicknames

The Il-2 acquired a long list of nicknames. Among Soviet troops it was named simply and tenderly "Ilyusha" after the works where it was produced, German soldiers christened it "Eiserner Gustav" ("Iron Gustav"), "Betonflugzeug" ("Concrete Airplane") and

"Fliegender Tod" ("Flying Death"). Changes to the cockpit aimed at improving visibility to the front earned it the sobriquet "Hunchback." In Finland it was even likened to an agricultural machine and indeed the name "Combine Harvester" graphically and aptly conveys the devastating effect of the Shturmovik on a battlefield.

Conceived as a ground-attack aircraft, the Il-2 Shturmovik was provided with the best possible armament for its task.

Heavy fighter

The Il-2 owed the name "Shturmovik" to its heavy armor and the ability this gave it to withstand fire. Pilot and engine were protected by an armored tub 0.2 to 0.3 in. (5–7 mm) thick. The radiator air inlet was located on the aircraft's nose but the vulnerable radiator assembly itself was positioned behind the engine, in other words amply protected by the armored tub. Protection to the front was so effective that normal .50 in.-caliber (12.7 mm) rounds were incapable of inflicting any real damage. Only cannon of .787 in.-caliber (20 mm) and above were capable of causing problems but the Shturmovik's armor could to a certain extent even withstand hits from weapons of this caliber. The front pane of the canopy wasn't easily destroyed either, as it was made from extremely tough K-4 bulletproof glass 2.5 in. (65 mm) thick.

The rear gunners did not benefit from this degree of protection, however, as the armor plating was only extended to the rear cockpit

Il-2s approaching their target for a typical low-level attack.

in later versions. It is hardly surprising, therefore, that four times as many rear gunners were lost as pilots.

One weakness of the Shturmovik was its oil cooler, which projected forward slightly from the underneath of the fuselage, in other words out of sight of the rear gunner.

The main danger to the Il-2 pilots lay in the nature of their missions. As a rule, they attacked from heights of less than 650 ft. (200 m) and frequently from treetop height. This put them within range of even the small-caliber arms of ground troops.

The Il-2's arsenal

Initial combat experience highlighted not only the importance of the rear gunner but also shortcomings in terms of armament. From model M3, therefore, the original .787 in. (20 mm) ShVAK cannon were replaced by two .90 in. (23 mm) cannon with a higher muzzle velocity.

Soviet crews line up in front of their *Shturmoviks* in preparation for their withdrawal from the German Democratic Republic (East Germany) in 1956.

A few aircraft were equipped with the 1.5 in. (37 mm) Nudelman-Suranov NS-37 cannon but the hefty recoil of this gun had an adverse impact on handling.

When protection was introduced for the rear gunner, the weight of the Shturmovik's armor rose to 1,984 lb. (900 kg).

In its internal bomb bays, the Il-2 carried either up to 192 armor-piercing PTAB bombs—small, hollow-charge bombs weighing 5.5 lb. (2.5 kg)—or up to 1,323 lb. (600 kg) of bombs of different sizes. The .50 in. (12.7 mm) UBT machine gun in the rear cockpit was swivel-mounted.

Other armament variants included eight 3.23 in. (82 mm) RS-82 or four 5.20 in. (132 mm) RS-132 rockets and the small, but according to Soviet reports highly effective, DAG-10 air mines. Descending slowly by parachute, these air mines could be deadly to a pursuing fighter.

Finally, the Shturmovik was also used as a torpedo bomber (Il-2T). Its armor had to be reduced in order to allow it to carry a 21 in. (533 mm) torpedo.

The tactics of the Shturmovik pilots

The Shturmovik pilots adopted a number of different basic tactics depending on the given situation. Against tank columns or stationary targets such as bunkers, dive-bombing brought the greatest success; against columns of infantry or trucks, low-level attack was preferred; and against armored divisions in attacking position, a special technique known as the "circle of death" was invented whereby the Shturmoviks would overfly the German Front in a chain of 12–18 aircraft and attack the enemy tanks from their most vulnerable point—the rear. They would then bank and attack again from the same position. This meant their targets came under more or less continual fire and suffered devastating losses as a consequence. At the Battle of Kursk, for example, it is believed the German 9th Panzer Division alone lost 70 tanks in just 20 minutes. Instead of leaving the battlefield after using up all their ammunition, providing the situation in the air allowed, the Soviet pilots would repeatedly dive at their opponents with the aim of demoralizing them and would only return to base after expending virtually all their fuel.

BOULTON PAUL DEFIANT

The Defiant was designed in the mid-1930s and was equipped with what was regarded as a revolutionary armament: a dorsal gun turret that rotated through 360 degrees. This turret was motor-driven and fired a veritable broadside from four Browning machine guns. Another peculiarity of the Defiant was that the rear gunner was also the commander of the aircraft—as during the early days of military aviation.

Development climate

The rear gunner and commander of the Boulton Paul Defiant, positioned in a dorsal turret, manned four Browning .303 in. (7.7 mm) machine guns.

Equipment specifications provide useful insights into the thinking of military strategists. In this case (specification F.9/35), it is clear that the Defiant arose out of a specific tactic devised by the air planners. The idea was that a fighter could approach unaccompanied bomber formations from the side or below and then attack with concentrated bursts of fire.

Fitting a motorized gun turret on an aircraft was truly innovative. With its Sidestrand bomber, British firm Boulton Paul was the market leader in the field at this time.

Carried away by the euphoria, fighters, as well as bombers, were equipped with motor-driven gun turrets. However, while they were right for bombers, turrets were not particularly appropriate as a fighter's main armament. Moreover, an important lesson seemed to have been forgotten: during the First World War, experience with the Bristol F.2 Fighter had shown that a rear gunner alone was not particularly effective. Only when the forward-firing machine gun was used as the main weapon did the F.2's kill rate improve.

The problem was that the Bolton Paul had no forward-firing gun and so the pilot was completely defenseless against frontal attack.

The element of surprise

Immediately after the Defiant entered service, its pilots achieved a number of kills by exploiting the element of surprise. The fighter bore a passing resemblance to the Hawker Hurricane and German pilots did not initially feel unduly threatened when what they took to be a Hurricane drew alongside or took up a position to the front. In this way the Defiant was able to fire at enemy aircraft from completely unexpected positions and for a brief period—during the Allied evacuation from Dunkirk—experienced a measure of success.

The element of surprise did not last long, however, and the Boulton sustained heavy losses when deployed in the UK. It was soon withdrawn from service as a day-fighter.

The Defiant as night-fighter

The Defiant was next deployed as a night-fighter and it was in this role that it proved most valuable. Equipped with radar, it continued to pose a serious threat to incoming German bombers until 1942, by which time its modest speed meant it could no longer intercept enemy aircraft. The night-fighter squadrons were therefore completely re-equipped. A number of Defiants were used to escort Allied bombers on missions to Germany, equipped with Moonshine or Mandrel radar jamming systems.

Subsequently, Defiants were used for sea rescue missions, carrying two dinghies in specially designed under-wing pods, or as target tugs with the initials TT appended to the model designation.

During the course of 1943, all Defiants were withdrawn from active service. A total of 1,060 were built

A common feature of bombers but highly unusual in a fighter: the fully rotating gun turret mounted on the Defiant's back was the fighter's only weapon but ultimately proved ineffective in combat.

Mascot animals (such as the dog being held here by the pilot) were a common sight at RAF airfields.

MESSER-SCHMITT Bf 110

This twin-engined "destroyer" from the Messerschmitt works was based on an offensive aerial warfare strategy that called for heavy fighters capable of penetrating deep into enemy territory. Although the Bf 110 was an extremely successful and adaptable design with outstanding maneuverability for a twin-engined aircraft, it became clear as early as the Battle of Britain in 1940 that it was unsuited to its original purpose. During the remaining years of the war, the Bf 110 was used successfully in a number of other roles—including that of radar-guided night-fighter.

**MESSERSCHMITT
BF 110G-4C/R3**
Two-seat day-fighter and night-fighter/fighter-bomber/
reconnaissance aircraft/military glider tug
Wingspan: 53 ft. 4 in. (16.25 m)
Length: 42 ft. 10 in. (13.05 m)
Height: 13 ft. 9 in. (4.18 m)
Empty weight: 11,222 lb. (5,090 kg)
Maximum take-off weight: 21,804 lb. (9,890 kg)
Power plant: 2 × Daimler-Benz DB 605B-1 liquid-cooled inverted V-12, 1,475 hp (1,085 kW) each
Maximum speed: 342 mph (550 km/h)
Operational ceiling: 26,247 ft. (8,000 m)
Range: 1,305 miles (2,100 km)
Armament: 2 × MK 108 1.18 in. (30 mm) cannon with 130 rounds each, 2 × nose-mounted MG 151/20 .787 in. (20 mm) machine guns, 1 × swivel-mounted .311 in. (7.9 mm) MG 81Z machine gun with 800 rounds (radio operator in rear cockpit) or 2 × dorsal MG 151/20 firing obliquely upwards (*schräge Musik*)

The twin-engined Messerschmitt Bf 110 heavy fighter during factory testing.

The Bf 110 as fighter

The planning departments of numerous air forces in the mid-1930s shared a widespread belief in the virtues of the so-called "destroyer" (*Zerstörer* in German) or heavy, long-range fighter. This led to the development of the Messerschmitt Bf 110 in Germany, the Bristol Blenheim in the UK, the Airacobra and Lockheed Lightning in the USA, and the Breguet 691 in France.

And, right at the start of the war, it seemed that the Messerschmitt would fulfill these expectations. In December 1939 a flight of Bf 110s encountered 24 British Vickers Wellington bombers over Heligoland Bight and managed to shoot down nine of them. The Bf 110's shortcomings only started to become clear during the German invasion of France. Although it was astonishingly agile for its size, in combat it was no match for a single-engined fighter.

The UK

During the Battle of Britain in the summer of 1940 the Bf 110 had to be withdrawn from direct combat operations once and for all as it had virtually no means of countering the attacking Hurricanes and Spitfires. In August alone the Luftwaffe lost 120 aircraft. In the end, the heavy fighters had to be escorted by single-engined Bf 109 fighters and, in Germany at least, the concept of the destroyer and heavy escort fighter had to be regarded as a failed experiment.

Fighter-bomber service over the Mediterranean

Two new combat roles were found for the Bf 110: as a fighter-bomber targeting British shipping and as a ground-attack aircraft, a role for which it was extremely well suited because of its heavy armor. A third operational area in which it was used was reconnaissance. Nevertheless, by 1942 the Bf 110 was essentially obsolete and was due to be replaced by the Me 210. The Me 210 was plagued by insoluble problems, however, and there was no alternative but to keep the Bf 110 in production. In conjunction with its versatility, this meant that it remained in service in ever new configurations through to the end of the war, by which time over 6,000 had been built.

Above left: A Bf 110's instrument panel with the control column temporarily removed.

Above right: The Bf 110 was briefly able to fulfill its intended role as a heavy fighter during the early days of the war.

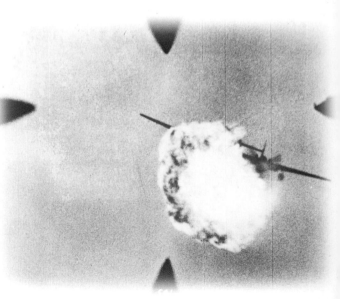

Bull's-eye! A fighter's gunsight camera captures the shooting down of a Messerschmitt Bf 110.

The external antennae of the Lichtenstein radar system generated considerable drag and impaired the Bf 110's performance.

A Bf 110 is shot down.

Schräge Musik

Defending Germany against the mighty British bomber formations of up to 1,000 aircraft was an impossible task. For every bomber shot down, another 20 got through to their targets. Nevertheless, the radar-enabled Messerschmitt Bf 110 was a very successful night-fighter.

The attacking bombers were by no means defenseless. The Avro Lancaster, for example, had up to ten machine guns including four in its rear dorsal gun turret.

Exhaust-flame baffle, auxiliary tank, and radar antennae—this is clearly a night-fighter version of the Bf 110.

Night-fighter operations—the Kammhuber Line and *Himmelbett* system

The devastating effects of the bombing campaign directed against Germany during the later stages of the war all too easily conceal the fact that during the early night-time raids of 1940, when radar was in its infancy, neither side was able to achieve a clear advantage over the other. One of the reasons for this state of relative equilibrium was the "Kammhuber Line," a line of air defenses named after its commander that ran from Denmark to the south of France. Initially the Kammhuber Line relied on searchlights alone but as the first radio location systems became available, it was transformed into an early warning and fighter guidance system. The Kammhuber Line was divided into individual, overlapping cells known as *Himmelbett* zones, measuring some 12 × 19 miles (20 × 30 km). Each zone comprised the following system components: a radio beacon serving as an absolute reference point, the control or command center, a Freya radar antenna—with a range of up to 95 miles (150 km)—for long-range scanning and the guiding of two more accurate Würzburg radar systems—range 23 miles (35 km); later 35–45 miles (60–70 km)—which tracked the enemy bombers and guided the German night-fighters. At the start of the night offensive, this system was so effective that, combined with the inaccuracy of bombsights and navigation in the early days, Britain's Bomber Command experienced serious difficulties and failed to inflict any major damage on German industry.

Perhaps the main shortcoming of the *Himmelbett* system was that only one or two night-fighters could be guided at once, which soon limited its effectiveness. The later switching of Allied tactics from bomber waves to bomber streams, along with new radar jamming techniques, eventually meant the end of the Kammhuber Line, which was effectively rendered obsolete.

In order to avoid presenting an easy target to the bomber's guns, the fighters attacked from below. Scoring a bull's eye, however, meant the fighter would fly right into a hail of debris—or worse, the exploding bomb load. The *schräge Musik* system increased the hit rate and improved pilot safety. It consisted of twin .787 in. (20 mm) cannon that fired forwards and upwards at an angle of 70 degrees. The pilot would position his Bf 110 underneath the bomber and then fire off the two cannon. This method of attack was so successful that to start with the RAF was unable to understand why it was losing so many bombers. Only after a close examination of the bullet holes in the damaged machines that made it home did the nature of the weapon and tactic become clear.

The German night-fighters had their greatest success during the RAF attack on Nuremberg in the night of March 30, 1944, when they shot down 95 bombers. During the late phase of the war, the RAF responded to the ongoing threat from the German night-fighters by interspersing their own night-fighters, predominantly the De Havilland Mosquito, among the bomber streams. These British night-fighters in turn attacked the attacking Bf 110 fighters—turning hunter into quarry.

After a combat mission, aircraft guns had to be cleaned and rearmed as quickly as possible.

1,800 rounds for the "fifties." The Mustang's .50 in. (12.7 mm) guns being rearmed.

NORTH AMERICAN P-51 MUSTANG

The P-51 can legitimately be regarded as the high point in the development of the piston-engined fighter. It was agile and responsive, with outstanding performance at all altitudes and a range that preordained it for a role escorting bombers deep into enemy territory. The Mustang protected US bomber formations during the final years of the war and made a decisive contribution to the outcome of the Second World War.

North American Aviation

In 1939, shortly before the outbreak of the Second World War, the UK's aircraft industry was operating at capacity. The RAF's purchasing commission therefore turned to the USA in its quest for a new fighter. It had already collaborated with North American Aviation (NAA), which had built a trainer for the RAF (the North American AT-6D Texan, known in Britain as the Harvard III). The British believed there was no time to initiate a completely new development process and planned at first to acquire an existing system. They looked at the Curtiss P-40, the Bell P-39, and various others with the idea that NAA should manufacture a licensed version of one of these aircraft, but James A. "Dutch" Kindelberger, president and chief

One of a number of possible construction methods: the wing and fuselage of the North American P-51 being fitted together as complete units.

designer of NAA, convinced the client that his development team could build a better fighter with increased performance, improved flying characteristics, and bigger guns. And he turned out to be right.

Ground attack: the P-51 in fighter-bomber guise attacking a column of tanks. It was able to carry around a ton of bombs or rockets in total.

NA-73X

Under the direction of Raymond H. Rice and Edgar Schmued, the NAA development department set to work and produced the first prototype (NA-73X) with astonishing speed—barely 130 days after the completion of the initial designs. Although different sources quote different times ranging from 102 to 170 days, one thing is certain: the development of the Mustang was a concerted and unparalleled feat of strength by NAA. The firm's enormous production capacity is illustrated by the fact that it was able to build as many as 850 P-51s in a single month.

An initial order for 320 aircraft—then still known as the NA-73—was received in spring 1940 (May 23), and the prototype flew on October 26. Two weeks later, the RAF informed NAA that the new aircraft's official name would be the "Mustang."

P-51A Mustang I and P-51D Mustang II

The first production model arrived in the UK on October 21, 1941. The British were enthusiastic about its flying characteristics and regarded the plane as an excellent fighter for low to medium altitudes. At this early stage in the Mustang's operational career, however, there was no way anyone could have had an inkling of the fighter's later superb combat effectiveness. The Allison V-1710 engine of this

engine were specially adapted for low-level attack and deployed as fighter-bombers and reconnaissance planes.

The modified Mustang entered service in October 1942. Fortunately, the airframe could be adapted without difficulty to accommodate the new engine, the Rolls-Royce Merlin—or more accurately the version of it built under license by Packard—which provided the P-51B Mustang II with a dramatic leap in performance. Other changes to this model included the introduction of a four-blade propeller and the shifting of the carburetor intake nozzles to the nose and of the machine guns from the nose to the wings.

The P-51D version—of which a total of 7,956 were built after its maiden flight on November 10, 1943—subsequently achieved its absolute maximum speed of 437 mph (703 km/h) at an altitude at which it had been unable to compete before—approximately 24,500 ft. (7,500 m).

Model H—the fastest wild horse of all

The P-51H represented the pinnacle of piston-engined, propeller-driven aircraft design. This ultra-light fighter was developed by NAA from prototypes XP-51F and XP-51G. Notable features of this version included its new body with a longer fuselage and larger tailplane and fin.

P-51 Mustangs of the Californian National Guard, with which the type served until well after the end of the war.

The Mustang P-51D achieved its absolute maximum speed of 437 mph (703 km/h) at approximately 24,500 ft. (7,500 m).

first model left so much to be desired in terms of high-altitude performance that to use the P-51 as a high-altitude interceptor seemed unthinkable at the time. Turbochargers, which helped other types powered by the same engine to achieve good high-altitude performance, could not be fitted to the Mustang. A supercharger had to be used instead. Those P-51s still powered by the Allison

Powered by the new Packard Merlin V-1650-9, the P-51H was capable of a top speed of 488 mph (785 km/h) at 24, 935 ft. (7,600 m). With water–methanol injection for short bursts of maximum power, the new engine was capable of developing up to 2,291 hp (1,685 kW). The P-51H (along with the P-47 Thunderbolt) was earmarked to form the backbone of the US Army Air Force (USAAF) for the imminent invasion of Japan, but the Second World War ended without this becoming necessary and only a quarter of the 2,000 aircraft ordered were delivered.

The wings

The NAA had designed a new type of wing for the P-51. It was to this wing, which was at its thickest in the rear section of the chord—further back than the norm—that the P-51 owed its speed and also the sophisticated, low-resistance lines of its entire airframe. This explains why with the same engine, and despite weighing more, the Mustang was around 28 mph (45 km/h) faster than the Curtiss P-40.

The first delivery

The USAAF had to approve the sale of the Mustang—still called the NA-73 at that point—to the UK in order for an export license to be granted. This it did, but under the condition that it was provided with two models for evaluation purposes—free of charge.

In tests, the Mustang was found so convincing that the USAAF claimed 57 of the initial version—the Mustang IA, destined for the UK—for itself and used them for tactical reconnaissance operations.

The Mustang as long-range fighter

In addition to its other strengths, the Mustang also had an enormous operational range. Even without auxiliary tanks, it was capable of flying previously unthinkable distances.

The Mustang's first mission as an RAF escort fighter was to provide protection to B-17 bombers on a trip from England to Kiel, Germany, and back in December 1943—a distance of nearly 1,000 miles (1,600 km)! The operational range of the Spitfire Mk.V, by comparison, was only half this. Reconnaissance missions deep into German territory now became possible. One of the first was a photo-reconnaissance mission over the Dortmund-Ems Canal in Germany's industrial heartland undertaken in October 1942. The Mustang's impressive range made it one of the RAF's few fighters capable of penetrating deep into the German Reich.

In response to the first appearance of a Mustang over the German capital Berlin, Hermann Goering, Field Marshal and Commander-in-Chief of the Luftwaffe, is supposed to have declared that the war was already lost—surely one of his few realistic assessments of the wartime situation.

A Mustang with the old-style canopy, prior to the introduction of the "bubble top."

MESSER-SCHMITT ME 262 SCHWALBE

MESSERSCHMITT ME 262A-1A SCHWALBE
Single-seat fighter/fast bomber/night-fighter
Wingspan: 41 ft. 6 in. (12.65 m)
Length: 34 ft. 9 in. (10.60 m)
Height: 9 ft. 2 in. (2.80 m)
Empty weight: 8,384 lb. (3,803 kg)
Maximum take-off weight: 14,764 lb. (6,697 kg)
Power plant: 2 × Junkers Jumo 004 B1 diesel-powered turbojets with 8-stage axial compressor, 1,978 lbf (8.8 kN) static thrust each
Maximum speed: 534 mph (860 km/h)
Operational ceiling: 37,566 ft. (11,450 m)
Range: 715 miles (1,150 km)
Armament (fighter version): 4 × nose-mounted MK 108 1.18 in. (30 mm) cannon with a total of 360 rounds, under-wing launch rails for 2 sets of 12 × 2.16 in. (55 mm) R4M "Orkan" rockets fired in salvos

There are very few aircraft of which it can be claimed that they mark the start of a new era in aerial warfare, but the Messerschmitt Me 262 is without doubt one of them. The Schwalbe (Swallow) was the first mass-produced operational jet aircraft in the world. It incorporated a number of revolutionary aerodynamic and propulsion concepts and was significantly faster than any Allied propeller aircraft. Introduced at the very last minute, the Me 262 could have changed the course of the Second World War but failed to because tactical and political mistakes prevented it from being used properly.

A Messerschmitt Me 262 with radar antennas. The price for an ability to track down foes was a reduction in speed.

The birth of the jet

Jet engines were developed independently in Germany and the UK in the mid-1930s. In Germany, Pabst von Ohain designed the world's first operable turbojet engine. This was then developed further at the BMW and Junkers plants.

In fall 1938, Messerschmitt was awarded a development contract for the construction of an aircraft designed specifically to accommodate the new BMW 003 turbojet, which produced 1,322 lbf (5.88 kN) of thrust. The original plan of attaching one of these engines to each of the wing roots was soon dropped and instead the power plants were fixed to the underside of the wings. As little was known at this time about the behavior of turbojets in flight, the aircraft designers were prepared for further changes to the jet engines, and the airframe was also designed to be capable of accommodating an increase in the size of the engines.

Messerschmitt's design was outstanding from an aerodynamic point of view, featuring relatively thin, swept wings suitable for high speed. Just how exceptional the Me 262's aerodynamics were is brought home by the following comparison: it was not until 1950, six years after the Schwalbe's maiden combat mission, that the first US jet, the F-84, achieved the same speed—albeit with an engine that produced double the thrust.

Early difficulties

The landing gear with tail wheel of the early prototypes caused initial problems. This arrangement caused the engines to slant downwards to the rear, directing their exhaust jet into the ground. The resulting thrust was insufficient for take-off.

As a result, the pilot was forced to touch the brakes at around 112 mph (180 km/h) in order to lift the tail wheel. This lifted the rear of the aircraft and allowed the thrust to take its full effect in a horizontal position. Messerschmitt remedied this specific thrust problem by fitting a tricycle landing gear, which also had the beneficial side-effect of improving visibility for the pilot.

The jet engine itself was the cause of further difficulties. The BMW turbojets were unreliable. They were prone to cutting out (flameout) and catching fire, but were also unsatisfactory in terms of performance.

This led to the absurd situation whereby, in order to test the airframe in 1941, a piston

The Messerschmitt Me 262—the world's first mass-produced jet.

engine with propeller had to be fitted in addition to the jet engines for safety reasons. However, the eventual production aircraft were powered by the more reliable Junkers Jumo 004 turbojet.

Raw materials shortage

The reason for these engine problems was not so much deficient engineering as a shortage of raw materials. The compressor vanes or blades operate under extreme mechanical and thermal loads that only special heat-resistant alloys can withstand on a permanent basis. The deposits of the rare raw materials needed for these alloys were all in British hands.

At least two Me 262s were equipped with the large-caliber Mk.214 1.97 in. (50 mm) cannon. It was hoped this long-range weapon would enable pilots to destroy US bombers from a greater distance.

The engineers at Junkers were therefore forced to make the turbojet engines out of steel. The cracking of the blades was taken account of with very short maintenance intervals. The Me 262's engines had to be dismantled and completely refitted after every ten hours of service. Furthermore, all jet engines until the 1950s were highly sensitive to sudden changes in load. Pilots had to handle the throttle control extremely carefully in order to avoid engines cutting out by themselves due to flameout. Many Me 262 kills resulted from engine failure of this kind.

Maiden flight

The first flight of an Me 262 powered exclusively by jet engines took place successfully on July 18, 1942. It is worth noting, however, that this was not the first-ever flight by a jet fighter. That honor went to the Me 262's competitor the He 280, designed by Ernst Heinkel.

Commander of the German fighter force Adolf Galland was able to fly the Me 262 for the first time in May 1943, and his verdict was euphoric. After its presentation to Hitler the aircraft was assigned number one development priority in November—albeit as a fast bomber rather than as a fighter.

The Me 262 as fast bomber

Contrary to Hitler's instructions, Karl Otto Saur, head of the Jägerstab, the committee in charge of fighter production, took the audacious step of having roughly every second Me 262 fitted as a fighter. Hitler's order still stood, however, and to discuss use of the Me 262 in any other role was out of the question.

This bad decision set the Me 262's development as a fighter back as much as nine months. Willi Messerschmitt himself was not entirely without blame for this situation. As recommended by his Luftwaffe adjutant, Nicolaus von Below, Hitler summoned Messerschmitt in September 1943 and asked whether the jet aircraft could also be used as a bomber. Messerschmitt answered in the affirmative and used the occasion to complain about Field Marshal Milch, Chief-of-Staff of the Luftwaffe and Chief of Aircraft Procurement and Supply, who, he claimed, was failing to provide him with enough workers. In November 1943, Messerschmitt went even further, assuring Goering that he could design the necessary electrical systems and bomb release mechanisms with two weeks.

The fast bomber was given the designation Me 262 A-2a and could carry either one 2,200 lb. (1,000 kg) bomb or two 1,100 lb. (500 kg) bombs under its fuselage. Its performance was disappointing. Moreover, the decision to turn the Me 262 into a bomber held back development and deployment of the existing Arado Ar 234 Blitz bomber.

Far too late, in September 1944, the Me 262 was reclassified as a fighter, but the shortage of

Jet engines

Jet engines generate thrust from a fast-moving stream of gases. A series of compressor blades—arranged perpendicular to the flow of air in an axial engine—in the air inlet boosts the pressure of the intake air and directs it into the combustion chambers. There, fuel is injected and continuous combustion takes place, significantly increasing the pressure and volume of the gas, which flows towards the turbines. The turbines drive the compressor blades by means of a driveshaft. The combustion gas then passes to the nozzle, through which the gas is expelled, and the resulting thrust drives the aircraft forward. In order to improve performance, an afterburner is sometimes fitted before or after the nozzle, creating additional thrust from a second combustion.

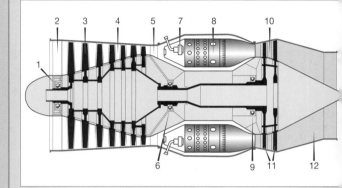

Diagram of a jet engine
1 Front chamber
2 Air inlet
3 Compressor blades
4 Stators (non-rotating blades)
5 Diffuser section
6 Middle chamber
7 Fuel injector nozzles
8 Combustion chambers
9 Rear chamber
10 Turbine blades
11 Two-stage turbine
12 Nozzle

two-seat trainers meant pilots received only minimal training.

Operational service with Jagdverband 44

The Me 262 first saw service as a fighter in July 1944 with Luftwaffe test unit Erprobungskommando 262 in Rechlin. In September 1944 this unit was transformed into "Kommando Nowotny" under the command of Walter Nowotny—283 aerial victories, died in combat November 8, 1944. Not until he became fully convinced of Allied air superiority, in

Alternative weapons systems

In addition to the standard armament of four 1.18 in. (30 mm) MK 108 cannon from which one hit was enough to inflict serious damage on a bomber and—according to Adolf Galland—three were enough to bring a bomber down, the Me 262 was also equipped with 2.16 in. (55 mm) R4M "Orkan" ("Hurricane") rockets. With these MK 108s and launch rails for twelve R4M rockets under each wing, the Me 262 had the most effective armament of any Second World War fighter. The 24 R4M rockets were fired in salvos of six rockets at 0.07-second intervals. They were outstandingly successful and the kill ratio of German fighters improved all of a sudden to 7:1 from 1:1! According to Adolf Galland, a single hit with an R4M rocket was enough to destroy a bomber! When attacking bomber formations, the rockets were fired from a range of around 5,000 ft. (1,500 m) and followed up with fire from the Messerschmitt's 1.18 in. (30 mm) cannon.

The Allied response

The sudden appearance of the Me 262 fighter in the skies above Germany caused the Allied pilots and their high command a considerable shock as the Schwalbe was nearly 125 mph (200 km/h) faster than Allied fighters. Before long, however, the pilots of the propeller aircraft of the US Eighth Air Force became familiar with and learned to exploit the Me 262's weaknesses. If it allowed itself to be lured into a duel, a Messerschmitt could be outmaneuvered. Furthermore, it was not unusual for the German fighter's jet turbines to cut out in such situations as pilots often failed in the heat of battle to treat the throttle control with the care it deserved. This made the Me 262 an easy target for the Allied fighters. From a tactical point of view, the Allied High Command reacted swiftly to the threat posed by the new jets. The first measure they introduced was to deploy fighters to permanently monitor the airspace above the Me 262 airfields. During take-off and landing, jets were all but defenseless against attacks by conventional fighters and many were shot down during these phases.

Pictures from a gunsight camera taken during an aerial battle capture the drama of the moment.

November 1944, did Hitler order the creation of Jagdgeschwader 7, the world's first jet fighter wing. In January 1945, Adolf Galland was ordered to form Jagdverband 44, another Me 262 unit. J.V. 44 developed into an elite unit for whose members the Ritterkreuz medal was almost part of the uniform. Among those who flew with it were aces such as Johannes Steinhoff, Heinrich Bär, Gerhard Barkhorn, and Walter Krupinski.

Due to its superiority in terms of speed, the Messerschmitt had the potential to win back air superiority for the Germans. Naturally its speed also brought undreamed-of problems. The Me 262 approached slow-moving enemy bombers so quickly that there was hardly time to aim. Johannes Steinhoff, later chief-of-staff of the West German air force, the Bundesluftwaffe, reported that enemy aircraft just seemed to hang motionless in the sky.

Further developments

A number of Me 262 A-1as were deployed with great success with night-fighter wing 10/NJG 11 as radar-guided night-fighters. Also planned was a two-seat night-fighter version with a longer fuselage based on the Me 262 B-2a trainer, but this progressed no further than the prototype stage. Another variant whose development was interrupted by the end of the war was the Me 262 model, which had an additional Walter rocket engine attached to the underneath of its fuselage. This was designed to accelerate the aircraft to interception altitude in the fastest possible time.

Tactical value

It is important not to overemphasize the operational success of the Me 262. Although a total of 1,430 had been built by the end of the war, due to the problems described above

The outcome is decided: an Me 262 is hit and goes into a dive with its engine blazing.

only around a quarter of them actually saw service. The bombing of the hydrogenation plants and the resulting fuel shortages took care of the rest.

Obstacles encountered during the development phase reduced the amount of time available to resolve teething troubles. Nevertheless, the Me 262 achieved over 700 aerial victories before the Allied invasion of Germany put an end to its operational history.

HEINKEL
HE 178

The experimental Heinkel He 178 occupies a very special place in the history of the fighter even though it never went into production. It was the first aircraft in the world to be powered by a jet engine and as such represented another significant leap forward in the development of aviation. There was no place in the National Socialists' war strategy for this pioneering aircraft, however, and the He 178 ended up in the Berlin Museum of Aviation, where it was destroyed in an air raid in 1943. The shortsightedness of the country's leaders had set back the development of the jet by years.

The Heinkel He 178 was the first aircraft in history to be powered by a jet engine but never went into production.

HEINKEL HE 178 V1
Experimental aircraft
Wingspan: 23 ft. 7 in. (7.20 m)
Length: 24 ft. 6 in. (7.48 m)
Height: 6 ft. 11 in. (2.10 m)
Empty weight: 3,638 lb. (1,650 kg)
Maximum take-off weight: 4,299 lb. (1,950 kg)
Power plant: 1 × Heinkel HeS3A turbojet with 1,012 lbf (4.5 kN) thrust, later the more powerful HeS3B with 1,101 lbf (4.9 kN) thrust
Maximum speed: 398 mph (640 km/h)
Range: 124 miles (200 km)

Ohain, Whittle, and Campini

In the early 1930s, substantial progress was made in jet engine research by these three designers in three different countries. In 1930, Frank Whittle had submitted a patent application for a turbine with a centrifugal compressor and it was a development of this that would later power the Gloster Meteor. In Italy, Secondo Campini had invented an engine that was actually a combination of piston engine and compressor with afterburner. This powered the first cross-country flight by a jet aircraft in 1940.

A fruitful partnership

In 1936, Ernst Heinkel, who had an abiding interest in technical innovation, was introduced by a former colleague, professor Pohl, to a 24-year-old scientist named Hans-Joachim Pabst von Ohain. The doctoral student was already working on his first jet engine and, following his meeting with Heinkel, he and his assistant Max Hahn were provided with the necessary financial resources and space (at the Heinkel aircraft works) to develop their invention to production readiness. A small hut outside the main Heinkel factory building in Rostock-Marienehe was fitted out as a research laboratory (Special Developments Department II) and the first HeS3A turbine was tested the very next year.

Through a process of continual improvement, Pabst von Ohain was able to increase the performance of his jet engine to such an extent that by spring 1938 it was already generating thrust of 1,012 lbf (4.5 kN). This was boosted further and then tested in flight. The staff involved in the development process were sworn to absolute secrecy. Only the Reich Air Ministry was kept informed of progress.

Interest in Heinkel's work

Unlike the government, the Air Ministry, to which the Luftwaffe was answerable, had been following the work being carried out at Heinkel with great interest and was convinced of the pioneering importance of the new engine. The country's leading manufacturers of aero-engines, Junkers in Dessau and BMW in Munich, were asked to develop their own jet engines, a request which gave rise a number of years later to the world's first mass-produced jet engines. the BMW 003 and the Junkers Jumo 004.

One of two Heinkel He 178 experimental aircraft. Neither has survived.

The He 178 V1 took its first short hop on August 24, 1939. The world's first confirmed jet-powered flight took place a few days later.

Testing in flight

The jet engine was initially tested on a propeller plane, specifically the He 118 V2 dive-bomber prototype, fitted to the underneath of the fuselage between the wings.

Following the complete loss of plane and engine during testing, Heinkel developed and built a new airframe, the He 178 V1, specifically for the purpose of testing the new engine. This test plane was designed as an all-metal—duralumin—high-wing cantilever monoplane with a span of just 23 ft. 6 in. (7.20 m) and a retractable undercarriage. It was powered by the second engine, the HeS3B, which had just been finished. This engine's compressor consisted of an axial pre-stage and a centrifugal main stage. At first the fuel used was kerosene, then normal aviation fuel. The He3SB was fitted lengthways into the fuselage with the air intake opening in the nose and an exhaust aperture in the rear. This design anticipated an idea later realized in a production context in the F-86 Sabre and MiG-15. In addition to the He 178 V1 (Experimental Type 1), a second version was also built with a 28 ft. (8.60 m) span and larger wings. Finally, on August 24, 1939, the He 178 V1 performed its first short hop during taxiing tests in Rostock-Marienehe with Heinkel test pilot Erich Warsitz at the controls. The world's first recognized flight of a jet followed on August 27, 1939, when two laps of the airfield lasting six minutes opened a new chapter in the history of aviation.

Jet engines—centrifugal and axial compressors
Before being mixed with the fuel in a jet engine's combustion chamber, the air flows through a compressor. The rotating blades provide the air with energy that is subsequently transformed into thrust. In the case of axial compressors the air flows through a series of compressor vanes arranged in parallel to the driveshaft, whereas in the case of centrifugal compressors the air is thrown outwards and—in multi-stage compressors—has to be redirected after each stage.

Both systems and also hybrid forms are used today.

Reactions

This sensational flight aroused surprisingly little attention in view of the significance of the achievement. However, the date must be taken into account: just five days after the first flight, Hitler's invasion of Poland marked the beginning of the Second World War and it is therefore hardly surprising that the Reich Air Ministry was preoccupied with other matters.

Moreover Ernst Udet, Chief of Aircraft Procurement and Supply at the time, who was responsible for Germany's military air planning, displayed a lack of foresight by taking little interest in the new form of aircraft propulsion.

Presentation

One month after the Polish surrender, another attempt was made to present the He 178 to the top brass with a demonstration flight of the He 178 V1 at the Rostock-Marienehe airfield on November 1, 1939. Present were Erhard Milch, State Secretary of the Reich Air Ministry, and Ernst Udet—who barely managed to conceal his lack of interest.

The main reason for this rejection of jet power lay in the relatively poor performance of the early jet engines relative to that of the by then highly developed piston engines. The Ohain/Heinkel HeS3B had an extremely high fuel consumption but gave only an average performance in the He 178 V1. It probably never flew much beyond 375 mph (600 km/h) and due to its high fuel consumption could only remain airborne for ten minutes at a time. Clearly the performance of both engine and aircraft could have been improved further, but Udet was only interested in the current state of development. The entire mindset of the military high command was geared up to a short war. The magic word was "production" and there was little or no interest any more in long-term development. In accordance with an order issued on September 2, 1939, Heinkel had to cease all research and development activity that was of no immediate benefit to Germany's war effort.

The end

Despite Heinkel's repeated pleas and arguments, development of the He 178 was terminated and the second of the two experimental planes (the V2) never flew. The He 178 was simply exhibited in the Berlin Museum of Aviation, where it was destroyed in an air raid in 1943.

Neither Heinkel nor Ohain allowed themselves to be disheartened by the official rejection and continued their development. Towards the end of the Second World War, what was probably the highest-performing jet engine of the war years, the He So11, was nearing completion but was never actually used.

Like many prominent scientists, Hans-Joachim Pabst von Ohain emigrated to the USA after the war, where he continued to work on the development of jet engines.

A modern jet engine

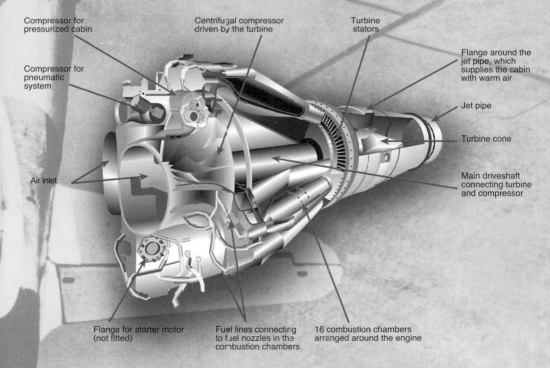

Compressor for pressurized cabin

Centrifugal compressor driven by the turbine

Turbine stators

Flange around the jet pipe, which supplies the cabin with warm air

Compressor for pneumatic system

Jet pipe

Turbine cone

Air inlet

Main driveshaft connecting turbine and compressor

Flange for starter motor (not fitted)

Fuel lines connecting to fuel nozzles in the combustion chambers

16 combustion chambers arranged around the engine

One of the earliest official photographs of the Lockheed F-80 Shooting Star. The aircraft was developed under the strictest secrecy.

LOCKHEED F-80 SHOOTING STAR

The Lockheed F-80 Shooting Star was the first jet to be used in overseas operations and the USA's first successful contribution to worldwide jet aircraft development. It appeared too late to see action in the Second World War but model F-80C bore the brunt of the air war in Korea.

LOCKHEED F-80C SHOOTING STAR
Single-seat fighter/fighter-bomber
Wingspan: 38 ft. 9 in. (11.81 m)
Length: 34 ft. 5 in. (10.49 m)
Height: 11 ft. 3 in. (3.43 m)
Empty weight: 8,419 lb. (3,819 kg)
Maximum take-off weight: 16,857 lb. (7,646 kg)
Power plant: 1 × Allison J33-A-23 jet engine with 4,595 lbf (20.44 kN) thrust, later J33-A-35 with 5,395 lbf (24 kN) thrust
Maximum speed: 594 mph (956 km/h)
Operational ceiling: 46,801 ft. (14,265 m)
Range: 1,379 miles (2,220 km)
Armament: 6 × M3 .50 in. (12.7 mm) machine guns, under-wing racks for 2 × 1,000 lb. (454 kg) bombs, 16 × unguided 5 in. (127 mm) rockets, napalm tank

Skunk Works and the XP-80

The first jet-powered aircraft developed in the USA, the Bell P-59 Airacomet (1942), never entered service because of its disappointing flying characteristics.

In 1943, Lockheed's chief designer, Clarence "Kelly" Johnson, was awarded a contract to design a completely new aircraft for the British Halford H.1B (Goblin) jet engine which had powered the prototype of the De Havilland Vampire.

Lockheed's "Skunk Works" development department underbid the deadline by 37 days and test flights with prototype XP-80, which featured lightly swept wings and a tricycle undercarriage, began in January 1944. The second prototype, the XP-80A, was powered by the first US jet engine with centrifugal compressor, the General Electric I-40, which was based on British designs. This in turn was replaced in XP-80B by the Allison J-33 with centrifugal compressor.

Deliveries commence before the end of the war

Machines were sent to the UK and Italy for testing but care was taken to keep them away from any fighting. As a result of its outstanding performance, the US government planned to purchase 5,000 P-80s, but after the end of the war this figure was drastically cut.

"P" for pursuit, "F" for fighter

On September 18, 1947, the National Security Act came into force, establishing the United States Air Force (USAF) as an independent arm of the US forces alongside the Army and the Navy. This led to a change in the designation of its various weapons systems. Its fighters, which had previously been designated "P" for "pursuit," were now given the abbreviation "F" for "fighter" and so the P-80 became the F-80 Shooting Star.

Korea

The USAF F-80Cs that took part in the early stages of the Korean War, which began in June 1950, were the first US jets ever to be sent into conflict. On the very first day of combat, four F-80s were victorious against a superior number of—albeit outdated—propeller aircraft. F-80Cs flying out of Japan attacked the North Korean

Army with machine gun fire, rockets, bombs, and—for the first time—napalm.

Jet versus jet

The entry of China into the war marked the beginning of a new chapter in the history of military aviation. For the first time ever, jet fighters encountered each other in combat as Chinese MiG-15s engaged US F-80s. On November 8, 1950, Lieutenant Russell J. Brown, in an F-80, shot down the first MiG-15 over North Korea. The battle lasted 30 seconds and ended in a US victory but this should not be taken as an indication of the Lockheed's superiority. Over a short distance at least, the MiG had a clear advantage.

Production span

The Lockheed F-80 Shooting Star remained in production until 1959. The T-33 two-seat trainer developed from the export version—the version built in the greatest numbers—became the most widely used and successful training aircraft for jet pilots in the world and remained in service for over 20 years.

More than 1,400 F-80 Shooting Stars served in every arm of the US forces for many years.

The "Acrojets," an aerobatic squadron of the US Air Force, flying in formation at around 625 mph (1,000 km/h).

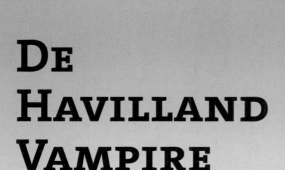

DE HAVILLAND VAMPIRE

Some experiments never get past the trial stage while others produce results that no one dared hope for. The Vampire belongs to the second category. It began life as an experimental aircraft designed in response to specification E.6/41 and went on to become an export success and the most versatile jet of the early years.

DE HAVILLAND VAMPIRE FB.5
Single-seat fighter/fighter-bomber
Wingspan: 38 ft. (11.58 m)
Length: 30 ft. 9 in. (9.37 m)
Height: 6 ft. 3 in. (1.91 m)
Empty weight: 7,253 lb. (3,290 kg)
Maximum take-off weight: 12,359 lb. (5,606 kg)
Power plant: 1 × De Havilland Goblin 2/2 turbojet with 4,400 lbf (19.57 kN) thrust
Maximum speed: 530 mph (853 km/h)
Operational ceiling: 41,010 ft. (12,500 m)
Range: 1,145 miles (1,842 km)
Armament: 4 × Hispano .787 (20 mm) cannon with 125 rounds each, 8 × 60 lb. (27 kg), 3 in. (76 mm) rockets and 2 × 500 lb. (227 kg) or 1,000 lb. (454 kg) bombs

Geoffrey de Havilland Jr.

The son of the aviation pioneer of the same name took off for the maiden flight of prototype LZ548/G on September 20, 1943, and 19 months later, on April 20, 1945, the first production aircraft left the factory. A total of 268 examples were built of the first model, the F.I.

Double fuselage

The Halford H.1 turbojet, named after its inventor Frank B. Halford and subsequently manufactured by De Havilland under the name "Goblin," produced thrust of around 2,698 lbf (12 kN). This necessitated an airframe that reduced drag to a minimum. The engineers at De Havilland opted for the twin-boom design that was characteristic of the firm—and was to remain so until the 1980s with the Vixen. In order to minimize loss of performance due to aerodynamic inefficiency, the turbojet's air inlets were sunk into the wing roots directly in front of the engine, obviating the need for long air ducts for the intake air.

Caught in the crosshairs: Britain's first jet, the De Havilland Vampire, in low-level flight.

Successor to the Mosquito

The Vampire's nose betrays the hand of its chief designer and progenitor of the Mosquito, R.E. Bishop. Another feature reminiscent of the Mosquito is the Vampire's molded plywood box fuselage. The wings—with slotted flaps and spoilers/air brakes— tail assembly, and booms were made of an aluminum alloy. Because of its twin booms, the Vampire had two fins and a long connecting horizontal stabilizer. The Vampire was the last high-performance military aircraft to be constructed using a hybrid wood–metal method.

Flying characteristics

The Vampire was without doubt one of the most agile of all jet fighters, with light, responsive controls—properties that made it particularly well suited to high-speed combat missions. Tight banking at low speeds and low altitudes could, however, be dangerous, and the Vampire was therefore one of the first aircraft to be fitted with an ejection seat. Another problem was that a sudden throttle movement could cause the turbojet to cut out (flameout). Without any possibility of restarting the engine, this made an emergency landing inevitable.

Another probable record is that of most widely used jet, as the Vampire served with over 30 air forces.

Last but not least, its length of service is also highly impressive. The Vampires ordered by the Swiss Air Force in 1946 remained in service until 1980 and trainer versions continued to be used by other air forces until even later.

The Vampire remained in service for over 30 years. A whole generation of jet pilots trained in it.

A record-breaker

The Vampire was the first British jet to break the 500 mph (805 km/h) barrier and at the end of the 1940s set a new world altitude record of over 59,055 ft. (18,000 m). In 1945 it aroused the interest of the Royal Navy when it became the first jet to land on an aircraft carrier. It was also the first single-engined jet to cross the Atlantic.

Production

The Vampire was a sales success with more than 20 basic versions and over 50 variants produced. A total of 1,979 specimens were built: 1,451 in the UK and the remainder under license in various other countries. The version built in the greatest numbers was the FB.5.

A jet pilot returns from a mission against insurgent Mau Mau guerillas in Kenya.

McDONNELL FH-1 PHANTOM

During the early stages in the development of the jet, US Navy chiefs sought a way of incorporating the new technology in a carrier fighter.

MCDONNELL FH-1 PHANTOM
Carrier-borne single-seat fighter
Wingspan: 40 ft. 9 in. (12.42 m)
Length: 37 ft. 3 in. (11.35 m)
Height: 14 ft. 2 in. (4.32 m)
Empty weight: 6,682 lb. (3,031 kg)
Maximum take-off weight: 12,035 lb. (5,459 kg)
Power plant: 2 × Westinghouse J30-WE-20 turbojets with 1,600 lbf (7.12 kN) thrust
Maximum speed: 479 mph (771 km/h)
Operational ceiling: 41,093 ft. (12,525 m)
Range: 695 miles (1,118 km)
Armament: 4 × .50 in. (12.7 mm) machine guns in nose

XFD-1, the Phantom 1 prototype, demonstrating the suitability of jets as carrier aircraft on board aircraft carrier Franklin D. Roosevelt.

Size as the main criterion

Space restrictions on the flight deck meant that large jet engines with centrifugal compressors were unsuitable for carrier operations. The firm of Westinghouse had been conducting government-funded research into axial compressors, which are considerably less bulky, and by 1943 it had developed a unit to production readiness.

McDonnell

In 1943, the new firm of McDonnell was asked by the Navy Bureau of Aeronautics to design a carrier-borne jet fighter around the Westinghouse turbojet.

To start with, a series of models was studied that were designed to accommodate up to eight of the smaller engines of 9.5 in. (240 mm) diameter. In the end, it was decided to construct prototype XFD-1 around two engines of 19 in. (480 mm) diameter.

Maiden flight and carrier landing
Due to supply problems, prototype XFD-1 completed its maiden flight on January 26, 1945, with only one 19XB—the future J30—engine. Despite this setback, two months later McDonnell received an order for 100 aircraft (reduced to 60 after the end of the war).

The XFD-1 performed its first landing on an aircraft carrier (USS *Franklin D. Roosevelt*) on July 21, 1946, against a backdrop of lined-up US Navy officers. The practicability of jet-powered carrier aircraft had thus been demonstrated in the USA too.

The first production aircraft
Another year went by before the first production of jets—powered by the Westinghouse J30—were delivered to the US Navy. In the meantime the aircraft's name had had to be changed from FD-1 to FH-1 Phantom because the letter "D" had already been allocated by the US Navy to the firm Douglas. In May 1948, VF-17A became the first carrier-borne fighter squadron to be equipped with Phantom jets.

The Phantom
The Phantom's airframe was a smooth, conservative design with straight wings. Its two axial J30 turbojets were integrated into the wing roots on either side of the fuselage. The short, broad, tricycle undercarriage retracted inwardly into the wings and fuselage.

The wings could be folded upwards in order to make optimum use of the limited space on an aircraft carrier.

Performance
The FH-1's two turbojets made it fast—it was the US Navy's first jet capable of over 500 mph (800 km/h)—but not extraordinarily fast. Moreover, with just four .50 in. (12.7 mm) machine guns—whereas during the Second World War .787 in. (20 mm) cannon had become the standard fighter armament—it could not be claimed that it was strongly armed.

Insights gained
In practical trials, the Phantom proved a robust aircraft fully capable of meeting the particular demands of carrier deployment.

However, developments in aircraft design soon demonstrated to the US Navy that the FH-1 could only be an interim solution. The plan was to use the Phantom to enable carrier crews and pilots to acquire experience of the new jet technology. In the meantime the Phantom's successor (F-2H Banshee) had become available and by 1953 all FH-1s had been retired.

The US Navy's first carrier-borne jet, the FH-1 Phantom, which had a top speed of over 450 mph (725 km/h).

The basic shape of this early jet, with its virtually straight wings, retains a certain similarity to its piston-engined predecessors.

GLOSTER METEOR

The UK's first jet fighter was the only Allied jet to see action during the Second World War. Having lost the race to become the world's first operational jet fighter by a hair's breadth, it went on to enjoy a far more successful career than its direct competitor.

No. 56 Squadron 56 flying Gloster Meteors in formation over southeast England.

GLOSTER METEOR F.MK IV
Single-seat fighter
Wingspan: 37 ft. 2 in. (11.32 m)
Length: 41 ft. (12.50 m)
Height: 13 ft. (3.96 m)
Empty weight: 11,217 lb. (5,088 kg)
Maximum take-off weight: 14,546 lb. (6,598 kg)
Power plant: 2 × Rolls-Royce Derwent turbojets with axial compressors, 3,507 lbf (15.6 kN) thrust each
Maximum speed: 585 mph (941 km/h)
Operational ceiling: 43,963 ft. (13,400 m)
Range: 994 miles (1,600 km)
Armament: 4 × British Hispano .787 (20 mm) cannon with 195 rounds each

From Thunderbolt to Meteor

Preliminary work on the Gloster Meteor was carried out in 1940. Building on Sir Frank Whittle's research, Gloster Aircraft and Whittle's firm Power Jets Ltd. began a collaboration to develop an experimental aircraft, the Gloster G.40, in response to specification E.28/39. This Meteor predecessor flew in May 1941. This gave rise to further prototypes and a small production run. The production model was originally going to be called the Thunderbolt but, to avoid confusion with the US Republic P-47, the name of the project was changed to Meteor in 1942.

Twelve prototypes

The number of prototypes gives an idea of the difficulties that attended the dawning of the jet age. The first aircraft to be designated a Meteor—the fifth prototype (DG 206/DG)—was fitted with two Halford H.1s for its first flight in 1943 but these turned out too underpowered to enable the new plane to be competitive. Other turbojets were tested, including the Metrovick F.2 and the Rolls-Royce Welland I. Finally, the Rolls-Royce W.2B/23C-Welland was chosen for production but was replaced by the Rolls-Royce Derwent from model F.Mk.III onwards. It is difficult to ascertain the intellectual ownership of the individual engines: ultimately the entire British jet engine industry was building on Whittle's original work.

George Carter, Gloster Aircraft's chief designer, had stuck to a conventional design for the airframe and wings. The Gloster was an all-metal construction with tricycle undercarriage,

an engine in the middle of each wing, and in order not to interfere with the exhaust gas, a high tailplane. The initial designs for aircraft E.28/39, meanwhile, had a double fuselage like the De Havilland Vampire.

> ### The speed of sound—Mach 1
> Mach is a dimensionless measure, a relative value indicating the relationship of the speed of a body to the speed of sound in the surrounding medium. This speed changes according to the pressure and composition of that medium (in this case air).
>
> An approximate or mean value for Mach is 767 mph (1,234 km/h) or 1,125 ft/s (343 m/s). This corresponds to the speed of sound at sea level in an ambient temperature of 68°F (20°C).

A Meteor takes shape: weapons technicians fit one of the aircraft's four .787 in. (20 mm) cannon.

No. 74 Squadron RAF photographed during an emergency drill in the 1950s.

An unobstructed view of compass and destination— the cockpit of the Gloster Meteor.

The early years of the jet

The jet engines that reached production stage in the early 1940s represented a whole new dimension in terms of high-altitude performance and speed.

This giant leap forward is well illustrated by the following comparison: whereas a propeller aircraft was considered extremely fast if it could achieve 435 mph (700 km/h) in level flight, production version F.Mk.IV of the Gloster Meteor was some 150 mph (250 km/h) faster.

The Meteor set two speed records, the first in 1945 and the second in 1946, when Captain Teddy Donaldson reached 616 mph (991 km/h) under official conditions. The order of velocity attained by the early jets brought completely new and unfamiliar problems and the Meteor was no exception.

Up to speeds of over 435 mph (700 km/h), the Gloster's controls were well balanced and effective. Beyond Mach 0.72 the degree of force needed to activate the control surfaces increased sharply. Tight banking during pursuit at speeds in excess of 450 mph (730 km/h) brought extreme forces on the ailerons, elevators, and rudder and impaired the Meteor's effectiveness as a fighter. Measures aimed at remedying this problem were introduced by Gloster Aircraft's development department during the course of F.Mk.IV production: the wings were shortened in order to improve the Meteor's maneuverability and roll speed.

Another problem was that the compressibility effect caused the airframe to vibrate. This made totally new demands on aerodynamics and the load-bearing capacities of materials.

Gloster Meteor Mk.I testing an auxiliary tank—being carried below the middle of the fuselage.

The engine gondolas

In order to reduce this vibration, the engine gondolas were modified in model F.3. Wind tunnel experiments had shown that the relatively short, thick housings were responsible for the movement. The new, more slender gondolas solved this problem up to a point and also increased speed by 75 mph (120 km/h) without any increase in engine performance.

Operational service

The first combat unit to be equipped with the new fighter was No. 616 Squadron, which received its first production aircraft in July 1944. For reasons of secrecy, they were initially used over the British Isles only—to destroy Fi 103 flying bombs. When the V1s were replaced by V2 rockets—against which fighters were helpless—this deployment was ended and the Meteors were transferred to Belgium.

There were no direct encounters between the Meteor and its direct rival the Messerschmitt Me 262, and the Second World War ended for the Meteor with a tally of 14 destroyed V1s and 46 German planes destroyed on the ground, with no losses in aerial combat.

The 1950s

Between 1950 and 1955 the Meteor formed the backbone of the RAF and was widely used in Korea by the British Commonwealth Forces. Initially the Meteor was deployed there as an air superiority fighter, but a direct comparison with the MiG-15s flown by China revealed it to be so inferior that it was redeployed as a reconnaissance plane and in a ground-support role as a fighter-bomber.

Variants

In addition to its role as a fighter there was a wide range of other tasks for which the Meteor was specially configured. These variants included:
- F.Mk.III with modified canopy, reduced wingspan, and Rolls-Royce Derwent I engine
- F.Mk.IV with Rolls-Royce Derwent 5
- T.Mk.7 two-seat trainer
- F.8, a development of the F.Mk.IV with a longer fuselage, larger fuel tank, and, for the first time, a Martin-Baker ejection seat

- FR.9 reconnaissance fighter developed from the F.8
- PR.10 high-altitude photographic reconnaissance variant with additional mounting for a tail camera
- NF.11 night-fighter with airborne radar
- NF.12 US night-fighter version with US radar
- NF.13 Tropics version of the NF.11
- U.16 drone derived from the F.8
- TT.20 high-speed target tug version of the NF.11

The Gloster Meteor remained in service with the RAF for over 17 years and with the New Zealand Navy until 1965. A few Meteors were also operated by Israel as the first jets in the Israeli armed forces. The British government was the only government prepared to issue an export license for Israel at the time.

POSTWAR FIGHTERS

DE HAVILLAND D.H. 103 HORNET

The Hornet and the Sea Hornet used by the British Navy were the fastest twin-engined single-seat fighters of the RAF and the Royal Navy. With a wooden fuselage and wings of mixed construction (light metal and wood), they were the last piston-engined planes from the De Havilland stable used militarily. At the beginning of the 1950s, the plane was still in service when the RAF changed over to jet fighters—the combat radius of the D.H. 103 was at this time not achievable with turbojet engines.

DE HAVILLAND D.H. 103 HORNET F.3
Single-seat fighter
Wingspan: 45 ft. (13.72 m)
Length: 36 ft. 8 in. (11.18 m)
Height: 14 ft. 2 in. (4.32 m)
Empty weight: 12.768 lb. (6,244 kg)
Maximum take-off weight: 20,875 lb. (9,467 kg)
Power plant: 2 × liquid-cooled parallel-feed 12 cylinder V-engine Rolls-Royce Merlin 130/131, each with 2,100 hp (1,544 kW)
Maximum speed: 472 mph (760 km/h)
Operational ceiling: 37,403 ft. (11,400 m)
Range: 2,981 miles (4,800 km)
Armament: standard, 4 × fixed in the lower front of the fuselage built-in .787 in. (20 mm) British-Hispano cannon with 190 rounds each, under-wing pylons (between engine and wingtip) for 2 × 1,001 lb. (454 kg) bombs or 8 × unguided 59.5 lb. (27 kg) RP-3 rockets or ventral tanks

The D.H. 103 Hornet, one of the last fighters with a piston engine, clearly bears the signature of the De Havilland designers

The long-range fighter

The Hornet was first a private risk venture and the F.12/43 specification was filed later. The task that the development department had set itself was a single-seat, twin-engined, long-range fighter for deployment in the Far East in the war with Japan over the Pacific.

At the De Havilland Company, a smaller and faster twin-engined fighter had been built from the proved and tested Mosquito—the similarity to the predecessor is unmistakable. The two Rolls-Royce Merlin engines rotated in opposite directions—to neutralize the rolling movement that would add up with two similarly rotating engines. The two different classifications in the "Technical Data" are explained by the use of different motors. The two contra-rotating propellers, moreover, lead to predictable and stable flight properties.

484 mph (780 km/h)

The prototype of the Hornet, which completed its first flight on July 28, 1944, reached 484 mph (780 km/h). At the end of the same year the production of the 12.5 mph (20 km/h)-slower mass-produced plane started. The Hornet was delivered from February 1945, and was put into service from 1946—too late to serve its planned deployment purpose. The only conflict the Hornet took part in was the Malaysia Uprising at the beginning of the 1950s. A struggle for air supremacy did not take place there, so it was used against ground targets for the suppression of unrest.

Sea Hornet

Alongside the 193 F.1 and F.3 models produced, which served in the front line of the British air force until 1951, 170 of the Sea Hornet version were built in total. The number of all planes of this type came to 382.

The very great range made the Hornet admirably suited to deployment as a carrier-borne long-range fighter. The prototype of this marine version (with propellers turning outwards!) flew for the first time in 1945. But it took three years for the mass-produced Sea Hornet F.20 to be handed to the Royal Navy.

Variants

The individual characteristics by mode of deployment:

- Hornet F.1—air supremacy and long-range fighter
- Hornet F.3—as F.1
- Hornet PR.2—photo-reconnaissance
- Hornet FR.4—spotter
- Sea Hornet F.20—first carrier-borne version, fighter plane
- Sea Hornet FR.20—carrier-borne spotter
- Sea Hornet NF.2—carrier-borne night-fighter
- Sea Hornet PR.22—carrier-borne photo-reconnaissance

The landing gear support beam of the Hornet unfolded forwards out of the engine pod.

The D.H. 103 was able to carry up to 2002 lb. (908 kg) external load. Here it is armed with rockets.

BELL P-59 AIRACOMET

The Bell P-59 Airacomet was, in 1942 on its first flight, the first American fighter plane with a jet engine. However, during the test the actual flight performance could not fulfill expectations, so the original order was cancelled and the Airacomet was mainly used for the training of jet pilots.

International co-operation

The development of this first American jet goes back to a visit by General Henry "Hap" Arnold, Chief of the US Army Air Corps, to Britain in spring 1941. There Arnold was able to watch the British Whittle turbine with centrifugal

The P-59 Airacomet was the first American military jet. Although it never achieved operative status, the Airacomet was very significant both technologically and in pilot training.

BELL P-59B-1 AIRACOMET
Single-seat fighter-bomber
Wingspan: 45 ft. 6 in. (13.87 m)
Length: 38 ft. 1 in. (11.62 m)
Height: 12 ft. 4 in. (3.76 m)
Empty weight: 7,904 lb. (3,601 kg)
Maximum take-off weight: 13,761 lb. (6,214 kg)
Power plant: 2 × General Electric J31-GE-3 (I-16) turbojet engines, maximum take-off performance each 2,000 lbf (8.9 kN) thrust
Maximum speed: 410 mph (661 km/h)
Operational ceiling: 46,196 ft. (14,080 m)
Combat radius: 522 miles (840 km)
Armament: 1 × M4 1.46 in. (37 mm) caliber with 44 rounds and 3 x bow-mounted .50 in. (12.7 mm) machine guns with 200 rounds each, under-wing pylons for 1,985 lb. (900 kg) bomb load

First flight

The flight performances of the first prototype XP-59A, which completed its maiden flight on October 1, 1942, were disappointing. Although the jet was pleasant to fly, the really big airframe and the low performance of the two turbines allowed no thrust in the maximum speed range above the 435 mph (700 km/h) mark. Their flight performances can most easily be compared with the Gloster Meteor developed at the same time in Great Britain and were similar to a Second World War piston-engined fighter.

Two planes of the Bell Company: an armed Airacomet and a Kingcobra (in the background).

A new field of operation

When the first twelve pre-production planes YP-59A were delivered for military trials in 1944, it then became clear that the Airacomet was unsuitable as a fighter. Even the mass-produced models, the P-59A and P-59B, with the greater thrust I-16 engine (General Electric J31-GE-3) were not convincing.

In the next few years they served as jet trainers for the training of air force and navy pilots who were thus introduced to the new jet technology. A few further YP-59A and P-59 Airacomets were later fitted with remote-control equipment and used as a towing aircraft for target-display until 1945.

Meeting of technologies: the first US jet together with the propeller-driven F4U Corsair.

compressor on a trial run and was very impressed by the novel airplane engine. After detailed consultation, an agreement was reached about the mutual exchange of technological advances. In the USA the British turbine was to be "Americanized" and a twin-engined fighter plane built with it. The General Electric Company became the contractor for the construction of the turbine, while Bell Aircraft Corporation was to design and build a jet fighter. Bell was given all of eight months development time from the day the contract was signed until the jet's first flight.

Behind closed doors

At Bell, under extreme secrecy, an all-metal mid-wing airplane with nose wheel undercarriage was designed with the jet engines fitted on either side of the fuselage under the wings. The turbines were positioned at the airplane's center of gravity and were easily accessible for maintenance and repair.

Timing

Bell managed to keep to the tight schedule for the jet's construction. However, General Electric was not able to deliver the engine until August 1942. These first jet engines, re-creations of the British Whittle W.1X, type General Electric I-A, caused additional difficulties for the development departments. They never worked smoothly and their performance, with a static thrust of only 1,102 lbf (500 kp), was by no means sufficient. Neither the first nor later improved versions of the turbine reached the originally expected performance.

HAWKER HUNTER

The Hawker Hunter is regarded by many experts as one of the best—and most elegant—jets flying at subsonic speed. In its function as an interceptor it served the RAF from 1954 to 1963; in other armed forces for much longer than that.

A Hawker Hunter on a works photo at Hawker Aircraft. The swept-back wings and tailplane document progress in the geometry of flight.

Sidney Camm

The legendary designer of the Hurricane, Sidney Camm, was also in the postwar period chief designer at Hawker Aircraft. His work found expression in the P.1067, an interceptor with swept-back wing unit and tailplane and also an axial-flow engine, and led to three prototypes (first flight July 20, 1951).

Three different engines with axial compressors were tested; included in the series were the Rolls-Royce Avon RA.7 and the Armstrong Siddeley Sapphire Mk.101.

The first plane of the 22 mass-produced Hunter F.1s completed—powered by an Avon engine—made its maiden flight on May 16, 1953, followed a little later by the first Hunter F.2s with Sapphire engines.

HAWKER HUNTER FGA.9
Single-seat fighter-bomber
Wingspan: 33 ft. 8 in. (10.25 m)
Length: 45 ft. 10 in. (13.98 m)
Height: 14 ft. (4.26 m)
Empty weight: 13,274 lb. (6,020 kg)
Maximum take-off weight: 24,001 lb. (10,885 kg)
Power plant: 1 × Rolls-Royce turbojet engine Avon 203 with axial compressor (alternative Avon 207) with 10,152 lbf (45.16 kN) take-off thrust
Maximum speed: 708 mph (1,140 km/h) (Mach 0.93)
Operational ceiling: 50,035 ft. (15,250 m)
Combat radius: 428 miles (689 km)
Armament: 4 × Aden cannon 1.18 in. (30 mm) caliber, under-wing stations for up to 3,594 lb. (1,630 kg) combat load: 992 lb. (450 kg) bombs and 2 × rocket launchers each for 12 unguided 3 in. (76 mm) rockets

Airframe and armament

The Hawker Hunter was a mid-wing airplane with a 35-degree swept-back wing unit and tailplane; the triangular air intakes were integrated into the wing roots on both sides of the fuselage. For maintenance work, the whole rear section of the fuselage could be easily removed—the same was true of the weapon system.

The Hunters displayed excellent flight performance, coupled with an enormously strong armament that in the initial stage of being put into service consisted of four 1.18 in. (30 mm) cannon. Later developments were also able to fire guided missiles such as the AIM-9 Sidewinder (air-to-air), the AGM-12 Bullpup (air-to-ground), the AGM-65 Maverick (air-to-ground), and 2.68 in. (68 mm) SNEB-type rockets. As an attack plane in the FGA version (Fighter/Ground Attack), they carried bombs or napalm containers under the wings.

First deployments

The first squadrons were equipped with the Hunter F.1 in July 1954 and there they revealed a serious deficiency in service: their internal fuel capacity was too low. Thus the jet was only able to stay in the air for a little more than an hour. Extra tanks under the wings containing up to 515 gal. (1,950 l) solved the problem.

Service record

With the later model F.7—introduced in 1957—the gap in performance was closed with respect to most contemporary fighters, but its performance could not match the newest supersonic fighters. So, it was already clear at the end of the 1950s that the time of the Hunter as an interceptor would be limited. Until the beginning of the 1960s, the Hawker Hunter still remained the front-line pursuit and attack plane of the RAF; however, with the arrival of the Lightning in 1963, its service as an interceptor ended. In the FGA version it continued to serve as a ground combat support plane in operative deployment and as trainer in the RAF. This service period was surpassed in the Swiss Air Force; there the last Hunters were taken out of service in 1993 after 37 years.

During the RAF maneuver "Stronghold" in 1956 a Hawker Hunter is being armed by the ground crew.

The Hawker Hunter weapons platform was impressive for its versatility.

GRUMMAN F9F PANTHER/ COUGAR

GRUMMAN F9F-5 PANTHER
Carrier-borne fighter-bomber
Wingspan: 38 ft. (11.58 m)
Length: 38 ft. 10 in. (11.83 m)
Height: 12 ft. 3 in. (3.73 m)
Empty weight: 10.158 lb. (4,607 kg)
Maximum take-off weight: 18,698 lb. (8,480 kg)
Power plant: 1 × Pratt & Whitney J48-2 radial-compressor turbojet engine with 6,991 lbf (31.1 kN) thrust
Maximum speed: 578 mph (931 km/h)
Operational ceiling: 42,837 ft. (13,060 m)
Range: 1,299 miles (2,092 km)
Armament: 4 × M20 cannon caliber .787 in. (20 mm); under-wing pylons for combat loads (bombs and rockets) up to 2,000 lb. (907 kg)

The F9F Panther—the first turbojet fighter built by Grumman Aircraft Engineering—was deployed from aircraft carriers as a fighter-bomber in the Korean War and during this period formed the flying backbone of the US Navy and the US Marine Corps. From the sixth series, the advanced F9F Cougar arose under the same identification but changed name.

On the flight deck. Immediately after take-off the next F9F of the US Navy is brought to the catapult.

The first Grumman jet

In 1945 the planning office of the Grumman Company began with the construction of the G-79 night-fighter, which was to be powered by four small Westinghouse axial turbines accommodated in the wings. During the development period an order from the US Navy was sent in April 1946 to build a carrier-borne jet-propelled fighter airplane. Grumman rejected the night-fighter and developed the prototype XF9F-1 Panther, which completed its first flight on November 24, 1947.

The engines originally planned were replaced by a Rolls-Royce Nene turbojet engine produced under license by Pratt & Whitney. These were not fitted in the wings as planned, but in the fuselage.

The prototype built under the new technical guidelines was a construction with straight wings and two air intakes for the turbines integrated into the wings on either side of the fuselage. The jet pipe in the rear lay directly under the high-mounted tail unit and an aerodynamically shaped supplementary fuel container was fixed on the wingtips. For steering the plane the leading edge of the wing was movable while the landing flaps and aileron were arranged on the trailing edge of the wing. The armament consisting of four .787 in. (20 mm) caliber MK M-2s was built into the underside of the nose.

Panther and Cougar

Because the flight characteristics and the carrier capability had proved excellent in tests, mass production of the F9F-2 Panther was begun in November 1948; the US Navy took delivery of the first planes by May 1949.

The F9F-3 to -5 versions were equipped with progressively more powerful engines, but ultimately still within the framework of model upgrading.

The F9F-6 to -8 model series were quite different; here it was a question of an advanced plane being developed from the most recent perspective, with wings swept back 35 degrees and swept-back control surfaces. Moreover, the fixed wingtip tanks disappeared. This jet—only similar to the Panther externally and in a limited way, and distinctly faster—received the designation Cougar and was delivered for the first time in December 1951.

The Panther can be recognized as a jet of the first generation by the wings which are not swept back and the tanks at the wingtips.

Valley Forge

F9F Panthers were the first jets of the US Navy that were deployed on July 3, 1950, in the Korean War. Two of the Panther units taking off from the aircraft carrier *Valley Forge* provided fighter protection for a group of British bombers whose mission consisted in the destruction of enemy airfields around the capital, Pyongyang. Ensign (Lieutenant) E.W. Brown succeeded in shooting down a Yak-9 with his Panther, thus achieving the first air victory for the US Navy in the Korean War. Later pilots with the Panther could even record air victories against the superior MiG-15s.

In conclusion, it can be said that the F9F Panther was a remarkably reliable and easy to maintain weapons platform.

Maintenance and on-board check on a US aircraft carrier off the Korean coast in the Korean War.

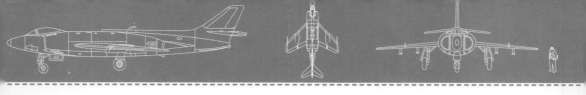

SUPERMARINE SCIMITAR

Shortly before landing: with extended arrestor hook, a Supermarine Scimitar glides on to the landing deck.

At the beginning of the 1950s, the Royal Navy investigated how a plane—with swept-back wings for high-speed flight—could be adapted to the particular conditions on aircraft carriers. The result, the Supermarine Scimitar, was in 1957 the first British naval fighter with swept-back wings—and the last warplane from the Supermarine stable. The service life of nine years was quite short—an unprecedented series of accidents led to its being withdrawn from service in 1966.

Innovations

The nameless Supermarine model 525, first flight April 28, 1954, was the second prototype with swept-back wings. It was mainly used to test the new landing flaps, and the steering system worked by hydraulics for the planned Scimitar. A special flap system for landing on aircraft carriers with boundary-layer override (compressed air from the turbine compressor is blown over the top surface of the flaps) holds the laminar boundary-layer flow longer on the wing. The result was a lower minimum speed, extremely important for carrier landings. The first model 544 final prototype called Scimitar made its maiden flight on January 20, 1956, followed on January 11, 1957, by the first of a total of 76 mass-produced planes.

SUPERMARINE SCIMITAR
Carrier-borne single-seat fighter-bomber
Wingspan: 37 ft. 2 in. (11.33 m)
Length: 55 ft. 4 in. (16.87 m)
Height: 17 ft. 4 in. (5.28 m)
Empty weight: 21,003 lb. (9,525 kg)
Maximum take-off weight: 34,211 lb. (15,515 kg)
Power plant: 2 × turbofan Rolls-Royce Avon 202 jet engines with 11,262 lbf (50.1 kN) static thrust
Max speed: 710 mph (1,143 km/h)
Operational ceiling: 50,002 ft. (15,240 m)
Combat radius: 600 miles (966 km)
Armament: 4 × Aden 1.18 in. (30 mm) caliber cannon, 4 × 1,000 lb. (454 kg) bombs, or 4 × Bullpup air-to-ground missiles (also suitable for anti-ship combat), or 4 × Sidewinder air-to-air missiles, or alternatively other external stores such as ventral tanks and tactical atomic weapons

---

The Beast

When introduced, the F.1 was the heaviest and most powerful warplane of the Fleet Air Arm (British naval air force), which subsequently was to bring a great deal of problems with it. The few Royal Navy aircraft carriers in those days were small and had short flight decks. Sufficient for propeller planes, they were not suitable for jets—because of the longer take-off and landing distance.

The Navy was the first to come up with the trick of allowing the flight decks at the end of the carriers to rise at a slight angle—like on a ski jump. However, this was still not enough for the weight of the Scimitar. Therefore in addition to the nose-wheel undercarriage, the jet was given a tail skid with bumper that the plane rested on at take-off and by which the approach angle and lift were increased: this enabled the Scimitar to take off. Nevertheless, take-off and landing on the small carriers was hazardous. Together with the design errors that persistently led to fires on board, the accidents accounted for a loss rate of F.1s of 51 percent in seven years.

These flight characteristics led the Supermarines' pilots to describe its behavior as "beastly", as the aircraft wasn't inclined to allow flight errors to go unpunished.

Role reversal

Although the Scimitar was armed as an interceptor, this function had now been taken over by the De Havilland Sea Vixen. As an attack plane, it was replaced by the Blackburn Buccaneer, and the Scimitars still in existence were used for secondary duties—as a refueling plane for the Buccaneer or for towing flak target banners and radar targets. The Scimitar was never used in combat operations, although in 1961 it helped avoid a war in the Persian Gulf by its appearance, preventing the Iraqi troops from marching into Kuwait.

The last Supermarine Scimitar F.1s were taken out of service with the Royal Navy in October 1966 (according to other sources 1969).

The service life of the Scimitar was, at nine years, relatively short. It was considered "beastly" and difficult to fly.

Resting on the tail bumper directly before take-off the Scimitar did not have contact with the ground with the nose wheel.

ENGLISH ELECTRIC LIGHTNING

In the 1950s the English Electric Company—which later merged into BAC—developed the first British jet fighter that reached twice the speed of sound. This plane—planned as an interim solution—stood the test so well in operational service that it was produced until 1972 and not withdrawn from service definitively until the late 1980s.

ENGLISH ELECTRIC LIGHTNING
Single-seat fighter
Wingspan: 34 ft. 10 in. (10.61 m)
Length: 55 ft. 3 in. (16.84 m)
Height: 19 ft. 7 in. (5.97 m)
Empty weight: 25,821 lb. (11,710 kg)
Maximum take-off weight: 41,708 lb. (18,915 kg)
Power plant: 2 × Rolls-Royce turbojet engines Avon 301, each with 12,676 lbf (56.39 kN) static thrust without and 16,231 lbf (72.20 kN) static thrust with afterburner
Maximum speed: 1,519 mph (2,446 km/h) (Mach 2.3)
Operational ceiling: over 59,058 ft. (18,000 m)
Combat radius: 373 miles (600 km)
Armament: 2 × Aden cannon 1.18 in. (30 mm) caliber with 120 rounds each (ventral pack) or cannon arm sets for 4 × Adens, two Red Top or Firestreak air-to-air missiles or 2 × rocket launchers with a total of 44 wing-stabilized unguided 2 in. (50.8 mm) rockets

The Lightning distinguished itself by excellent lift performance and speed

English Electric Company

With the design of the Lightning, the English Electric Company was reacting to an invitation to bid from the British Procurement Office from 1947 seeking a faster interceptor.

The prototype P.1A flew for the first time on August 4, 1954. The jet broke the sound barrier in horizontal flight on the third test run and thus became the first British supersonic plane. In July 1957, a P.1B prototype flew at Mach 1.72, unofficially a new record.

From 1960 the first RAF squadrons were equipped with the Lightning F.1 Series model, in 1961 Series F.2 followed, and in 1962 Series F.3. From July 1965 came Series F.6 with improved range to remove the greatest drawback in the Lightning as, despite excellent handling and spectacular flight characteristics, the Lightning was only rarely able to go further than 100–150 miles (160–240 km) away from its base without in-flight refueling.

Maintaining tradition: Two generations of jets, a Lightning and a Tornado, in the special livery for the 75-year jubilee of No 65 Squadron RAF.

Unusual solutions

The climbing performance and final speed of the new interceptor were unrivaled in Europe. In the construction unusual paths had been followed to reach this performance. A markedly slimmer, stretched-out oval fuselage, wings swept back at 60 degrees, and very little head resistance contributed to the Lightning's success.

The arrangement of the engines is the striking construction feature—the two turbines were arranged one above the other in the fuselage behind the pilot's seat and were both supplied with inlet air through the air intake in the nose.

Fuel

The disadvantage of this construction method was the fact that there was hardly any room left over in the fuselage for tanks. So every available place for fuel containers—including the free space in the wings and even in the flaps—had to be used.

In comparison

The speed and climbing ability of the Lightning were excellent and this was true not only for the 1960s but also in comparison with contemporary warplanes. Even the operational ceiling was quite extraordinary. Its operational altitude lay above 59,058 ft. (18,000 m)—in areas, therefore, normally only achieved by specially built jets.

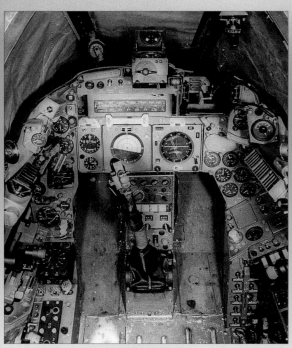

The end of the Lightning

The new generation of fighter planes in the 1960s made the Lightning increasingly superfluous, and from 1974 a changeover to the Phantom F4-F occurred, which was completed in 1988.

Cockpit of a Lightning from 1965.

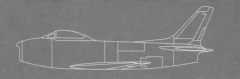

NORTH AMERICAN SABRE

The North American F-86 was a second-generation jet, and combined American and German developments into the outstanding Western fighter plane at the time of the Korean War.

The instrument panel of a North American F-86 H Sabre.

NORTH AMERICAN F-86D SABRE

All-weather single-seat fighter
Wingspan: 37 ft. 1 in. (11.31 m)
Length: 40 ft. 3 in. (12.27 m)
Height: 14 ft. 8 in. (4.47 m)
Empty weight: 13,501 lb. (6,123 kg)
Maximum take-off weight: 19,980 lb. (9,061 kg)
Power plant: 1 × General Electric J47-GE-17 turbojet engine with axial compressor and afterburner, 7,643 lbf (34 kN) thrust
Maximum speed: 702 mph (1,130 km/h)
Operational ceiling: 50,002 ft. (15,240 m)
Range: 850 miles (1,369 km)
Armament: 24 × "Mighty Mouse" 2.75 in. (70 mm) folding-fin rockets with 7.5 lb. (3.4 kg) warhead carried in extendable boxes in the under-front fuselage or 16 × HVAR rockets under the wings

The high-set tailplane, the swept-back wings and the air intake on the plane nose were identifying features of the F-86 Sabre.

The 1950s jet

The North American F-86 Sabre can justifiably be called the most important American fighter plane of the new generation. Its development goes back to a call for bids for a jet fighter plane from the US Army Air Force (USAAF) and the US Navy in 1944. In this bid the Sabre was still being requested as a conventional construction with straight wings.

of swept-back wings led the Sabre to become the first American jet to receive swept-back wings. For reasons of space-saving and performance it was decided to go for an engine with axial compressor. The engine air intakes were situated in the nose, the turbojet engine in the fuselage behind the pilot, and the thrust jet in the rear. From the original standard design, two separate jets were now developed at North American: the F-86 Sabre for the USAAF and the aircraft carrier-capable FJ-1 Fury for the Navy and the Marine Corps.

An F-86 shoots 5 in (127 mm) caliber unguided rockets in practice shooting at Nellis Air Force Base.

NORTH AMERICAN F-100F SUPER SABRE
Single-seat fighter-bomber
Wingspan: 38 ft. 9 in. (11.81 m)
Length: 52 ft. 6 in. (16.00 m)
Height: 16 ft. 3 in. (4.96 m)
Empty weight: 22,304 lb. (10,115 kg)
Maximum take-off weight: 30,705 lb. (13,925 kg)
Power plant: 1 × Pratt & Whitney J57-21A turbojet engine with afterburner with 16,936 lbf (75.34 kN) thrust
Maximum speed: 863 mph (1,390 km/h)
Operational ceiling: 45,015 ft. (13,720 m)
Range: 1,500 miles (2,415 km)
Armament: 2 × .787 in. (20 mm) M39-E cannon with 200 rounds each; maximum combat payload of bombs and rockets 6,002 lb. (2,722 kg)

Development help

With the defeat of Germany the Me 262 jet fighter and large quantities of scientific documentation on turbines and wings fell into the hands of the Americans. The research results of the wind-tunnel tests by German researchers on air current characteristics

The slimmer nose and stronger back-sweep of the tailplane and wings distinguish the F-100 Super Sabre from its predecessors.

General Electric

The newly designed prototype for the USAAF, the XP-86 Sabre, flew for the first time on November 27, 1946, with the quite simple TG-180 turbine built by Chevrolet. The first production model, the F-86A, was delivered to the US Air Force (USAF) in December 1948 with the improved General Electric J47-1 jet engine with 4,844 lbf (21.55 kN) thrust. An almost standard F-86A then established a new world speed record at 671 mph (1,080 km/h) in 1949.

New paths in construction

With the F-86, new paths were being trodden in airplane construction. Alongside the swept-back shape already mentioned a new production method was used for the wings: each wing was assembled from two aluminum sheets using a "sandwich" technique.

The rear of the plane could be detached completely from the fuselage, making the engine easily accessible for maintenance and repair work.

Improvements

The weakness of the armament and the targeting equipment turned out to be shortcomings of the F-86—with its otherwise excellent flight characteristics. Their six .50 in. (12.7 mm) machine guns did not have the firepower to inflict lasting damage on a MiG-15 in the short time of a combat engagement. The request of the pilots for more thrust, stronger armament, and better targeting equipment was fulfilled in 1952 with the Model F-86F—which had direct influence on air combat sorties. In each month after its introduction at least 25 MiG-15s were shot down.

MiG Alley

The Sabre received its baptism of fire in the Korean War in 1950, which, at the beginning, was primarily fought by the F-86E model series. The F-86 acquired its real fame in combat against Chinese MiG-15s over the so-called "MiG Alley," the airspace over the Yalu River, which marked the northwest border between North Korea and Chinese Manchuria. The Sabre flew on Yalu patrol and had the task of intercepting MiG-15s flying in from China.

The MiG-15 was built by the Russians Mikoyan and Gurevich on the basis of captured German jet fighters and research documents and a Rolls-Royce turbine, and delivered to Red China. It was so similar to the F-86 Sabre in profile that in the heat of the battle the pilot often had difficulty in distinguishing the two models.

While the Sabre distinguished itself by its outstanding agility and its stability as a weapons platform, the MiG-15 had a greater operational ceiling and could climb faster. So, as a rule, the MiG-15s attacked the American bomber formations, pouncing from a great height at top speed. Because, unlike the MiG-15s, the Sabres were stationed a long way from the border river, their combat time was limited by long flight penetration into the combat area. Therefore all the advantages were on the side of the MiGs, apart from one. From the middle of October until the end of March, the prevailing wind blew from westerly and northwesterly directions (over 29,529 ft./9,000 m altitude at more than 99 mph/160 km/h!) and allowed the Sabre with very little fuel reserves to break off air combats and still get back to base. Then the greater agility of the F-86, its higher stability, and the better training of the US pilots could come to bear.

On December 17, 1950 Lt. Col. Bruce H. Hinton was the first Sabre pilot to shoot down the first MiG-15. In the same month the Sabre reached the strike/loss ratio of 8:1. On May 20, 1951, Captain of the USAF James Jabara became the first ace of the jet age when he shot down his fifth and sixth MiG-15s in his F-86. In the month of June 1953 alone, US pilots destroyed 77 MiG-15s in this way and damaged a further eleven without losing a single Sabre.

On the most-built model of the Sabre, the F-86D, an all-weather interceptor with increased thrust performance, the armament was further developed. Instead of the usual six machine guns, the F-86D had a radar-steered fire-control system for the 24×2.72 in. (69 mm) caliber rockets carried in the extendable box under the front fuselage.

F-100 Super Sabre

Already planned in 1949, the F-100 Super Sabre was the successor to the F-86. All the experiences with this type led directly to the development of the F-100.

The combination of the Pratt & Whitney J57 high-performance two-shaft jet engine with afterburner with even more swept-back wings—45 degrees as opposed to the 35 degrees of the F-86—made the F-100 enormously fast. It was the first worldwide standard jet to break the sound barrier in horizontal flight.

The Super Sabre received an oval engine air intake, which gave it the characteristic appearance from the front. As armament with .50 in. (12.7 mm) caliber machine guns had turned out to be insufficient, the F-100A

received four .787 in. (20 mm) cannon, and also several pylons for various types of rockets and bombs. A radar and various electronic positioning and identification systems were now installed as standard and thus made the F-100 Super Sabre the precursor of the modern fighter.

In the Vietnam War the Super Sabre proved itself markedly successful, both in low-level flight attack and also as an escort and high-altitude fighter.

Super Sabres were withdrawn from service in the USAF in 1972 and in the National Guard from 1980.

The landing after the successfully completed maiden flight of the XF100, the prototype of the Super Sabre.

Three F-86D Sabres. The model, which with 2,054 exemplars was the most produced, formed the backbone of the US air defense of its time.

MIKOYAN-GUREVICH MIG-15/ MIG-19

A MiG-15, NATO code name "Fagot," on the American Nellis Air Force Base in Nevada.

Together with its direct opponent the F-86 Sabre, the MiG-15 stands for a giant leap forward, and both are rightly considered to be the first representatives of the second generation of combat jets. That the MiG-15 had so little success in the Korean War, despite unsurpassed performance in climb rate, altitude performance, and final speed, is explained by its conception and the poor state of training of the Chinese pilots.

MIKOYAN-GUREVICH MIG-15BIS
Single-seat fighter
Wingspan: 33 ft. 1 in. (10.08 m)
Length: 36 ft. 3 in. (11.05 m)
Height: 11 ft. 2 in. (3.40 m)
Empty weight: 8,117 lb. (3,681 kg)
Max. take-off weight: 13,329 lb. (6,045 kg)
Power plant: based on the Rolls-Royce Nene developed Klimov turbojet engineVK-1 with 5,957 lbf (26.5 kN) static thrust
Max. speed: 668 mph (1,075 km/h) (Mach 1.3)
Operational ceiling: 50,856 ft. (15,500 m)
Range: 1,155 miles (1,860 km)
Armament: 1 × 1.46 in. (37 mm) NR-37 cannon or 2 × .9 in. (23 mm) NS-23 or NR-23 cannon and up to 1,103 lb. (500 kg) of diverse combat load or ventral tanks on under-wing pylons

The foundations of the development

In the 1940s German scientists were leading worldwide in jet technology and high-speed flight—comprehensive documentation about the aerodynamic advantages of swept-back wings had been compiled—and after the war this material was accessible to the victorious powers. The findings from this research had lasting influence on the development of jet airplanes and supersonic flight.

OKB Mikoyan-Gurevich

Building on the captured material, the construction team in the Soviet Union under Artem Mikoyan and Mikhail Gurevich started with the planning of a new jet plane with turbojet engine and swept-back wings. As propulsion they used the RD-45 jet turbine, a Rolls-Royce Nene radial engine copied in the OKB Klimov. This was only possible because in 1947 in Great Britain the new Labour government had allowed the sale of the engine long before this engine was to be built into a British jet.

The result, the MiG-15, which was presented unofficially for the first time in 1948 at the Soviet Flying Day and officially at the parade on May 1, 1949, alarmed the military all over the world—no one had suspected such a progressive state of development in the Soviet Union.

The then-revolutionary MiG-15 had the engine intake in the aircraft nose, the engine in the fuselage, and the thrust nozzle under the tail fin. The nose wheel undercarriage and the swept-back surfaces on all sides (wings and tailplane) were—in combination with the efficient and maintenance-friendly armament it was equipped with—typical characteristics of a modern fighter plane.

"Farmer" was the codename for the MiG-19 in the air forces of the Western Alliance.

License with and without fee

The MiG-15 and the RD-45 turbine went very quickly into production—without license fees for the engine ever being paid to Rolls-Royce, however—with the result that the first jets were able to be delivered by 1949. The production of the MiG-15 proceeded at such a pace that in only five years 8,000 were produced in the Soviet Union alone—more than for every other fighter plane of its time. In addition factories came into existence in Poland, Czechoslovakia, and China, producing the MiG-15 under license.

Spoiler

The numerically largest share fell to the MiG-15bis model, which had a better performing turbine, stronger armament, perforated Fowler flaps, and adapted air brakes (spoilers) on the rear fuselage. These air brakes were absolutely essential: they extended automatically when a certain speed was reached and thus prevented the pilot of the MiG-15 flying faster than Mach 0.93. Above this speed the jet was no longer stable, tended to swerve uncontrollably, and go into a tailspin from which it could no longer be pulled out. It left the pilot with no choice but to eject. The tendency to uncontrolled tailspin probably cost more MiG pilots their lives than combat losses caused by the US Air Force.

The split air intake for the two turbines in the plane nose is a typical technical detail of the MiG-19.

Mikoyan-Gurevich MiG-19
(NATO code name "Farmer")

The MiG-19 was the first Soviet plane to fly at supersonic speed. It combined high speed, very good maneuverability, and a mighty fire power and was in its time an impressive warplane. It was still being used in the late 1970s.

Addition to the family

Artem Mikoyan's new warplane, the MiG-19, was already designed on the drawing board before the beginning of the Korean War. Although externally there was a slight similarity to the MiG-15, it was, however, a completely independent design. Only the arrangement as a mid-wing airplane with the engine air intake in the nose and a nose-wheel undercarriage was carried over from the MiG-15 and MiG-17.

The sound barrier falls

The split engine air intake in the nose of the MiG-19 supplied two jet turbines lying parallel to each other in the fuselage behind the cockpit. Their exhausts were also released separately in the rear under the tail fin. Although the empennage and wings were at

55 degrees, very sharply swept-back boundary-layer fences on each of the wings and Fowler flaps between aileron and fuselage allowed a satisfactory handling of the plane even at lower speeds. The high-performance Klimov RD-9B turbojet engine with afterburner made the MiG-19 the first Soviet jet able to fly faster than sound in horizontal flight and the second worldwide. The armament was impressive with three 1.18 in. (30 mm) cannon and air-to-air guided missiles.

The first prototype flew on May 27, 1952, followed by the production prototype on January 5, 1954. Like the MiG-15 and MiG-17, the MiG-19 was also built in large numbers. Outside the Soviet Union there were licensed productions in Poland, Czechoslovakia, and China. Possibly, all in all, more than 10,000 MiG-19s were built.

Vietnam and the Near East

The MiG-19 was used in combat in the Vietnam War and in the Arab–Israeli Six-Day War. In the Vietnam War the jet was mainly used—with success—as a defensive weapon in the air combat against penetrating American F-4 Phantom and F-105 Thunderchief

In service in the Soviet brother nations: a Polish formation of MiG-15s.

fighter-bombers. Here the co-operation and co-ordination between the crews of the North Vietnamese anti-aircraft defense, armed with 1.46 in. (37 mm) twin anti-aircraft guns and SA-2 anti-aircraft rockets, and the pilots of the MiG-19s was indispensable.

In the Six-Day War, the air forces of Syria and Egypt were armed with MiG-19s and MiG-21s; Egypt alone had four squadrons of MiG-19 warplanes. Most of them were destroyed on the morning of June 5, 1967, in a surprise attack by Israel within a short period of time while they were on the ground. The few MiG-19s that succeeded in challenging the Israeli jets to air combat mostly fell victim to the Dassault Mirage III used by the Israelis, which was superior to the MiG. Finally, MiG-19s were probably used by the Syrian air force in 1979 in the wake of the Lebanon conflict. In an air battle, eight Syrian MiG-19s fought with six Israeli F-15 Eagles and Kfirs (the Israeli version of the Mirage V). Very rapidly, five MiG-19s were shot down, and the rest escaped to safety. With that, the time of the MiG-19, a design from the 1950s, was, in 1979, definitively at an end.

From the test flights with the MiG-15 of the defector Ro Kum Suk the US Air Force gained important knowledge about the potential of the MiG-15.

Ro Kum Suk

Information about Soviet airplanes was subject to the most stringent secrecy, though the flight properties of the MiG-15 could be studied in detail in the air combat during the Korean War. The Americans obtained the most important information about the jet in 1953 from the North Korean defector Lieutenant Ro Kum Suk, who landed with his MiG-15 on a South Korean airfield near Seoul. From February 1954 the first two US Air Force test pilots, Chuck Yeager and Tom Collins, were able to test this plane intensively. Although the MiG-15 showed itself to be a good warplane, it lacked the refined American technology. It was a basic and incomplete design. Because of insufficient heating, it was always very cold in the cockpit at high-altitude flight. The windscreen and the cockpit glazing became covered on the inside with hoar frost that could only be scratched off with difficulty. The MiG-15 also did not have the automatic pressure control system usually found in American jets. Instead, the pilot had to constantly readjust the cabin pressure during the climb by hand on a control wheel.

The target camera of a pursuing fighter captures the shooting down of a MiG-15 during the Korean War.

CONVAIR F-102 DELTA DAGGER

For the first time, with the Convair F-102 Delta Dagger, a jet-propelled delta wing plane was constructed on which it was not the actual flight performance but the characteristics as a carrier of the complex weapon system that was seen as the most important requirement.

The first delta wing plane

At the Convair company at the end of the 1940s, development of a delta wing plane was begun in co-operation with the German delta wing pioneer Alexander Lippisch. This was part of a US Air Force program that was to lead to the development of a supersonic fighter. The XF-92A arising from this was, in 1948, the first plane in the world with a delta wing.

Hughes MX-1179

At the beginning of the 1950s, the MX-1179, a fire-control system that was revolutionary for its time, was developed at the Hughes Company. To go with this system, the US Air Force required an all-weather interceptor. However—diverging from the usual procedure—the fire-control system was to be made ready to go into production first and then the aircraft was to be developed.

The F-102, one of the first delta wing planes and the first of this build constructed according to Whitcomb's area rule. The "pinched waist" is clearly recognizable.

230

YF-102A

The delta wing plane YF-102, designed at Convair for this bid, flew for the first time on October 24, 1953. The jet was disappointing, however, insofar as it created too much air resistance and was not able to reach to the supersonic range. Fortunately, the aerodynamics expert Richard T. Whitcomb, during wind-tunnel tests at NACA (National Advisory Committee for Aeronautics, later NASA), remembered the area rule which had been formulated in 1944. It stated that the increase in resistance during supersonic flight decreases when the total cross-sectional area of the fuselage plus surfaces from nose to tail corresponds to the cross-section of a streamlined body. Paying attention to this area rule, the fuselage was given a "pinched waist," and completed its maiden flight on December 20, 1954 as the YF-102A. With Mach 1.2, the sound barrier was broken with no problem, and the fighter went into mass production as the F-102A.

New tasks for the pilot

The Convair F-102A Delta Dagger was an imposing plane with a small cockpit. As the whole plane was conceived as a weapons platform, the pilot had to follow a new system of working—using two steering columns, one for the flight steering and one for the radar. In search mode, the pilot strained his eyes against the viewing hood of his radar screen and flew the jet with one hand on each control stick.

In semi-automatic mode, guided missiles were automatically extended from the shaft in the fuselage and, by means of the target search and track computer, fired at exactly the right time.

Convair F-106 Delta Dart

From the original series as the F-102A Delta Dagger, the designated F-102B was given the designation F-106 Delta Dart because of its numerous design improvements and armament with the new Hughes MA-1 fire-control system. The fuselage of the Delta Dart, with an even more pronounced "pinched waist" in combination with a stronger thrust engine and a larger trapezoid fin, made for an almost twofold increase in final speed compared with the Delta Dagger and could be refueled mid-air.

Strategically, the Delta Dart was integrated into the USA national early warning and air defense system as an interceptor carrying nuclear weapons (unguided MB-1 Genie rockets). The Hughes MA-1 fire-control system was integrated via a digital data connection to the air defense control system SAGE (Semi-Automatic Ground Environment).

The considerably improved successor, the F-106 Delta Dart, on a works photo of the manufacturer Convair belonging to General Dynamics.

An F-102 of the Quick Reaction Alert of the North American Air Defense Command (NORAD) is being manned to intercept an unidentified aircraft.

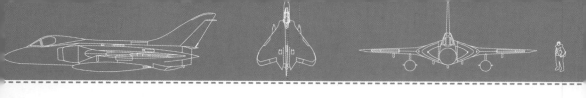

Douglas F4D Skyray

In the late 1950s and early 1960s the Douglas F4D—which had already set world records in the test stage—was a particularly favored carrier-borne interceptor among the pilots of the US Navy and Marine Corps because of its maneuverability, agility, and reliability.

Douglas F4D Skyray. The rounded transition from wing root to fuselage demonstrates the progress in aircraft construction.

DOUGLAS F4D SKYRAY
Carrier-borne single-seat fighter
Wingspan: 33 ft. 6 in. (10.21 m)
Length: 45 ft. 5 in. (13.84 m)
Height: 13 ft. (3.96 m)
Empty weight: 16,026 lb. (7,268 kg)
Maximum take-off weight: 27,011 lb. (12,250 kg)
Power plant: 1 × J57-P-8A Pratt & Whitney turbojet engine with afterburner and 15,983 lbf (71.1 kN) thrust
Maximum speed: 725 mph (1,167 km/h)
Operational ceiling: 54,990 ft. (16,760 m)
Range: 950 miles (1,530 km)
Armament: 2 × M-12 .787 in. (20 mm) caliber twin cannon each with 70 rounds per tube in the outer wings, 6 × under-wing pylons for combat load of up to 4,000 lb. (1,814 kg) in bombs, 2 × Sidewinder AIM-9 N-7 air-to-air missiles or rocket containers each with 7 × 2.72 in. (69 mm) projectiles, or 4 × containers each with 19 unguided rockets of a smaller caliber, supplementary tanks

The airframe and the delta wing

The development of the F4D Skyray is based on the research of German Dr. Alexander Lippisch on airplanes with delta wings. Building on captured German archive material Ed Heinemann at Douglas designed a fighter with large delta-shaped wings. This delta wing was expected to give the plane good maneuverability in combat with minimal structural loading. Also, the leading edge of the wings was not straight but flowed in a rolling curve to the base of the delta. The straight trailing edge of the wing was in contrast angled and attached on both sides to the thrust nozzle—the missing tailplane is a peculiarity of the F4D. The engine air intakes on either side of the fuselage were integrated into the wings and supplied a jet turbine with afterburner.

Innovations

At the first flight of the prototype XF4D-1 on January 23, 1951, the Skyray already seemed considerably further advanced than any other navy fighter. One of these advances was the hydraulically activated flight steering, which was accessed via the pilot's steering column. However, the model also possessed a purely manually controlled reserve steering system. For this the pilot had to release the locking device of the steering column and lengthen it manually—for better leverage. A further peculiarity was the so-called sandwich outer skin, a double cladding of the wings. Unfortunately, the sandwich outer skin did not turn out to be a complete success as it led to the formation of bulges and thus to inferior flight performance.

The world record holder

Climbing performance had the highest priority in the conception of the Skyray. The planned mode of deployment was interception of high-flying bombers but even the other flight characteristics were extraordinary: on October 3, 1953, a F4D flew at a new world speed record of 753 mph (1,212 km/h). Another all-time high concerned the climbing performance— from take-off to a height of 50,002 ft. (15,240 m) in 2.6 minutes; that corresponds to almost 330 ft/s (100 m/s)!

The geometry of the Skyray. Elevator and aileron are both on the trailing edge of the rolling delta wing.

Westinghouse and Allison

Technical problems with the projected Westinghouse J40-WE-8 jet turbine with afterburner delayed the start of production by three years. Therefore, the production aircraft were given the Pratt & Whitney J57 jet engine; delivery began on April 16, 1956.

A works photo of the Douglas Aircraft Company shows one of the first Skyrays from the series production.

VOUGHT F-8U CRUSADER

The Vought F-8U Crusader is one of the most successful carrier-borne jets in history. It was delivered for the first time to the US Navy in 1957, and—being continually improved—it was still in service there 25 years later.

VOUGHT F-8 CRUSADER
Carrier-borne single-seat fighter-bomber
Wingspan: 35 ft. 8 in. (10.87 m)
Length: 54 ft. 3 in. (16.53 m)
Height: 15 ft. 9 in. (4.80 m)
Empty weight: 19,702 lb. (8,935 kg)
Maximum take-off weight (series C): 34,001 lb. (15,420 kg)
Power plant: (series C, K): 1 × J57-16 Pratt & Whitney turbo jet engine with afterburner with 16,882 lbf (75.1 kN) thrust
Maximum speed: 1,230 mph (1,980 km/h)
Operational ceiling: 42,981 ft. (13,100 m)
Combat radius: 455 miles (732 km)
Armament: 4 × .787 in. (20 mm) caliber Colt Mk.12 cannon each with 84 rounds, 2 × "Sidewinder" air-to-air guided missiles, and 32 × 2.76 in. (70 mm) unguided rockets in extendable rocket cases under the fuselage

An unusual arrangement: the four Sidewinder guided weapons of the F-8U Crusader D were carried not under the wings but on the fuselage.

F-8U and F-8

Although the Vought F-8U Crusader is easily recognizable on the basis of its characteristic central air intakes on the underside of the fuselage nose, because of its similar build it is easy to confuse it with a later fighter-bomber, the Vought A-7 Corsair II. Vought won a

US Navy call for bids with the F-8U Crusader in 1953 for a fighter and fighter-bomber operating from aircraft carriers and flying at supersonic speed. The Crusader was an outstanding aircraft that even outperformed the North American F-100 Super Sabre of the US Air Force, although both planes were powered by the same jet turbine. On its very first flight on March 25, 1955, as the XF8U-1, the Crusader broke the sound barrier. Subsequently the Crusader set up new records. It was the first carrier-borne plane in the world that flew faster than 1,180 mph (1,900 km/h) and the first plane to cross the North American continent at supersonic speed. Two years after the maiden

flight, the first Crusader fighter squadron, the VF-32, was formed. During the course of the code changeover in 1962 all F-8Us of the US Navy and the US Marine Corps were renamed F-8s. The last delivery of F-8 Crusader fighters went to the fleet in 1965.

Model upgrade

The Crusader was one of those outstanding designs that could be used over a long period of time by continually updating the series. The improvements affected the radar, the autopilot, the weapons system, the structure, and the engine. The Pratt & Whitney J57 jet engine that was developed in the first series with

On the right wing of the F-8U-2N (F-8D) the dog tooth on the leading edge is clearly recognizable.

The only two-seat trainer in the Crusader series.

afterburner and 16,156 lb. (7,327 kg) thrust was replaced in the course of time by the Pratt & Whitney TF300-P-420 with an afterburner thrust performance of 19,602 lb. (8,890 kg). The fuel was largely carried in internal tanks.

Product recall

Between 1967 and 1971, Crusaders from series B, C, and E were converted in the factory to the most up-to-date state of technology and returned to service as series J, K, and L. The RF-8 spotter from series A was likewise updated and was given improved photo and electronic equipment. Re-named the RF-8G, it was transferred back to the fleet. All in all, in this way more than a third of all Crusaders were improved and their withdrawal from service continually delayed.

At the beginning of the 1980s there was still a unit in the US Navy, the VFP-63 reconnaissance squadron, that was equipped with RF-8Gs—resulting in a service life of over 25 years. In the French Navy, the last Crusaders (Croisés) were not taken out of service until December 1999—45 years after the first flight of the prototypes.

Firepower

Four .787 in. (20 mm) cannon and two "Sidewinder" air-to-air guided missiles already gave series A to C enormous firepower. Then the F-8D carried alongside the four cannon four "Sidewinders." In addition to this armament the F-8 of series E, H, and J were also able to carry 12 Mk-81 bombs, or eight "Zuni" rockets, or two AGM-12B Bullpups.

Vietnam

The F-8 experienced their first deployments during the Cuban Crisis in 1962. In combat operations, the Crusader is inseparably linked

with the aerial warfare in Vietnam. In the first four years of the conflict, F-8 fighters and fighter-bombers accounted for more than half of all carrier planes of the US Navy and the US Marine Corps stationed in the Gulf of Tonkin. On August 2, 1964, the US Navy was first involved in combat within the framework of the "Maddox" incident. Four F-8 Crusaders from the aircraft carrier *Ticonderoga* attacked North Vietnamese patrol boats and sank one of them. In the further course of the war the F-8s were deployed both for pursuit missions and also for bombing, during which, for the first time, 2,000 lb. (907 kg) bombs were dropped by Crusaders. Commander Jim Stockdale carried out pioneering work here by taking off from the carrier catapult in an overladen F-8 with only minimal fuel supplies. The actual fueling took place after take-off in mid-air by means of a tanker plane.

Marines

The Crusaders of the US Marine Corps intervened directly in ground combat in Vietnam. They provided ground combat support on request for their own ground troops. During the Vietnam War the Crusaders earned their reputation as the best of the fighter planes armed with a cannon ("best gun fighter"). Their pilots were credited with 19 air victories over North Vietnamese MiG fighters, most of them with Sidewinder AIM-9s.

Reconnaissance

A particular significance in the Vietnam War was attributed to the photo-reconnaissance Crusader RF-8. With the airborne reconnaissance it provided, potential targets were picked out and the resulting damage documented after an attack. On such reconnaissance flights, which as a rule were only carried out at a height of 4,003 ft. (1,220 m), the RF-8s were each covered by an escort fighter. Nevertheless, the missions were extremely dangerous as, for photographic reconnaissance, the pilot had to keep a straight course at constant speed—easy prey for anti-aircraft fire. The aircraft carrier operational group was thus kept continuously updated about newly built anti-aircraft rocket batteries in North Vietnam—but the price was high. On reconnaissance flights alone, 20 RF-8s were shot down, almost a quarter of all Crusader losses in the Vietnam War.

With the Sixth Fleet in the Mediterranean: formation flight of Crusaders that were stationed on the USS Forrestal.

With the Dassault Ouragan, France had found entry into the development and building of combat jets. The Super Mystère shown here meant a further big step.

DASSAULT SUPER MYSTÈRE

The Mystère is at the same time both the beginning and end. On a par with the F-100 Super Sabre and the MiG-19 from the point of view of performance, it was the first supersonic plane of Western Europe that made it into mass production. As the last daylight-fighter before the arrival of the radar-controlled Mirage III, it marked the end of daytime pursuit by sight. And it stands at the end of a generation of fighter planes and, furthermore, the generation that in the 1950s began to fly faster than sound.

DASSAULT SUPER MYSTÈRE
Fighter-bomber
Wingspan: 35 ft. 6 in. (10.52 m)
Length: 45 ft. 9 in. (13.95 m)
Height: 14 ft. 11 in. (4.55 m)
Empty weight: 15,285 lb. (6,932 kg)
Maximum take-off weight: 22,050 lb. (10,000 kg)
Power plant: 1 × SNECMA Atar G-2 turbo jet engine with afterburner with 7,418 lbf (33 kN) static thrust without and 9,914 lbf (44.1 kN) thrust with afterburner
Maximum speed: 742 mph (1,195 km/h) (Mach 1.12)
Operational ceiling: 55,777 ft. (17,000 m)
Range: 540 miles (870 km)
Armament: 2 × 1.18 in. (30 mm) caliber DEFA 551 cannon, 2 × Matra 511 air-to-air guided missiles, and 35 × 2.68 in. (68 mm) SNEB unguided air-to-air rockets in a retractable rocket case under the fuselage, under-wing pylons for 2 × rocket containers each with 19 air-to-air rockets, or 2 × 1,103 lb. (500 kg) bombs, or 2 × 127 gal. (480 l) napalm bombs, or 12 × anti-ship missiles

The external appearance

To look at the Super Mystère, the similarity with other fighters of its time is striking. As with many of them, the engine drew its intake air from a splayed opening in the flattened fuselage nose, and the sweeping back of the wings by 45 degrees reflected the fact that in the 1950s this wing type became standard for high-speed flight.

The fighter-bomber

The early Dassault jet planes were able to reach the speed of sound, though only in a flat nose dive. With the Super Mystère this limit was removed. The first prototype B.1 already reached Mach 1 directly after its first flight on March 2, 1955 in horizontal flight—with the Rolls-Royce Avon RA afterburner engine. The first serial model B.2 was—unlike the prototype—driven by a SNECMA Atar 101 G-2; production began in 1957. The original order comprised 400 exemplars and in 1958— because of the changeover to a stronger thrust engine—the higher performance B.4 was to be created. At that time, however, the series-production readiness of the in-house competition was announced—the Mirage III, which was expected to fly at twice the speed

From a good family

Marcel Bloch was one of the pioneers of flight in France; by 1918 he had manufactured propellers. Even if one does not immediately connect him with Dassault, he was the driving force behind Dassault Aviation, though at first under another name. During the occupation of France by Germany in the Second World War, Bloch was interned in a concentration camp and survived this imprisonment only with the help of prominent advocates. After his return to France he changed his name to Marcel Dassault—the name used by his brother in the French Resistance—and began to build planes again. The Curagan, the first French jet, became an early success and, with the Mystère and the Mirage, it brought France back to where it had been in the pioneering days—a world leader in airplane construction.

of sound. For this reason, the government contract was cancelled after the delivery of 180 Mystères and thus a promising production came to a premature end.

The highly set tailplane and the half oval air intake on the nose are two distinguishing features of the Mystère.

The swept wing

The compressibility—the compaction under pressure—of the air creates unfavorable pressure ratios on the wing with increasing speed. A zone of high pressure builds up in front of the leading edge of the wing that eases off in sudden rhythmic bursts. That leads to vibrations—which can be so strong that the plane becomes uncontrollable or breaks apart in the air. In the middle of the 1930s Adolf Busemann developed the swept-back wing as a countermeasure. Looking in the direction of the longitudinal axis of the plane or the direction of flight, it can be seen that the wingtips do not stand at right angles to the longitudinal axis but are pushed back opposite the wing root. This causes the pressure zones on the leading edge of the wing to flow back much more evenly without the pressure equalization leading to vibrations. The degree of sweeping is dependent on the expected maximum speed

and the type of operation of the planned plane. High speeds demand a strong swept-back shape, which, however creates less lift than an unswept-back wing. The technical solutions for this dilemma can be either movable wings with variable back-sweeping or the leading edge not following a straight line but a curved one.

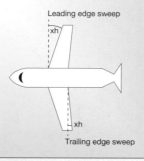

Leading edge sweep

xh

xh

Trailing edge sweep

Six-Day War

Of the 180 mass-produced Mystères, 36 were sold to Israel—18 of them from the original order and a further 18 from those in the service of the French Air Force. They were equal opponents for the MiG-17s of the Arab countries but achieved their greatest success in the support of the ground troops and not in the planned use as interceptors. The French weapons embargo—after the Israeli attack on Beirut airport—and the problems of supply of spare parts arising from this, led to the Mystère being modified.

In 1973 it was again updated to the state-of-the-art technology with new engines—Pratt & Whitney J52-P-8A—and its performance enhanced. This revised model had its maiden flight on February 13, 1969, and took part in the Yom Kippur War in 1973. No reliable statements can be made about the end of its service life in Israel; all that is certain is that the Israeli air force sold twelve of their Dassaults to Honduras in 1977 where they were in service until 1989—among other things in the war against drug smuggling. In France itself, the last planes of this type were taken out of service in 1977.

The Mystère was the first jet from Dassault that was faster than sound in horizontal flight.

In a Dassault Mystère, Jacqueline Auriol became one of the first pilots to fly at supersonic speed; in 1953 she set a world record with the model.

Jacqueline Auriol—the First Lady of French Aviation

Jacqueline Auriol was a society lady but clearly bored by the duties of official functions. At the age of 30 she decided to learn to fly—that was the beginning of an unprecedented career. Within six years she obtained six pilot's licenses and was licensed to fly almost anything with wings. That was not enough for her and she became the first female test pilot outside the Eastern Bloc. Her career was overshadowed by a serious accident as a co-pilot, as a consequence of which she had to undergo numerous operations. She used the time in her sickbed to acquaint herself with the theoretical and mathematical backgrounds of aviation. Directly after undergoing, in the USA, the last cosmetic operation on her face (which had been disfigured by the accident) she completed her helicopter pilot exam in record time and made the acquaintance of the American flight record-holder Jacqueline Cochran. Although they both admired each other, there was fierce competition between the two ladies of speed for the world speed record, which for several years passed back and forth between the two. In the summer of 1953 Jacqueline Auriol gained the world record for the third time when she broke the sound barrier in a Mystère—as one of the very first pilots to do so.

DASSAULT-BREGUET MIRAGE F1

With the Mirage III Dassault-Breguet had built the first Western European interceptor that achieved Mach 2. The Mirage F1 was conceived to be just as fast but to improve the flight performance of its predecessor. For this reason the delta wing was changed into a conventional swept-back wing and, unlike its predecessor, the F1 again possessed an elevator unit—which made it into a completely new fighter that only had its name in common with the Mirage III.

DASSAULT-BREGUET MIRAGE F1
All-weather single-seat fighter
Wingspan: 27 ft. 7 in. (8.40 m)
Length: 49 ft. 3 in. (15.00 m)
Height: 14 ft. 9 in. (4.50 m)
Empty weight: 16,317 lb. (7,400 kg)
Maximum take-off weight: 32,855 lb. (14,900 kg)
Power plant: 1 × SNECMA Atar 9K-50 turbojet with 10,993 lbf (48.9 kN) thrust without and 15,828 lbf (70.41 kN) thrust with afterburner
Maximum speed: 1,450 mph (2,335 km/h) (Mach 2.2)
Operational ceiling: 65,620 ft. (20,000 m)
Combat radius: 621 miles (1,000 km)
Armament: 2 × 1.18 in. (30 mm) caliber DEFA 552A cannon with 125 rounds each, five universal external pylons with two rocket launchers on the wingtips for AIM-9 Sidewinder and/or Matra R.530/550 Magic air-to-air guided missiles; version for ground combat supports up to 8,820 lb. (4,000 kg) external stores, for bombs, air-to-ground rockets, napalm containers

Development advances: On the Mirage F1, there was a move away from the concept of the delta wing and back to the swept wing.

The limitations of the delta wing

In the search for the wing geometry with the best characteristics in supersonic flight, Dassault chose, for the Mirage III, the delta wing without empennage, the wing that is really best suited for straight-ahead flight faster than Mach 1. With respect to the speed the aim had been achieved—at the price of more moderate characteristics in slow flight, a high landing speed, and insufficient maneuverability.

Therefore, the Mirage F1 model was arranged as a conventional shoulder-wing airplane and displayed significantly improved flight characteristics. The take-off strip could be shortened for the new fighter, the combat range was doubled, and both the maneuverability and also the slow flight characteristics of the F1 were clearly superior to those of its predecessor.

The birth of the Mirage F1

The development brief of Dassault-Breguet from the year 1964 contained the development of an all-weather interceptor as a replacement for the Mirage III.

The design of the new type that only had the fuselage in common with the old Mirage took so much time that the first flight of the prototype Mirage F1-01 was delayed until December 1966—the result of the test justified the long construction time. Already on one of the first flights in January 1967, the SNECMA Atar 9K engine accelerated the prototype to double the speed of sound.

However, the F1-01 did not go into production. In May 1967 the plane crashed, and the test pilot was killed. The new revised test

version F1-02 and two further pre-series versions were flown for the first time in 1969.

The first mass-production Mirage F1 was produced in February 1973, delivered a month later to the Armée de l'Air, and in December of the same year was put into service.

The technology

The fuselage of the Mirage F1 is constructed in a semi-shell form and carries on its tip a bow probe (pitot tube) and radar turret (radome). Fire-control radar and radar antennae are installed in front of the cockpit pressure frame.

Behind the cockpit with its Martin Baker Mk.4 ejector seat is the main equipment bay for the avionics equipment. The two half-circular engine air intakes are arranged to the left and right of the fuselage exterior. The fuel tank holding 1,125 gal. (4,260 l) is placed in the middle of the fuselage behind the cockpit.

The wings of the self-supporting shoulder-wing airplane F1 display a backwards sweep of 50 degrees and a negative V-formation of 5 degrees.

The leading edge of the wing is conceived with the outer third displaying a projection (dog tooth). Two-thirds of the trailing edge of

Twice the speed of sound was already possible in 1967 with the Dassault Mirage F1.

An elegant appearance: Clear lines and the very large vertical tail characterize the Mirage F1.

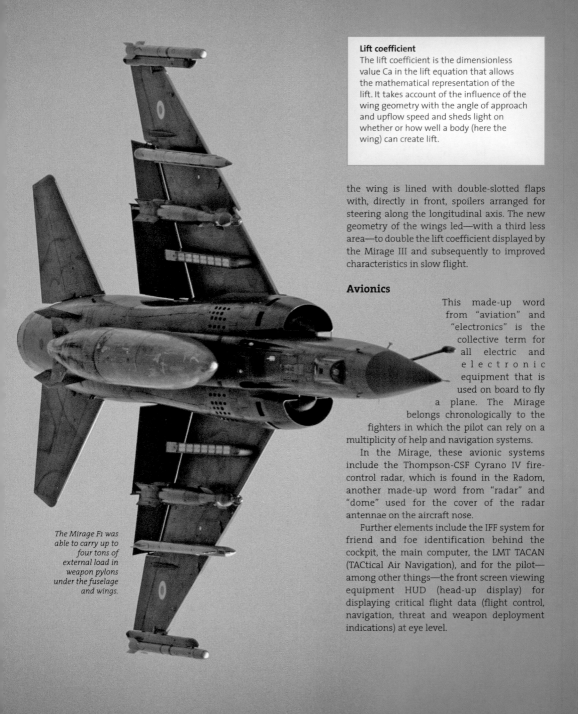

the wing is lined with double-slotted flaps with, directly in front, spoilers arranged for steering along the longitudinal axis. The new geometry of the wings led—with a third less area—to double the lift coefficient displayed by the Mirage III and subsequently to improved characteristics in slow flight.

Avionics

This made-up word from "aviation" and "electronics" is the collective term for all electric and electronic equipment that is used on board to fly a plane. The Mirage belongs chronologically to the fighters in which the pilot can rely on a multiplicity of help and navigation systems.

In the Mirage, these avionic systems include the Thompson-CSF Cyrano IV fire-control radar, which is found in the Radom, another made-up word from "radar" and "dome" used for the cover of the radar antennae on the aircraft nose.

Further elements include the IFF system for friend and foe identification behind the cockpit, the main computer, the LMT TACAN (TACtical Air Navigation), and for the pilot—among other things—the front screen viewing equipment HUD (head-up display) for displaying critical flight data (flight control, navigation, threat and weapon deployment indications) at eye level.

The Mirage F1 was able to carry up to four tons of external load in weapon pylons under the fuselage and wings.

Deployment in the Gulf

Of the approximately 770 Mirage F1s built, almost two-thirds were exported and only 270 remained in France. In many states without their own aircraft industry they were in the service of the military—directly after the start of production Spain, South Africa, Greece, and Kuwait had already ordered over 200 aircraft in total. Thus, in 1991 it came to the absurd situation that Mirages were fighting against each other on the two opposing sides—in the Gulf War. Earlier, in the Iran–Iraq War of 1987, the frigate USS *Stark* had been attacked by an Iraqi Mirage F1 and seriously damaged by two Exocet guided missiles. After the Gulf War, 24 ex-Iraqi F1s came to be in Iran. In Spain, 72 of the series F1B, F1C, and F1E are likewise still in service.

The grand seigneur of French aviation: Marcel Dassault critically watching a test flight.

Turbojet/turbofan

In both forms, turbine jet engines are used to drive the plane with the backthrust of pressurized combustion gases. The difference between the two engine types is the control of the air. The jet turbines of the first generation were without exception turbojets (turbine air jet engine). In turbojets, all the air that flows in through the engine air intake reaches the combustion chamber and is combusted there. This creates extremely high engine temperatures that put tight limits on the service life of such an engine. The turbofan—or turbofan engine—draws only a small part of the air mass in through the engine core (central chamber). A large part of the air mass flows past the engine core and delivers the largest part of the thrust (cold part of the aggregate). The engine core (hot part) serves as the drive for the air intake fan. This leads to a two-wave construction in which the high-pressure components and the lower-pressure elements turn on their own drive wave. The higher the ratio of the two air streams (outside to inside; bypass flow ratio), the more efficient the engine will be. This construction is significantly more economical and today is widespread.

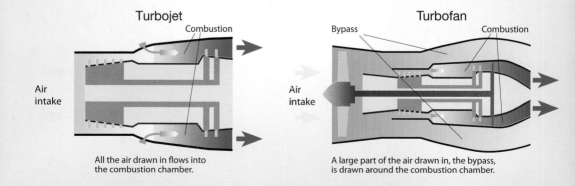

Turbojet

Combustion

Air intake

All the air drawn in flows into the combustion chamber.

Turbofan

Bypass   Combustion

Air intake

A large part of the air drawn in, the bypass, is drawn around the combustion chamber.

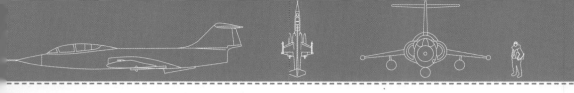

LOCKHEED F-104 STARFIGHTER

The Starfighter suffered from the consequences of its conception. In the USA it was planned as a fine-weather interceptor with great emphasis on climbing performance and maximum speed; in NATO, overloaded with additional equipment, it became the most controversial all-weather fighter of the North Atlantic Pact.

A Lockheed F-104S destined for the Italian air forces. At this period, the Starfighter was in service in 13 nations.

LOCKHEED F-104G STARFIGHTER

Single-seat fighter-bomber
Wingspan: 21 ft. 11 in. (6.68 m)
Length: 54 ft. 9 in. (16.69 m)
Height: 13 ft. 6 in. (4.11 m)
Empty weight: 13,997 lb. (6,348 kg)
Max. take-off weight: 29,042 lb. (13,171 kg)
Power plant: 1 × General Electric J79-GE-11A turbojet with 15,579 lbf (69.3 kN) afterburner thrust
Max. speed: 1,327 mph (2,137 km/h) (Mach 1.7)
Operational ceiling: 50,002 ft. (15,240 m)
Combat radius: 509 miles (819 km)
Armament: 1 × M61A1 six-tube rapid-fire cannon based on the Gatling function principle, manufacturer General Electric, .787 in. (20 mm) caliber with 750 rounds, explosive orcnance payload 4,807 lb. (2,180 kg)

From the experiences in Korea

In 1951 Clarence L. "Kelly" Johnson, Chief Designer and head of the Lockheed Advanced Development Projects "Skunk Works," asked pilots for their special wishes and ideas about an optimal fighter plane. At that time, from their experiences in Korea the pilots asked for a

jet with superior speed, climbing performance, and armament, even at the expense of payload.

Twice the speed of sound

The prototype XF-104 flew for the first time on February 28, 1954. It was a radical design for that time, arranged for top speed—the F-104 was the first Mach 2 warplane in the world—and climbing performance combined with maximum firepower. In addition, the

Starfighter was the first plane in the world that was able to break the sound barrier even in a climb. The extremely small and thin wings set very far back and the enormous climbing performance gave it the disposition of a manned rocket. The wings were so thin that there was only a construction space of 1 in. (2.5 cm) left for the aileron.

J79 Turbojet

The Starfighter was driven by the General Electric J79 turbojet with an afterburner thrust performance of 14,792 lbf (65.8 kN)—that became one of the most sold engines, with 17,000 exemplars built. The M61 rapid-fire cannon with six rotating muzzles—still the standard armament of American fighters today—provided excellent firepower.

In addition, the jet could carry "Sidewinder" air-to-air guided missiles and supplementary tanks. However, any additional payload was very limited because of the small wings. A curiosity of the Starfighter was the pilot's ejector seat, which ejected downwards.

USA

The result of concentration on sheer performance was a jet that reacted extremely sensitively and was not easy to fly. The F-104 was one of those planes that are unforgiving to pilots' mistakes. Also—although it carried a small radar set in the plane nose—the Starfighter was limited to daylight missions and its all-weather suitability was limited. The F-104A was therefore only ordered in small numbers by the US Air Force.

NATO

The majority of the F-104s were in the Lockheed Series G, equipped as multi-purpose warplanes, and delivered to NATO partners. The largest customers were the Canadian Air Force—for their three squadrons stationed in Europe, the Bundesluftwaffe (Federal German Air Force), and the Japanese and Italian air forces.

Statistics

From sources in the German Luftwaffe it emerges that on average the Starfighter statistically recorded a crash every 6,765 flight hours. The evaluation of the F-104 as a "widow-maker" came about to a large extent by judgments of the media—there the Starfighter, after the affair in the Bundestag (Federal Parliament) of the same name, was always worth a report.

In the US Air Force, the Starfighter was deployed as a fine-weather interceptor under conditions of flying by sight.

A Starfighter of the Royal Canadian Air Force in camouflage colors.

The most expensive prop in the world: The film Top Gun made the Grumman F-14 Tomcat world-famous even in civilian circles.

GRUMMAN F-14 TOMCAT

When it was put into service in the middle of the 1970s, the Grumman F-14 Tomcat was the perfect carrier-borne multi-purpose plane—heavily armed, with exceptional acceleration, and extraordinarily agile in dogfights. And that is true almost up to the present—the last Tomcat of the US Navy was only withdrawn from service on September 22, 2006.

GRUMMAN F-14A TOMCAT
Two-seat carrier-borne multi-purpose warplane
Wingspan: 64 ft. (19.54 m), at 68° normal wing sweep 38 ft. (11.63 m), at 75° maximum wing sweep 33 ft. (10.15 m)
Length: 62 ft. (18.89 m)
Height: 16 ft. (4.88 m)
Empty weight: 37,507 lb. (17,010 kg)
Maximum take-off weight: 72,015 lb. (32,660 kg)
Power plant: originally 2 × Pratt & Whitney TF30-412A turbofan engines, with 20,929 lbf (93.1 kN) thrust, afterburner thrust 41,813 lbf (186 kN) each; replaced by 2 x TF30-414As with the same performance
Maximum speed: 1,543 mph (2,485 km/h)
Operational ceiling: 50,002 ft. (15,240 m)
Range: 2,000 miles (3,220 km)
Combat radius: 745 miles (1,200 km)
Armament: 1 × M61A1 Gatling system .787 in. (20 mm) six-tube rapid-fire cannon in the fuselage, 4 × AIM-7 Sparrow and 4–8 × AIM-9 Sidewinder air-to-air guided missiles or up to 6 × AIM-54 Phoenix and 2 × AIM-9 Sidewinders, external stores up to 14,505 lb. (6,577 kg)

Development

Originally, the General Dynamics F-111B was intended as the new carrier-borne fighter for the US Navy for the 1970s and 1980s. It turned out that these were unsuitable for carrier use—so the US Navy called for bids in July 1968. A plane was stipulated to fulfill every military requirement right into the 1990s.

The winner was the Grumman Company. In January 1969 it received the contract for the development and construction of twelve prototypes—the maiden flight took place as early as December 21, 1970.

The Tomcat concept

The Tomcat is a two-seat multi-purpose swing wing aircraft with double tail fin. Take-off and landing is carried out with fully extended wings swept back at an angle of 20 degrees. For high-speed flight the wings are continually adjusted until they are in the final position of 68 degrees. In this position main and rear wings almost form a delta wing—during the flight the wing position is automatically adapted and continually optimized by the on-board computer.

Air combat

With this configuration, it was possible to fulfill several contradictory requirements. The jet was suited to classical air combat, for combat at high speeds, and for low-level attacks against ground and sea targets. But above all the F-14 Tomcat is carrier-friendly as it can approach the aircraft carrier at low speed and land—and to accommodate it on the aircraft carriers, the two halves of the wings

can be folded up at 75 degrees 'beyond the back sweep." The drop-shaped canopy glazing gives the crew excellent all-round vision—a further important aspect for carrier aircraft. For a jet that was conceived at the end of the 1960s, the F-14 had a very advanced airframe design. Other advanced design features, alongside the swing wings already mentioned, include the covering of the horizontal stabilizers with a composite material and the tail fins arranged over the engines.

With any combination of Phoenix, Sidewinder, and Sparrow guided missiles, the F-14 can attack up to six targets at the same time.

The drop-shaped glazing of the canopy gives the pilot very good all-round vision.

The costs

The weak dollar and the increasing complexity of aircraft technology drove the price of the Tomcat up to 17 million US dollars each and brought Grumman Industries to the edge of ruin.

The issue of contention with the Navy was the delivery contract originally negotiated. The US Navy insisted on the fixed prices stated therein for the delivery, while Grumman argued that the rules fixed when the deal was made were no longer valid, that the inflation of the dollar was eating up practically all the profits, and that the company was on the brink of bankruptcy. At one point Grumman even refused to carry on with the F-14 construction program as the existing contracts would lead to a financial loss of 105 million dollars.

For this reason, Grumman only built one prototype of the improved F-14B with a more powerful engine and stopped any further development. After heated discussions, they arrived at a refinancing of the program, and delivery could be continued. At the beginning of the 1980s there were then 18 fighter squadrons of the US Navy on seven aircraft carriers equipped with the Tomcat.

Fire and forget

The highly efficient Hughes AWG-9 fire-control radar built into the F-14 made the Tomcat, in combination with the up to six AIM-54 Phoenix (AIM = Air Interception Missile = US term for air-to-air missiles) one of the first warplanes to activate target-seeking missiles. By means of the radar the pilot was in the position to register up to 24 targets from a distance of over 125 miles (200 km), to pick out up to six from among them, and fire the Phoenix. After firing, the missile followed the target with its own radar. After the firing of the first missile, the pilot was able to concentrate on another target. This system was unique at the time—and extremely expensive. The individual price of an AIM 54 Phoenix was over a million US dollars.

Alongside the Phoenix guided missiles, the Tomcat was also able to carry the AIM-7 Sparrow for medium ranges between 31 and 62 miles (50 and 100 km) and the AIM-9 Sidewinder for ranges between 6.2 and 11 miles (10 and 18 km). Neither of them are target-seeking missiles with active radar homing but air-to-air weapons, and they had to be guided to the target by the crew of the Tomcat by means of on-board radar. The seeker warheads of the Sparrow and Sidewinder (built as different variants) then react to the emissions of the opposing planes and destroy it. The Sidewinders on board the F-14 were an improved, extremely sensitively reacting version with an infra-red seeker head that could be fired in any position. However, these guided missiles could be outmaneuvered by a pilot with strong nerves if his on-board radar displayed the exact approach flight.

The Grumman F-14 Tomcat in its original application as a carrier-borne multi-purpose combat airplane.

Rapid-fire cannon

Guided missiles were supposed to make classical air combat redundant—however, the experience from Vietnam showed that jets also had to be suitable for this sort of combat. The versions of the Sparrow used in this war were very unreliable—so afterwards air combat was continued with the machine guns. In its fuselage the F-14 carried a six-tube M61A1 rapid-fire cannon designed on the Gatling principle and electrically operated with a fire speed up to 7,200 rounds/minute. Added to that the fact that in situations in which extreme agility mattered, the F-14 was unsurpassed. Because the swing wings could be automatically adjusted according to the flight situation, it was able to outmaneuver every jet then known and was ideal in dogfights.

To operate the whole weapon system the pilot had a HUD (head-up display), eye-level front screen vision equipment that gave him all-important threat and weapon indications (e.g. distance from the target, approach speed, fire readiness, and quantity of available missiles and munitions).

USS *Enterprise*

In October 1972 the F-14 was tested for the first time by the US Navy by VF-124 Squadron on aircraft carriers. The task of this squadron was education and training of further carrier-borne fighter squadrons on the Tomcat. The first two fully operational Navy units with the F-14 were then the VF-1 and VF-2 squadrons on board the aircraft carrier USS *Enterprise* in late summer of 1974—the crew were consistently enthusiastic. Over 500 F-14 Tomcats were

An F-14 with a full payload of six Phoenix guided missiles, one under each wing, two under each side of the fuselage. Recognizable under the nose is the IRST (Infra-Red Search and Track system).

At the beginning of its service life probably the best carrier-borne warplane in the world: the Grumman F-14.

Incident in the Mediterranean

On August 19, 1981, Tomcats were on a combat mission for the first time from the aircraft carrier *Nimitz* during a maneuver in the Mediterranean. The carrier group had already been approached several times by Libyan jets—on this day the situation escalated.

Two F-14 Tomcats and two Libyan Sukhoi Su-22s were involved. From a distance of 984 ft. (300 m) one of the Libyan jets fired a rocket at the leading Tomcat but the pilot was able to evade it by a rapid maneuver. The Tomcat outmaneuvered its opponents and positioned itself behind the Sukhoi Su-22 in a firing position. Both US pilots fired off a Sidewinder and destroyed the Libyan jets.

The maximum wing sweep with the Grumman F-14 Tomcat was 75 degrees.

in 1983 had the improved P-414A version of the Pratt & Whitney TF30 engine and also improved electronic equipment. This comprised more modern radar (AGP-71), a new IFF system (Identification Friend or Foe), and a built-in Northrop AXX-1 (TCS) TV camera system with a wide range for visual target identification, a laser inertia navigation system, and a completely newly designed cockpit display. Furthermore, the F-14C was given a new warning system and an internal self-protection jamming transmitter.

A special version of the Tomcat is the RF-14A, a photo-reconnaissance plane that replaced the Vought RF-8G Crusaders of the US Navy which were getting old. In total, 49 of the RF-14A were manufactured, equipped with the TARPS (Tactical Air Reconnaissance Pod System), a container-supported tactical air reconnaissance system consisting of optical cameras and an infra-red sensor.

At the end of the 1980s the F-14A was given the higher-performance General Electric F110 engine with 28,965 lbf (128.85 kN) thrust and this led to the series being renamed F-14A+ (or F-14A plus). The F-14D of the 1990s had the same engine but improved weapons and electronic equipment. It had devices for recording both from the TCS camera system and also the IRST (Infra-Red Search and Track system).

Operational deployment

At the time of the introduction of the Tomcat, Eastern and Western powers were still opposing each other and unreconciled. The original deployment concept must be looked at from this perspective.

In the event of a conflict between the two military powers the main focus would have lain with the carrier fleet stationed in the Atlantic. An approach of enemy ships or aircraft would have been announced by the E-2 Hawkeye early warning planes. The F-14A Tomcats were to intercept the air targets from a greater distance with the AIM-54 Phoenix guided missiles, a weapon to which the enemy jets at that time had nothing comparable—this scenario has fortunately never come about.

delivered to the US Navy by Grumman until 1985. Between 1976 and 1977, a further 80 went to the Iranian air force.

Further advances

The F-14 of the 1980s was basically the same one that had been put into service in the mid-1970s—apart from the electronics and the engine. The C series of the Tomcat introduced

Above: The Tomcat was tested by the US Navy on aircraft carriers for the first time in October 1972.

Below: The crew of the F-14 comprises pilot and Radar Intercept Officer (RIO).

LT.JG MICHAEL SEIP
TB

LT.JG TIM MYERS
NIEDER

103

AN SMART
MILAN, IL

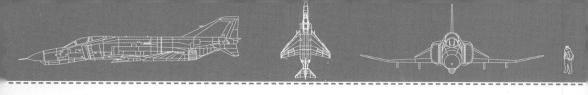

McDonnell F-4 Phantom II

This 1950s design became the standard NATO fighter in the 1970s and can now look back on a service life of almost 50 years. The number of 5,211 fighters and fighter-bombers built places the F-4 in the leading group of the most successful military aircraft—the record flights demonstrate the performance.

MCDONNELL F-4E PHANTOM II

Multi-purpose warplane
Wingspan: 38 ft. 7 in. (11.77 m)
Length: 63 ft. (19.20 m)
Height: 16 ft. 6 in. (5.02 m)
Empty weight: 30,334 lb. (13,757 kg)
Maximum take-off weight: 61,806 lb. (28,030 kg)
Power plant: 2 × General Electric J79-GE-17A turbojets each with 17,917 lbf (79.7 kN) thrust with afterburner, 11,080 lbf (49.29 kN) thrust without afterburner; in the German version 2 × General Electric J79-GE-17A turbojets produced under license at the MTU company with the same afterburner thrust and 11,689 lbf (52 kN) thrust without afterburner
Maximum speed: 1,438 mph (2,300 km/h) (Mach 2+)
Operational ceiling: 70,049 ft. (21,350 m)
Range: 1,490 miles (2,400 km)
Combat radius: 786 miles (1,265 km)
Armament: 1 × M61A1 Vulcan .787 in. (20 mm) caliber rapid-fire cannon, AIM-9L Sidewinder air-to-air missiles, AIM-120 AMRAAM medium-range air-to-air missiles

From the Navy to the Air Force

For decades the McDonnell Phantom II was the standard fighter for NATO partners.

The most frequent course of development of a fighter plane for use in fleet defense is when an existing model is adapted for use on an aircraft carrier—the F-4 is an exception to this. The US Navy called for bids for the construction of the Phantom and after that handed over a model to the USAAF (US Army Air Force) for testing—the model was found so good that the carrier plane was converted to a ground-supported multi-purpose warplane (long-distance high-level interceptor and low-level attack plane).

Four years in development

In 1954, the US Navy ordered two prototypes as part of a running program—these YAH-1s can be considered to be the first predecessors of the Phantom. The final specifications for the construction of the new two-seat marine fighter appeared in 1955 and led to some changes on the test model: a second seat for the radar observer and fire-control officer was created, the J-79 turbojet engine was made available by General Electric, and the armament of the first planes was limited to four Sparrow air-to-air missiles. Under the new designation XF4H-1 the prototype completed its first flight on May 27, 1958.

The roots

Although the new jet bore the same name as the predecessor McDonnell FH-1 Phantom from 1945, there is no similarity apart from the name. The short period of use of the Phantom

FH-1 had pushed the less successful fighter so far out of general thinking that the F-4 was, and to a large extent still is, thought of as the only Phantom. The development of the first test model of the Phantom II was based on the unpopular McDonnell F3H Demon, but the production model displays hardly any similar features.

Testing and the first production models

From the prototype, 23 further pre-series models were built and the first 45 F4H-1 mass-produced models were ready for delivery in 1961. The first fully deployable squadron—VF-114—received their Phantoms in October that year. With the standardization of the designations of all US armed forces, the Phantom II was given the official designation F-4 Phantom II in 1962. In 1960, the world speed record was set up at 1,389 mph (2,236 km/h) in

With an operational ceiling of over 12.5 miles (20 km) the Phantom II qualified as an interceptor, with a broad battery of guided weapons as a ground-attack plane.

The negative V-arrangement of the tailplane, and the wings starting level and the outer wing panel in a positive V-arrangement, give the Phantom II an unmistakable appearance.

Catapult take-off:
a carrier-borne
Phantom II takes
off from the flight
deck of the
British aircraft
carrier Ark Royal.

an F-4A, which only a year later was improved by 217 mph (349 km/h) again in an F-4.

Airframe

Few planes are so obviously recognizable as the F-4. The bent wing begins at the fuselage with

The cover of the
plane nose of
the McDonnell F4
accommodates
among other things
the radar antennae.

an angle of incidence of zero degrees, from where the wing bends, the outer wing assembly points upwards at an angle of 12 degrees (i.e. in a positive V-shape). The wing is swept back at an angle of 45 degrees along the whole of its length. Over the whole of the leading edge, slats are stretched, divided at the bend, forming a "dog tooth"; the ailerons are limited to the straight trailing edge.

The similarly swept-back tailplane displays a considerable 23-degree negative (downward) V-shape.

The air intakes of the two engines arranged on either side of the fuselage are placed at a height between the two cockpit seats with the outer edges shaped as rounded right angles.

The weapons

Depending on the type of operation, the F-4 can be armed in various configurations. In the interceptor and air supremacy fighter version, the General Electric M61 rapid-fire cannon should be mentioned first. From the experiences in the Second World War, the USA had learned that the machine gun armament of its fighters could not keep up with the models of the Allies and its opponents—as far as fire speed and range were concerned. The M61 changed this.

The Vietnam War provided a painful realization about the cannon. Because the leadership of the US Air Force (USAF) considered tube weapons superfluous in dogfights in times of missile technology, the first F-4 Phantom models that came into operation in Vietnam were equipped neither with a machine gun nor with the rapid-fire cannon. How wrong the strategists were with this appraisal is shown by the high numbers of losses at the beginning of the war.

Avionics

As with the armament, the on-board computers of the Phantom II are to be found in differing variants. For example, in the German version, the AN/APG-65 on-board radar is in operation, the same as in the F-18 Hornet. The gray covering of the radar antennae camouflage in the plane nose led to the nickname "Gray Nose," as opposed to the conventional "Black Nose."

In the USAF the Phantom was equipped with the AN/ASQ-22 navigation computer and the AN/ASQ-91 fire-control system. A small number were fitted with the AN/ARN-92 LORAN.

On all fronts

A dark chapter of air combat began for the USA and for Vietnam in the Gulf of Tonkin. The F-4 took part from the start with all the armed forces. The first combat operations were in summer 1964, and from the beginning of 1965—with the beginning of the "Rolling Thunder" bomb attacks—Phantom IIs were increasingly involved in air combat.

The lack of an on-board cannon represented a serious handicap, though the pilots of the Phantoms tried to compensate for this with superior speed. The first confirmed air victory

In the UK, Phantom IIs replaced the obsolete models of the RAF under the designations FGR.1 and FGR.2.

From the Gatling cannon to the intelligent guided missile

The requirement for a new weapon had already been expressed in 1946; from 1950 General Electric began work on a multi-barrel rapid-fire cannon that still today is part of the standard armament of American fighters. In 1862 Richard J. Gatling had patented a first rapid-fire cannon—named after him. In such a weapon, several tubes turn like the barrels of a revolver and can thus reach a previously impossible firing speed. Building on Gatling's principle, the General Electric Company began the development of the M61 cannon—this first

rapid-fire cannon for operation in warplanes bore the name M61 "Vulcan" and was tested with an F-104 Starfighter. Thus the Starfighter became the first fighter that was armed with the M61 as standard.

Sidewinder

The A M-9 Sidewinder air-to-air guided missile became the second standard weapon of US warplanes from the end of the 1950s, an early but by then very reliable and cheap weapon system. The Sidewinder has an infra-red target-seeking head that recognizes a target on the basis of its heat emission and directs the missile to this target. Missiles for use in the

Phantom are to a large extent the AIM-7 Sparrows, a supersonic, radar-guided, medium-range air-to-air missile and the advanced AIM-120 AMRAAM (Advanced Medium-Range Air-to-Air Missile) with radar target-seeking head. The AMRAAM can also be used in poor visibility or outside the vision of the pilot and comes very close to the idea of a self-seeking missile. The key words are "fire and forget."

for the USAF occurred in June 1965 when two F-4s of the 45th Tactical Fighter Squadron destroyed two MiG-17s with AIM-7 Sparrow medium-range air-to-air guided missiles.

The tactical use of the F-4 compared with the MiG on the opposing side cannot be unequivocally assessed. Even when the decision to fly without on-board cannon was later revoked and the Phantom was again armed with the M61 rapid-fire cannon, the pilots achieved no better a strike/loss rate than 1:2 against the MiG-21s.

At least at night, the Phantom was superior to the MiG-17s and MiG-19s that bore the main burden of the combat in this conflict. The much better instrumentation of the McDonnell almost certainly doomed the MiGs in the night—if they were found.

One domain of the Phantom IIs became the so-called "Wild Weasel" attacks. In F-4s specially equipped for this purpose (mostly from Series G), the pilots searched for the emissions of the opposing fire-control radar and then tried to destroy the transmitting stations. For this mission they had special anti-radar missiles (ARM = Anti Radiation Missile) the seeker heads of which followed the detected opposing radar signals and destroyed the radar installations.

LORAN

LORAN is a long-range wireless navigation procedure that was maintained in the Second World War by the US Coast Guard for border protection and afterwards made available for civilian users. The name is an acronym formed from "Long-Range Air Navigation." To be able to determine a fixed point, the LORAN system needs a network or a chain of at least three stations. One of them is the main station; the others (at least two) are secondary stations. The main station transmits an uninterrupted sequence of impulses in the low frequency range that cause the secondary stations to broadcast similar signals. The LORAN receiver on board the plane or the ship decodes all the signals, separates the main from the secondary signals, takes account of the time lag to activation of the secondary signals, and determines the coordinates of the receiving station.

LORAN-A was replaced in 1977 by LORAN-C because of the much greater ranges, and became indispensable until the introduction of satellite navigation.

Further combat areas of the McDonnell included the war of attrition in Israel 1969–1970, the Yom Kippur War in Israel 1973, the Iran–Iraq War 1980–1988, the war between Israel and Lebanon 1982, and the operations "Desert Storm" and "Southern Watch" in the Gulf War 1991–1998.

McDonnell F-4 Phantoms were deployed—within the US Navy, US Air Force, and US Marine Corps—as well as in the air forces of Australia, Egypt, Germany, Greece, Great Britain, Iran, Israel, Japan, South Korea, Spain, and Turkey.

Until the Gulf War in 1998, Phantom IIs flew combat missions for the US Air Force and US Navy.

30 years after the first flight in 1958, the Phantom II was still an effective weapon system.

MIKOYAN-GUREVICH MIG-29

With the reunification of the two German states in 1990, a whole squadron of the former Nationale Volksarmee (NVA) (East German Army) was transferred to the ownership of the Federal Republic of Germany. For the first time, Western military experts had the opportunity of studying this Soviet aircraft in detail—and were appalled. Some aspects of the performance capability of this air supremacy fighter were not achievable by NATO fighter planes at that time. Only the newest combat jets could carry out fight maneuvers that were possible with the MiG jet, which was by this time already 30 years old.

Until into the 1990s, the MiG-29 demonstrated the Soviet superiority in aircraft construction.

MIKOYAN-GUREVICH MIG-29
One or two-seat air supremacy fighter
Wingspan: 37 ft. 3 in. (11.36 m)
Length: 56 ft. 10 in. (17.32 m)
Height: 15 ft. 6 in. (4.73 m)
Empty weight: 24,035 lb. (10,900 kg)
Maximum take-off weight: 40,748 lb. (18,480 kg)
Power plant: 2 × Klimov RD-33 turbofan engines each with 11,100 lbf (49.38 kN) thrust without and 18,281 lbf (81.32 kN) thrust with afterburner
Maximum speed: 1,521 mph (2,450 km/h) (Mach 2.3)
Operational ceiling: 57,418 ft. (17,500 m)
Combat radius: 466 miles (750 km)
Armament: 1 × GSh-301 1.18 in. (30 mm) caliber cannon with 100–150 rounds of ammunition, firing rate 1,500 rounds/minute; 7 × external pylons for air-to-air guided missiles, 8 × 551 or 1,102 lb. (250 or 500 kg) bombs, napalm and submunitions containers, unguided rockets

The future "light front-line fighter"

That was what the MiG-29 was called in the planning phase. The aircraft was conceived in the USSR as a replacement for the obsolete MiG-21/23 and Su-15, and also as an answer to the developments of the US FX and LFW projects, which produced among other things the McDonnell Douglas F-15.

The standards for the new, light front-line fighter were superior maneuverability, suitability for air-to-ground capability (ground combat use), and independence from intact structures (i.e. the capacity to operate from auxiliary airfields).

Product 9

The NVA designated the first test model handed over to it with the harmless-sounding term "Product 9." A total of 19 prototypes were built—both one- and two-seaters. The first of them took off on its maiden flight on October 6, 1977, from Zhukovsky near Moscow. US spy satellites picked up the MiG-29 for the first time in 1979 on the parking area in Zhukovsky (usually called "Ramenskoye" after the next village to the west). In NATO code the unknown plane received the name "RAM-L." The designation "Fulcrum," introduced later, distinguished the MiG as a fighter with the initial letter "F" for "fighter."

Initial problems and the crashing of two prototypes led to a relatively long development period of eight years from the beginning of the detailed planning in 1974. In 1982 series production began, building on product (*Izdeliye*) 9.12. The training center of the Red Army received the first planes in spring 1983, and the MiG-29 reached operative status at the beginning of 1985. From April 1988 deliveries to Soviet "brother lands" began—the first recipient being East Germany.

Thrust vectoring and other refinements

In consideration of the newest generation of NATO warplanes in the 1970s, maneuverability was given the highest priority in the development of the MiG-29, and it was achieved. The characteristics of the Fulcrum in slow flight, which

in a dogfight determines the outcome of the skirmish, are outstanding even by 2007 standards. The wing geometry, or rather the whole design, are largely responsible for this, as the MiG-29 obtains 40 percent of the lift with the fuselage—the wing roots are spread out wide and blend into the fuselage. The latest versions of the MiG-29 from 2003 display so-called thrust vectoring (a thrust nozzle movable in all directions with which the exhaust stream of the turbines is controlled), and the agility of the fighter in dogfights is once again improved.

The tactical value

At short distances and low speed, the Russian aircraft is a serious opponent even for the most modern fighters of today when comparing combat abilities. The pilot is in a position to carry out flight

The MiG-29, NATO code name "Fulcrum," was primarily to fulfill tasks in land defense.

The latest models of the MiG-29 have access to thrust vectoring that allows the aircraft to undertake flight maneuvers that were considered impossible before this invention.

maneuvers that completely confuse the opponent; for example, pointing the plane nose in a direction other than that of the flight direction or standing for a short period on the thrust stream of the engine. A further design prerequisite for this maneuver is offered by the air intakes of the turbines. The MiG-29 draws the air for the turbines from several intake openings. Hydraulically operated flaps close-off the air intakes as long as the plane is on the ground (taxiing and take-off) and—particularly on auxiliary runways—prevent foreign bodies being sucked in and damaging the engine. The engines then draw their air from openings in the top of the fuselage. In unusual maneuvers, the variable air intakes prevent the engine from stalling from lack of oxygen, when it is no longer being supplied by the slipstream.

Electronics and targeting

The avionics of the Mikoyan-Gurevich was—with some small faults—at the peak of its time. In the meantime, other essential components had been replaced and modernized because it turned out that in this respect the MiG was inferior to comparable Western fighters.

The American F-15 had at its disposal a weapons system for air combat beyond visual range (BVR)—but the MiG-29 could essentially only operate within these limits. It achieved its best performance in close combat—the

preferred tactic of Soviet pilots was to involve the opponent in a dogfight. The helmet visor, as part of the weapons system, was one of the most dangerous inventions it possessed; the pilot was able to switch on targets in the display installed in his helmet, and fire the Wimpel R-73 air-to-air missile independently of the flight position and directly to the target.

The fire-control system of the MiG-29 did not have its equal in the world of that time! One of the receiver devices was the RP-29 impulse Doppler radar (NATO code "Slot Back"). Thanks to this RP-29, higher flying targets could be locked on to at a distance of more than 50 miles (80 km) and lower flying objects attacked at 31 miles (50 km) from elevated positions. For additional targeting channels for air combat, an IRST (Infra-Red Search and Track system) and also a laser rangefinder were used. The IRST can pick up and attack a target without the prey realizing it. The radar stays in passive operational readiness without transmitting its own signal until the fire-control system has fired the guided missile. The radar warning device of the target plane does not respond until the radar controlled guided weapon is set off—mostly too late for countermeasures.

Other parts of the computer-controlled avionics were a head-up display (HUD) that projected flight and threat data into the field of vision of the pilot and the plane's own on-

Even 30 years after its maiden flight, over short distances the MiG-29 is still a dangerous opponent.

Distribution and variants

Although the MiG-29 is already aging a bit, the model is still being built—but being constantly updated to the newest state of technology. The model was an out and out sales success. MiG-29s are operational in no less than 23 air forces worldwide—in Europe, Asia, and Africa—and it is said that the US Air Force has bought and used planes of this type from Moldavia for practice purposes.

MiG-29s can be found in Algeria and India. In Iran, former Iraqi MiG-29s, whose pilots flew there during the Gulf War, are operational. The Iranians are so taken with the model that they are refusing the originally intended restitution.

In Serbia-Montenegro, five of 16 machines delivered in 1987/88 are still in service; the rest were destroyed by NATO troops. From October 1989 Cuba received ten MiG-29s; however, it is not known if any of them are still serviceable.

In total, 1,500 of the MiG-29s were built.

The outstanding flight characteristics of the MiG-29 predestine it for aerobatic and formation flying.

From the planning point of view comparable to the American F-15, the MiG-29 displays similar design characteristics.

board Aekran fault diagnosis equipment—and, despite all the computer technology, there were also still numerous conventional dial instruments in the cockpit.

The arsenal

The MiG-29 could be equipped with a variety of weapons. Alongside the cannon, it carried a great variety of guided missiles, including the following:

- For short-range air target combat, six Wimpel R-73 or infra-red-controlled Molniya R-60M (NATO code AA-8 Aphid) air-to-air guided missiles.
- For longer distances, radar-controlled R-27REs or R-27TEs (with infra-red seeker head).
- For combating ground targets, up to 9,923 lb. (4,500 kg) bombs or air-to-ground guided missiles (X-25 ML/MP with laser target seeker head or as anti-radar version) or X-29LT/TD (TV seeker head), and for anti-ship combat radar-controlled X-31A/P.

The double tail fin
of the MiG-29
displays a rudder
on each one.

Left page: The strake or hybrid wing has been the measure of things in aircraft construction since the 1970s—to this day.

Jagdfliegergeschwader (JG) (fighter squadron) 3 Victor Komarov in Preschen

At the beginning of the 1990s, there were 24 MiG-29s in service in this unit of the LSK/LV (Luftstreitkräfte/Luftverteidigung = air force/air defense) that were transferred into the possession of the Federal Republic of Germany on reunification. Thus, before the eastern expansion of NATO, Germany became the only North Atlantic Pact country to have these planes. The chance to measure up under maneuver conditions against one of the most powerful weapons of the Eastern Bloc made the pilots of the MiG-29 testing squadron—as the JG 3 was called after the changeover—welcome guests at comparative demonstration flights and maneuvers.

In the meantime, the squadron was combined with Jabo squadron 35 and, on September 18, 1997, was officially given the title Jagdgeschwader 73, "Steinhoff" (JG 73 "S"), after the First World War flying ace and later first inspector general of the Luftwaffe, Johannes Steinhoff. After the testing phase, the planes were re-equipped up to NATO standards—by the then DASA—and under the new designation MiG-29G or MiG-29G⁻ (two-seat trainer) became the responsibility of the German Luftwaffe. The planes served under NATO Supreme Command, among other things in air surveillance, as pairs on alert. With the beginning of the introduction of the Euro-fighter, on June 24, 2003, an agreement was signed between Germany and Poland in which the remaining MiG-29s would be handed over to Poland for a token price of one euro each. From September 2003 the handing over of the planes began and on August 4, 2004, the last nine MiG-29s of the German Luftwaffe took off from the Laage airbase for Bydgoszcz in Poland.

Daily routine:
A pilot on the
internal check
of his plane.

SUKHOI SU-27

Military information from the Soviet Union was subject to the most stringent secrecy, but with the opening up to the West that was to change. At the 1989 Paris Air Show, the Sukhoi Su-27 was presented to the public for the first time—and caused a sensation. The introduction of the plane not only astounded the experts, but the flight maneuver demonstrated on this occasion—the Pugachev Cobra—made it clear even to the uninitiated that this plane redefined the term maneuverability.

SUKHOI SU-27
One or two-seat long-distance fighter
Wingspan: 48 ft. 3 in. (14.70 m)
Length: 71 ft. (21.94 m)
Height: 19 ft. 6 in. (5.93 m)
Empty weight: 36, 118 lb. (16,380 kg)
Maximum take-off weight: 84,452 lb. (38,300 kg)
Power plant: 2 × Saturn/Lyulka AL-31F turbofan engines each with 27,560 lbf (122.6 kN) thrust
Maximum speed: 1,553 mph (2,500 km/h) (Mach 2.35)
Operational ceiling: 59,058 ft. (18,000 m)
Combat radius: 932 miles (1,500 km)
Armament: 1 × internal GSh-30-1 Gryazev-Shipunov) 1.18 in. (30 mm) cannon with 150 rounds, 10 or 12 × external pylons for a variety of air-to-air and air-to-ground weapons

With the Sukhoi Su-27, the then Soviet Union possessed a warplane that stood for 20 years at the peak of development.

A long way

It was a long way from the heavy, future front-line plane, as the Sukhoi was called in the planning phase—from which the MiG-29 also developed—to the Paris Air Show in Le Bourget. From the first conception to the production readiness of this amazing air supremacy interceptor, it took a decade.

With a formulation similar to the American duo F-15 and F-16, the new fighter was to complement the MiG-29. The specifications for maneuverability were the same as for the medium-range fighter, which manifests itself in the very similar wing geometry. Beyond that, the Sukhoi was to have a good altitude performance for pursuit and an extensive range for deep penetration into enemy territory.

For this reason the design department at Sukhoi created the new jet approximately a third bigger than the MiG, to make enough room for equipment and fuel. At this time in the Soviet Union, refueling in the air was not always guaranteed, and so was not planned for in the first series.

T-10 the first prototype

In 1977, after several years' development time, the Sukhoi OKB had reason to assume that mass production was about to start. The first of ten prototypes was being tested and a start had already been made with the setting-up of assembly lines.

The prototype of the Su-27, the T-10, took off on May 20, 1977, with test pilot Vladimir Ilyushin—the son of the famous designer—on its first flight, considerably earlier than the MiG-29 prototype.

During the test phase it became clear that the design and performance specifications were not to be fulfilled with the test models; in some ways they failed the set expectations considerably. Furthermore, during this series of tests two of the jets crashed, and these two accidents overshadowed this time.

The operating temperatures of the turbojets reached values that made a markedly short service life for the components more than likely. Apart from that, the specifications for weight and range were not achievable with this model; the avionics needed so much room that the fuel tanks could not have the required volumes.

T-10S the new design

On the basis of the specifications not achieved in the first prototype, at Sukhoi OKB under the leadership of Head Designer Mikhail Simonov, the design was re-addressed and a completely new plane was built—while the testing of the avionics continued in parallel with the first model.

The result was the T-10S, which became the standard model for the long-range interceptor. The T-10S was driven by a different type of turbine, a turbofan engine that considerably

Increasingly, even in Russia, the dial instruments were being replaced by screens. On the upper edge of the picture, the half-transparent head-up display can be seen.

For design reasons
the nose points
downwards and
thus guarantees
excellent all-round
visibility.

reduced the strain on its components. This prototype finally completed its first flight on April 20, 1981, just short of ten years after the beginning of the detailed planning stage, and can be regarded as the first version of the later Su-27 that was ready for series production.

It was the first time that the USSR had consistently backed electronic steering. The Su-27 was the first serially produced Soviet plane with a "fly by wire" system. This system is quadruple redundant, and in addition the rudder and aileron functions could be manually secured. As the Su-27 is aerodynamically laid out in an unstable format, the flight envelope is normally automatically limited. For high angles of approach, these limits can, however, be deactivated at the push of a button.

Also in other ways the Su-27 was, technically speaking, at the latest state of the art at the beginning of the 1980s. The HOTAS principle generally used today (Hands On Throttle And Stick), whereby all important operating elements were to be found on the thrust control lever and the joystick, was then new.

Because of its elegantly rolling front fuselage and its hanging nose, many pilots call the Su-27 the "crane." The construction method, however, serves rather more practical reasons

than aesthetic ones. It guarantees, among other things, all-round vision of 360 degrees from the cockpit. The whole geometry of the Su-27 not only resembles the MiG-29 but also the American models of this period; the strake or hybrid wings were at this time just becoming standard. After years of research on unswept— as in the MiG-9—via delta wings of the Sukhoi Su-9, and the swing wings of the MiG-23, the same conclusion had been reached at the same time worldwide: the combination of sharp and gentle wing sweep promised the best results.

Combat loads

Alongside its remarkable maneuverability, the Su-27, has a range of up to 2,285 miles (3,680 km). This performance is reached thanks to a maximum fuel quantity of about 3,110 gal. (11,775 l)—if it is operated with the largest possible take-off mass. The weight is at the expense of the flight characteristics but, by the time the Sukhoi has reached its planned location, the consumption en route has evened out this handicap. The strategic advantage of this extreme range is deep penetration into enemy territory for targeted interruption of the airspace surveillance, for example of the Western AWACS system. The Russians demonstrated this range in 1992 in a very

The strake wing

The strake or hybrid wing is striking because of the varying sweep. At its root (join to the fuselage) the wing is strongly swept back. The wing roots tapering in the direction of flight reach right under the cockpit. The outer area of the wing, after the bend, is moderately swept back at 43 degrees. This wing is one of the answers to the problems of high-speed flight; similarly to the swing wing, the sharp sweep improves stability in supersonic flight and prevents the appearance of the rhythmic shock waves from the compressibility effect. The gentle sweep in combination with the lift-creating fuselage provides maneuverability and control at low speed. Wings of this construction method create air turbulence that is difficult to control (see diagram). The lift gained by this is in any case worth the effort and stalling happens—compared with a delta wing—only with much greater angles of approach.

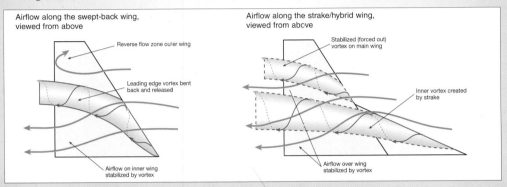

Airflow along the swept-back wing, viewed from above

Reverse flow zone outer wing

Leading edge vortex bent back and released

Airflow on inner wing stabilized by vortex

Airflow along the strake/hybrid wing, viewed from above

Stabilized (forced out) vortex on main wing

Inner vortex created by strake

Airflow over wing stabilized by vortex

media-effective way when the new Su-35, based on the Su-27 and first of all designated Su-27M—NATO code "Flanker D"—flew non-stop from Moscow to the British Isles for the Farnborough Air Show—and only with the contents of the internal tank without in-flight refueling.

Thrust vectoring

A further impressive capability of the Su-27 is thrust vectoring. The principle of this technique rests on the diversion of the thrust stream at the exit—of the thrust nozzle—of the turbine. This steering further widens the range of possible flight maneuvers and directly affects agility and mobility. The disadvantage of this innovation is an increase in fuel consumption and shortened service life of some of the components of the turbine. Therefore, thrust vectoring finds application exclusively in the military field.

Guided missiles and others

The Su-27 was to ensure the protection of the air space and interception of penetrating enemy aircraft at great heights; the armament

is adapted for that. The on-board cannon for short-range target combat is installed in the starboard wing root. The Gryazev-Shipunov GSch-30-1 is a single-barreled, gas-operated 1.18 in. (30 mm) cannon that in contrast to Western multi-barreled standard weapon means a clear weight-saving. It compensates for the relatively slow fire speed of 1,800 rounds per minute with such an effective projectile force that only a few strikes are necessary to destroy a plane—even if according to the manufacturer the barrel only has a service life of less than 2,000 rounds. The optimum range of the cannon lies between 3,281 and 6,562 ft. (1,000 and 2,000 m).

For medium-range air targets, the Su-27 carries, among other things, the Wimpel R-27 air-to-air guided missile (NATO code AA-10 Alamo). This is a medium-range weapon that is guided either by infra-red or radar guided seeker pulses in active mode.

The helmet visor

The Su-27 is fitted with Wimpel R-73 short-range air-to-air guided missiles

(NATO-Code AA-11 Archer). They can be deployed in an area from a few hundred yards/meters up to 18.6 miles (30 km). The guided missile finds its target either on its own, with a heat-seeking infra-red seeker which can accommodate an angle of up to 60 degrees from the flight axis, or is guided by the pilot with radar via the helmet visor. When the target can be picked up in the viewing glass of the pilot's helmet, the rocket finds its way there irrespective of the flight attitude of the plane.

The Wimpel R-73 is considered to be the most effective weapon of this type—and to be superior to the comparable NATO "Sidewinder" guided missile.

The sensors

"Slot Back" is the name given by NATO to the Sukhoi radar originally used, a Pulse-Doppler Radar with the capability of distinguishing deep-lying targets from background interference.

In the fuselage nose of the Su-27 is the IRST, an infra-red supported search and track system with a range of 43 miles (70 km). It can be operated independently or as part of the radar. In a passive mode, it is possible to make out an enemy target without transmitting one's own signal. Not until the mid-range rockets are fired does it begin to transmit pulses in active mode. The radar

Thrust vectoring enables flight figures that make the Sukhoi the spectacular highlight of numerous air shows and flight days.

The Pugachev Cobra

This maneuver from air combat tactics is one of the more recent flight maneuvers, first demonstrated by the Soviet pilot Victor Pugachev with a Su-27 at the 38th Le Bourget Air Show in 1989. The name graphically describes the procedure: just as the cobra raises its head for attack, the pilot takes the plane nose even higher in a climb until at an approach angle of over 100 degrees—the plane nose then stands vertically behind the tail—it is slowed down by the air resistance and comes abruptly to a standstill. Literally. For a short time the plane rides on its own exhaust stream until the pilot lowers the nose again, allows the plane to fall back down slowly, and resumes the flight. The tactical use of this is that a pursuer is surprised and flies past the Su-27 at high speed and puts itself in the firing line.

In the 1990s—on the side of the Western powers—only the Lockheed F/A-22 Raptor was able to carry out this maneuver.

warning device of the target in sight does not pick up the danger until after switching—then it can already be too late.

Furthermore the IRST controls the cannon with greater precision than would be possible with radar.

The strake wing with variable geometry was introduced worldwide almost simultaneously.

The port side of the tailplane fin of an SU-27.

DASSAULT SUPER ÉTENDARD

Since the beginning of the 1960s the Dassault Étendard has been the standard fighter of the French Navy. In the middle of the 1970s, this successful series was extended with the Super Étendard and its combat effectiveness considerably improved. The superiority of the Super Étendard can be seen from the fact that, in the modernized version SEM—alias Modernisé—it is still today in service on the *Charles de Gaulle*, the flagship of the French Navy—together with its successor, the Rafale, which will replace it in the foreseeable future.

DASSAULT SUPER ÉTENDARD
Carrier-borne interceptor and air supremacy fighter/fighter-bomber
Wingspan: 31 ft. 6 in. (9.60 m)
Length: 46 ft. 11 in. (14.31 m)
Height: 12 ft. 8 in. (3.86 m)
Empty weight: 14,333 lb. (6,500 kg)
Maximum take-off weight: 27,342 lb. (12,400 kg)
Power plant: 1 × turbojet SNECMA Atar 8K-50 jet engine with 11,015 lbf (49 kN) static thrust
Maximum speed: 857 mph (1,380 km/h) (Mach 1.3)
Operational ceiling: 45,000 ft. (13,715 m)
Combat radius: 522 miles (840 km)
Armament: 2 × DEFA 533 cannon 1.18 in. (30 mm) caliber 125 rounds each and up to 4,631 lb. (2,100 kg) external stores, an under-fuselage and 4 × under-wing bomb stations, air-to-air Matra Magic guided missiles, rocket launcher or Aérospatiale Exocet AM39 anti-ship missiles

A Super Étendard with extended undercarriage.

Its predecessors

The first Étendards were delivered to the French Navy at the beginning of 1962 and completed over 180,000 flight hours and over 25,000 carrier landings until their withdrawal from service in July 1991. In 1973, these pursuit planes were to be replaced; with the Vought A-7 and the Anglo-French co-production SEPECAT Jaguar M to choose from. The representatives of the Dassault Company had a better suggestion—an improved version of the Étendard. Dassault's arguments were convincing. If they remained to a large extent with the existing model, that would have significant advantages with respect to costs, spare-parts economy, and servicing. And last but not least, this plane was a purely French product. The Navy agreed.

Concept

The specifications for the first Étendard as a light interceptor were quickly extended. The new specifications demanded a light tactical bomber that was also able to guarantee air supremacy—this range of duty has been taken on by the Super Étendard for the Aéronavale, the French Navy Air Force, to the present day. The whole range of deployment includes airspace protection of the fleet, protection of the fleet against ships (anti-ship combat), support in ground combat, and photo-reconnaissance.

The maiden flight of the SEM took place on December 28, 1974; on June 23, 1978, deliveries of the mass-produced planes began.

Changes

The intention of using nine-tenths of the original Étendard as a basis for the succeeding model seems to have fallen into oblivion. With the new single-wave turbojet engine Atar 8K-50, a fundamentally changed airframe, and an entirely new avionics at the end of the development, the Super Étendard has become an almost completely different aircraft

Super Étendard with extended air-refueling probe—ready for refueling.

On board an aircraft carrier. The Super Étendard is engaged in the catapult equipment and the ground crew authorize take-off.

from the one originally planned. The new engine, a version of the turbine from the Mirage F.1, achieves 11,015 lbf (49 kN), even without afterburner, about 10 percent more than the previous model Atar 8—and also with lower fuel consumption. The increased operational radius of 522 miles (840 km) is a direct consequence of this and of the increase in the fuel tank capacity to 864 gal. (3,270 l).

The Super Étendard carries auxiliary tanks of various sizes depending on the configuration and bomb load. Armed with the Exocet, it could only carry one of 290 gal. (1,100 l) capacity; otherwise it could carry two under the wings or else the 158 gal. (600 l) auxiliary tank under the fuselage, already used on the previous model.

The wings were adapted to the increased take-off weight. Although they are similar to those of the Étendard, they have an extended wing root, a somewhat stronger sweep, and extendible flaps that reach over the whole length of the leading edge. The flaps on the trailing edge of the wing are designed as a double-slotted flap.

Combat effectiveness

Particular emphasis was laid on the electronic fitting of the SEM in the development; the Agave Radar, a joint development of Thomson-CSF and Electronique Marcel Dassault EMD, is mounted in the nose and has a range of up to 68.3 miles (110 km), for the recognition and identification of ship targets and a range of 18.6 miles (30 km) in air-to-air mode. Other modes of operation of the Agave are pursuit/range-finding of ground and air targets, ground display, and target-marking for attacks with Exocet anti-ship missiles.

The Agave was supplemented by the SAGEM-Kearfott ETNA navigation and attack system that was able to lead the pilot accurately to the target with values that were entered before take-off—the deviation was only 1.4 miles/flight hour (2.2 km./flight hour).

Also very modern for the early 1970s were the head-up display (HUD) VE120 from the Thomson-CSF company and a TRT radio altimeter. Mention should also be made of an IFF on-board radar for the identification of friend and foe from the LMT Company and the Micro-TACAN (TACtical Air Navigation), a

An impressive silhouette of an armed Dassault Super Étendard M.

tactical navigation aid that provides the pilot with distance and bearing values that are obtained by using ground beacons. The antennas for the civil variant, the Socrates omnidirectional radio beacon, a VHF navigation aid for short and medium range were installed like the radar warning receiver on the side of the tailplane fin.

The avionics were completed by a Crouzet 97 navigation screen, weapon selection and deployment equipment, and the Crouzet 66 air data calculator. Together with considerable advantages in aerial combat, the improved avionics of the Super Étendard Modernisé mean that now even night carrier landings are possible, which for a carrier-borne pursuit plane is one of the most difficult operations of all.

To this day, the Super Étendard attracts numerous visitors at air shows.

HMS *Sheffield*

Even in circles that otherwise do not concern themselves with military questions, the anti-ship missile Aérospatiale AM39 Exocet has achieved a certain fame because of the Super Étendard. With these Exocet guided missiles, Argentinian Air Force Étendards sank two British warships in the war for the Malvinas or the Falkland Islands as they are called in Great Britain. The only orders for the export version of the Super Étendard had come in 1981 from Argentina. At the beginning of the combat operations with the Royal Navy, the French government did stop the delivery, but five planes had already been delivered and were ready for service. On May 4, 1982, Super Étendards launched one Exocet at the guided missile destroyer HMS *Sheffield* and on May 25 two at the supply ship *Atlantic Conveyor* and sank both—although it was never wholly clarified whether the Exocet that hit the *Sheffield* actually exploded. On the one hand, it made the fighting spirit of the Argentinians clear, on the other hand it is a proof of the strike capability of the Étendard.

Matra magic

Alongside the two 1.18 in. (30 mm) caliber DEFA2 cannon the SEM carries a comprehensive arsenal of guided weapons—also with atomic warheads—such as the air-to-air guided weapons Matra 550 Magic and the AM39 Exocet for anti-ship combat.

The wings of the Super Étandard were adapted to the increased take-off weight compared with its predecessors.

Iran and Iraq

The Super Étendard is still in the service of the French Navy today.

A number of Super Étendards served in the first Gulf War between Iran and Iraq—as a loan. Although Saddam Hussein had bought Exocets from France, he was not able to use them. The reason was that in his air force there were no fighter planes with the appropriate delivery systems. So Aéronavale lent Iraq five Super

Étendards until the Mirage F.1s with the appropriate weapon systems ordered could be delivered. The planes took part in combat missions from 1984 and flew mainly in attacks against oil tankers. After the war they were handed back to France.

Operation Trident was another conflict in which SEM was utilized on board the aircraft carrier *Foch*. Between January and June 1999, 18 Super Étendards of the French Navy flew 450 missions over Kosovo and dropped 268 GBU-12 laser-guided bombs.

Exocet

The tactical value of an anti-ship guided missile was considered to be quite small up to the 1950s. The idea that a rocket—fired from on board an airplane or a ship— could damage the armor plates of a heavy warship seemed unrealistic. Nevertheless, during this period, attempts were started, and in Sweden and the Soviet Union these weapons were ready for action by the mid-1960s. It was also at this time, in 1967, that Styx anti-ship missiles of Soviet origin sank an Israeli destroyer and started a rethink in the ranks of the strategists. France was among those at the forefront of development; there, the Exocet was already in the arsenal in 1967.

The functioning mode of the Exocet is adapted to its combat mission. Guided by its active radar, it attacks with a speed of Mach 0.93 close over the waves (about 8 ft. 4 in. or 2.50 m high) and hits the ships just above the waterline—where it causes maximum damage. As the target data are fed in before take-off, the pilot has completed his mission with the launch. Because of their low flight path, Exocets can almost only be successfully combated with radio interference equipment or anti-radar guided missiles.

Representatives of the Royal Navy evaluated the Super Étendard and the Exocet as their most dangerous threat in the Falklands War—although the Argentinians had only five Exocets altogether at their disposal.

EXOCET AM39

Anti-ship missile with two-stage solid propellant motor

Length: 15 ft. 5 in. (4.69 m)
Diameter: 14 in. (35 cm)
Maximum take-off weight: 1,444 lb. (655 kg)
Warhead: 364 lb. (165 kg)
Flight time (engine shutdown): 2 seconds with take-off motor, with booster motor 150 seconds
Speed: 696 mph (1,120 km/h) (Mach 0.93)
Approach altitude: under 49 ft. (15.00 m)
Attack altitude: 8.2 ft. (2.50 m)
Range: 32–43 miles (52–70 km)
Detonator: Proximity or delay-fused

HAWKER SIDDELEY HARRIER

The British Harrier was, and still is, the only tactically and economically successful warplane with steep, vertical or short take-off capability and also the shortest landing. It is rightly considered to be one of the greatest innovations in the history of flight and was used together with the Sea Harrier with great success in the Falklands War.

The most successful jet with V/STOL capabilities—the Hawker Harrier here in the Sea Harrier version.

HAWKER SIDDELEY HARRIER GR3

Tactical warplane
Wingspan: 25 ft. 3 in. (7.70 m)
Length: 45 ft. 7 in. (13.89 m)
Height: 11 ft. 11 in. (3.63 m)
Empty weight: 12,304 lb. (5,580 kg)
Vertical take-off weight (VTOL): 18,004 lb. (8,165 kg)
Short take-off weight (STOL): 23,009 lb. (10,435 kg)
Maximum take-off weight: 25,203 lb. (11,430 kg)
Power plant: 1 × turbofan Rolls-Royce Pegasus 103 jet engine with 21,500 lbf (95.64 kN) thrust
Maximum speed: 730 mph (1,176 km/h) (Mach 0.95)
Operational ceiling: 51,184 ft. (15,600 m)
Combat radius: 416 miles (670 km)
Air surveillance: 115 miles (185 km) 1½ hours
Armament: 2 × 1.18 in. (30 mm) Aden cannon in two under-fuselage containers; 4 × under-wing pylons for a total loading of 5,292 lb. (2,400 kg) that can comprise bombs, unguided rockets, flare throwers, anti-radar missiles AS.37 Martel, and AIM-9 Sidewinder air-to-air guided missiles; in total 35 different combinations of weapons and other equipment can be carried

Sidney Camm time and again

In 1957 Sidney Camm began his design for a vertical take-off aircraft at the firm Hawker Aircraft. His concept rested on the deflection of the jet airflow of the so-called vectored thrusting—without turbines, swiveling engines, or twistable wings. This concept was to prove to be the most successful in the course of time.

V/STOL or VSTOL, STOL, STO(V)L or STOVL

The abbreviations for the bewildering array of possibilities for vertical or short take-off planes are many and varied: for example, V/STOL or VSTOL for "Vertical or short take-off and landing," STOL for "Short take-off and landing," and STO(V)L or STCVL for "Short take-off or vertical landing."

Just as extraordinary as the jet is the undercarriage, with three wheels under the fuselage and support landing gear under each of the wingtips.

Sidney Camm conceived the vertical take-off.

To allow for balance when hovering, the engine of the Harrier is installed at the center of gravity of the plane in the center of the fuselage.

The first vertical take-off aircraft at Hawker, with the works number P.1127, came into being under Sidney Camm's leadership. It completed its first hover flight on October 21, 1960, albeit a very limited one because of safety ropes. As a result of a long and difficult test phase, and after the fusion of Hawker and Siddeley, nine Kestrel F(GA)1s were built which were later used to train Harrier pilots.

In 1966, Hawker Siddeley received the first order to build 67 further-developed Kestrels, six of which were presented as P.1127RAFs and 61 as Harrier GR1s.

Powered by a Rolls-Royce 6 (Mk.101), the first Harrier GR1 completed its maiden flight on December 28, 1967, and on April 1, 1969, the RAF took delivery of the first planes. Additionally, for training purposes the two-seat Trainer T2 was developed and mass-produced.

The AV-8A variant developed for the US Marine Corps and the Spanish Navy was very similar to the Harrier GR1.

With the Harrier GR3, Hawker Siddeley brought out a significantly improved variant— externally recognizable by its pointed and extended nose housing in which a new laser rangefinder was accommodated. The GR3 was probably the best model of the first generation.

A Harrier II of the US Marine Corps begins to land on an aircraft carrier.

Sea Harrier

The Sea Harrier was developed for naval operations. It could take-off without the help of a catapult from the relatively small British aircraft carriers or vertically from the deck of a cruiser. The first Sea Harrier flew on August 21, 1978, and by June 1979 the first jets were delivered to the Royal Navy.

At the end of the 1970s, the second generation of the Harrier family was specially developed for the US Marine Corps in co-operation with McDonnell Douglas. Of these the AV-8B is the best known model.

Ground engaging

The Hawker Harrier is a high-wing airplane with a negative angle of incidence and an unusual undercarriage. The nose wheel is under the front fuselage and the double wheels of the main landing gear are on the fuselage middle line—approximately on a line with the wings. After take-off, the nose wheel and the main landing gear are retracted into the fuselage or lowered for landing. On both wingtips there is an outrigger landing gear for take-off and landing with a very small tire. After take-off, the support undercarriages are folded under the wings and covered with a secure, aerodynamically shaped cowling. Wings and tailplane are swept back and the leading edges of the wings are rounded. The two very large jet engine air intakes are arranged on either side of the cockpit at the front of the fuselage.

Thrust vectoring

The Rolls-Royce Pegasus of the Harrier is a turbojet engine, the emissions of which the pilot can variably adjust, within certain limits, by means of swiveling nozzles.

The two-jet engine air intakes are arranged on either side of the fuselage at the height of the cockpit. However, the exhausts (here also called jets or nozzles and not to be confused with the jet engine) for the emissions are not integrated into the rear as in conventional construction but in the fuselage, the first pair under the leading edges of the wings and the second underneath the middle of the wings. Each of these four thrust jets can be swiveled through 98 degrees. With a separate lever next to the thrust performance level, the pilot can adjust the nozzles and divert the airstream.

For take-off and landing, the nozzles point downwards. The vectors (direction) of incoming air and emissions are thus at an angle of 90 degrees to each other. To change over into horizontal flight, the pilot continually adjusts all four nozzles to the point at which they are pointing to the rear until the vector of air flowing in and exhaust emissions is identical and the Harrier transforms the thrust into acceleration. Additionally, the jet plane can decelerate with the nozzles during a conventional landing and, within limits, fly backwards. Thus the Harrier is capable of landing within a circle of 66 ft. (20 m) diameter.

The second generation Harrier: a Harrier II AV-8B in the service of the US Marine Corps.

Tactical applications

Originally, thrust vectoring was only intended for take-off and landing. After the Harrier had been taken into service by the RAF and the US Marine Corps, a USMC pilot recognized the VIFF potential of the Harrier. VIFF stands for "Vectoring In Forward Flight" and means that by rapid swiveling of the jets the flight direction can be changed, and climbing and decelerating at lightning speed is possible. VIFF is also an astounding flight maneuver that gives the Harrier a unique agility and can make the difference between victory and defeat in air combat. A pursuing opponent must of necessity overtake the Harrier and changes from the pursuer to the pursued.

The Falklands

Theoretically the advantages of a vertical take-off are obvious and, in the disputes between Argentina and the UK, they were put to the test.

Both the Harrier GR3 and the Sea Harrier were used in the Falklands War for air defense, intelligence, and land combat support—and achieved an excellent strike rate. Despite the low maximum speed of only 727 mph (1,170 km/h), the pilots of the 38 Harriers and Sea Harriers succeeded in shooting down 31 Argentine jets, 19 of which were supersonic Mirages, without any losses themselves. This took place under the extreme weather conditions of the South Atlantic, in the sort of weather that would have made a conventional deployment from aircraft carriers impossible.

The second generation

The AV-8B Harrier II was developed from the original Harrier by McDonnell Douglas in co-operation with British Aerospace. In many respects it was a new design providing a general improvement in the range and the scope of the weapons used, and the flight performance. McDonnell Douglas brought to the new design the expertise that had been gained in the development of the F-15 Eagle and the F-18 Hornet. The prototype, the YAV-8B, flew for the first time on November 9, 1978, and the first production models of the AV-8B were delivered to the US Marine Corps in 1983. Additionally, for training purposes the two-seat Trainer TAV-8B was developed.

One of the disadvantages of the "old" Harrier was its classic 1960s cockpit. This cockpit was redesigned for the Harrier II. It was modernized and equipped in a more user-friendly way, given a drop-shaped canopy, and offered—now being placed higher up—excellent all-round vision. Furthermore, the new larger wingspans are immediately striking, though their weight has been kept low by the use of carbon-fiber composite materials and they are almost unbreakable. They now not only give more lift but also have enlarged internal fuel tanks with the result that the Harrier II now has a 50 percent higher fuel capacity. As propulsion, it has a turbojet engine with adjustable nozzles, the Rolls-Royce Pegasus 11-21 Mk.105 (US designation: F402-RR-406). Its static thrust performance of 21,178 lbf (94.21 kN) accelerates the Harrier II to 668 mph (1,075 km/h) maximum speed.

External stores

Under each wing there are three pylons. Two of these are intended for auxiliary tanks with 300 gal. (1,136 l) capacity but can, if necessary, also be loaded with Mk 82 bombs. On the two other weapon stations are carried AIM-9 Sidewinder air-to-air guided missiles. A further, seventh weapon station can be found under the fuselage and is normally loaded with two pods; one contains the 1 in. (25 mm) cannon GAU-12/U and the other 300 rounds of ammunition. These pods are aerodynamically shaped and give the jet additional lift. For vertical take-off the Harrier II can carry a maximum external additional load of 7,000 lb. (3,175 kg) and has a range in combat operations of 748 miles (1,204 km); a significant improvement on the Harrier I. If refueling in the air is necessary, the AV-8B can be fitted with a hydraulically extendable air-refueling arm above the left air intake.

Data management

The joint venture of British Aerospace and McDonnell Douglas built the Harrier II to conform to the most up-to-date standards both for the flight servo-system and also weapon guidance systems and the targeting equipment. The whole system is controlled by a digital computer via glass-fiber data bus cables. The central weapon system installed is the Hughes ARBS (Angle Rate Bombing System) with TV and laser targeting, and in addition there is a comprehensive defensive system of radar warning receivers and EW (electronic warfare) systems. The pilot receives all important threat, weapon deployment, and flight data via a head-up display (HUD).

Harriers of the first generation are still being deployed in small numbers and the new versions will probably remain in service for a while yet—a real replacement for the vertical take-off is not in view.

The command center of the Harrier. The inclined viewing glass (top middle) is an early head-up display on which flight data are displayed.

Harrier in ground-support. The possibility of operating from extremely short runways is a decisive tactical advantage.

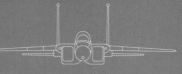

McDonnell Douglas F-15 Eagle

In the USA there had not been another outstanding long-range air supremacy fighter since the days of the P-51 Mustang—in the Vietnam War this became a clear tactical disadvantage. From this experience, as early as March 1966, within the framework of the FX project, first study briefs were granted—the winner of the subsequent bid at the end of 1969 was McDonnell Douglas and the new fighter became the F-15. The heavy fighter dominated development for years and is still being used today. Since McDonnell Douglas was merged into Boeing in 1997, the F-15 has been produced under the new company name.

MCDONNELL DOUGLAS F-15A EAGLE

Single-seat long-range air supremacy fighter
Wingspan: 42 ft. 10 in. (13.05 m)
Length: 63 ft. 9 in. (19.43 m)
Height: 18 ft. 6 in. (5.63 m)
Empty weight: 28,605 lb. (12,973 kg)
Maximum take-off weight: 56,008 lb. (25,401 kg)
Power plant: 2 × Pratt & Whitney F100-PW-100 turbofan, maximum thrust 25,459 lbf (113.25 kN) with afterburner
Maximum speed: 1,517 mph (2,443 km/h) (Mach 2.3)
Operational ceiling: 62,995 ft. (19,200 m)
Combat radius: 1,199 miles (1,930 km)
Armament: 1 × M61A-1 Vulcan .787 in. (20 mm) rapid-fire cannon with 940 rounds (in the starboard wing roots), 4 × AIM-7M Sparrow air-to-air guided missiles on the outside of the fuselage, 4 × AIM-9M Sidewinder air-to-air guided missiles on the upper side of the under-wing pylons or 4 × AIM-120 AMRAAM air-to-air guided missiles; in the configuration as fighter-bomber up to 16,004 lb. (7,258 kg) bomb load

Waiting for the all-clear—an F-15 pilot just before take-off.

Air supremacy

During the development period of the F-15, the Western secret services had little or no knowledge about its potential opponent, the MiG-25, which was the most modern warplane at this time in the Soviet Union. So, to be on the safe side, they reckoned on the greatest possible superiority in all aspects. In the first place was maneuverability in dogfights and the extensive range planned in order to be able to operate in a superior situation deep inside enemy territory. Acceleration and final speed were ranked as indispensable and achieved with a good performance weight (i.e. the ratio between thrust and weight)—the low surface loading and the geometry of the delta wing with recoiling wingtips provided mobility.

The weapons system and the weapons control system were optimum at that time and are partly still in use today. In the F-15A and C versions, the flight performance and the avionics enabled a single pilot to use a complex plane safely and effectively.

When in 1976 the plane of the Soviet defector W.I. Belenko was tested for the first time—a MiG-25 P, the plane against which the F-15 had been developed—it turned out that the objective had been more than fulfilled.

Today the USA's F-15 is still regarded as the superior warplane that it certainly was for a long time, although the Eagle has long since been outclassed by the Eurofighter, the Sukhoi Su-35, and others. In a dogfight the F-15 was

unequal to the Sukhoi Su-27, but could at least obtain a draw with its advanced and superior avionics in combat outside visual range.

FX—Fighter eXperimental

The tactical fighter from the FX project in the USA was brought to mass production readiness under great time pressure. If the complexity of the new fighter and the numerous new developments brought into use are taken into account, the development time is unbelievably short. The FX specifications date from 1966, McDonnell Douglas won the bid on December 23, 1969, and only two and a half years later, on July 27, 1972, the F-15A made its maiden flight. The first two-seat planes, the F-15Bs, were ready for training use in 1973, and in May 1976 the first squadron of the US Air Force reported ready for duty with the F-15.

The two engines of the F-15 develop with afterburner a thrust of 25,459 lbf (113.25 kN) each.

With the F-15 Eagle McDonnell Douglas had developed a long-range fighter in excellent shape.

The avionics of the F-15 Eagle set standards in aircraft construction in the 1970s.

Still dial instruments: angle of approach and g forces were displayed to the pilot in analogue form.

Update

Three years after the beginning of service life, the improved F-15C model was produced with extended range and improved avionics. The original, interference-prone Hughes APG-63 multi-purpose pulse Doppler radar was replaced by the APG 70 that was produced under the company name Raytheon after the fusion of the two companies in 1997.

The range of the F-15 is still 2,760 miles (4,445 km), with a maximum lift-off weight double that of a "heavy" Second World War bomber, at around 35 tons—and that is despite an increase during the course of the development by around 10 tons to the intended total weight. Both the single-seat model and the two-seat counterpart were, with the PEP-2000 (Production Eagle Package-2000), given an internal tank capacity greater by 2,000 lb. (907 kg) and two external tanks, that can literally carry it off.

CFT—Conformal Fuel Tank

Under this name auxiliary tanks were developed that no longer have much in common with the torpedo-shaped Second World War fuel drums—apart from the contents.

These low-resistance containers are attached within the transition area between the wing and the fuselage on either side and thanks to their highly developed aerodynamics do not impair flight behavior. The number of external stores is not reduced and the CFT themselves can also serve as weapons stations for guided missiles. The volume of the tanks at about 790 gal. (3,000 l) each allows the F-15 to cross the Atlantic with its own fuel.

Strike Eagle F-15E/D

As is so often the case, the F-15 was converted in the course of its career to a fighter-bomber for air-to-ground missions. F-15C, D, and E were the versions that were used in large numbers in combat operations. In the Near East, in the Gulf War in the operations of Desert Storm and surveillance of the no-fly zone—Southern Watch—the F-15 achieved an excellent performance against mobile rocket stations and in other combats. One would have to go a long way to find a fighter that could show a similar strike/loss ratio: in all combats in which it took part the F-15 was credited with 101 air victories—with no losses.

Avionics in the example of the F-15K

The Model K built for the South Korean market possesses a variety of control and navigation systems for electronic warfare (EW): seven colored liquid crystal displays for flight and weapons data, the JHMCS pilot helmet with integrated visor for targeting of guided missiles, and a wide-angle front head-up display (HUD).

For protection against attacks, there was a Northrop-Grumman ALQ-135 jamming transmitter and the Lockheed Martin ALR-56C Loral radar warning device.

The radar is provided by the Raytheon company, and consists of an AN/APG-63 (no longer used in the USA) that can pursue air targets in air-to-air mode or ground targets in air-to-ground mode. Targets are picked up using the Forward-Looking Infra-Red device (FLIR) and the IRST (Infra-Red Search and Track system).

Purchase decision

The F-15 Eagle was also a success from an economic point of view. Beside the USA, it is also flown in the armed forces of Israel, Saudi Arabia, and South Korea. Japan received 223 planes built by Mitsubishi under license. Singapore has recently decided to buy the system and South Korea has been receiving the Model K since 2005.

It may be assumed that, with the most recent decisions to buy a product that is really outdated, it is not only the plane itself that is uppermost in customers' minds. According to press reports, US politicians are said—at least in South Korea—to have actively influenced the decision.

The McDonnell F-15 is still in service today.

The F-16 Fighting Falcon is, with over 4,000 planes produced, one of the most successful jet fighters worldwide.

GENERAL DYNAMICS F-16 FIGHTING FALCON

The F-16 Fighting Falcon represents the first fighter in mass production that is completely electronically steered. Conceived at the beginning of the 1970s from the FX project as a relatively cheap and small light fighter, in the course of its working life it has become one of the most powerful multi-purpose warplanes in the world.

**GENERAL DYNAMICS
F-16 FIGHTING FALCON**
Single-seat multi-purpose warplane
Wingspan: 31 ft. (9.45 m)
Length: 49 ft. 3 in. (15.01 m)
Height: 16 ft. 8 in. (5.09 m)
Empty weight: 16,238 lb. (7,364 kg)
Maximum take-off weight: 34,508 lb. (15,650 kg)
Power plant: 1 × F100-PW-200 23,829 lbf (106 kN) thrust Pratt & Whitney turbojet engine with afterburner
Maximum speed: 1,349 mph (2,173 km/h) (Mach 2.05)
Operational ceiling: 50,002 ft. (15,240 m)
Range: 546 miles (880 km)
Combat radius: 776 miles (1,250 km)
Armament: 1 × six-barrel M61A-1 .787 in. (20 mm) rapid-fire cannon with 515 rounds, 4 to 6 × AIM-9 Sidewinder air-to-air guided missiles, under-wing and under-fuselage pylons for up to 12,002 lb. (5,443 kg) external weapons load and auxiliary tanks

Numbers

According to numbers from Lockheed Martin— where the jet is now being built—the four thousandth plane was delivered in 2000. Up to 1997, the USA alone had completed over

Flight safety

Two units of the US Air Force received the "Gerald John J. Pesch" prize for outstanding flight safety in 2004. Since the changeover of these squadrons to the F-16, there have been no accidents in 65,000 flight hours. The total flight hours and the number of accidents during them give a result of a rate of fewer than four accidents of the first category for the new versions from Block 50/52. That means four fatal accidents or planes lost in 100,000 flight hours—reason enough to describe the Fighting Falcon as the safest single-seat fighter ever.

Fly by wire

The so-called "fly by wire" (FBW) steering system that was installed worldwide for the first time in mass production in the Fighting Falcon does not need conventional hydraulics to regulate the flaps. Instead of that, on the F-16 the joystick is connected directly to the on-board computer. The computer receives the steering commands from the pilot and passes these on by electronic signals to the drive of the switch units on the movable parts (rudder and flaps).

At a flight demonstration, smoke dischargers at the ends of the wings provide a dramatic entrance of the F-16.

Patrol flight: F-16s survey the air space; armed with, among other things, Sidewinder short- and medium-range guided missiles.

five million flight hours with this model—alongside a strike/loss ratio of 71:0, counting only air victories, and a figure of 13,500 missions flown, a record of versatility.

LWF Lightweight Fighter

The F-16 is compactly built, relatively light, and all in all quite cheap—Models A and B still cost under ten million US dollars. The low cost and the easing of US weapons policy led to the F-16 developing into a real export hit. Above all, the air forces of the Western-oriented countries bought Series A (fighter) and B (two-seat trainer) of the Fighting Falcon. In addition the F-16 was produced under license in various countries. As demand for a cheap and competitive warplane still continues, the possibility exists that the Fighting Falcon will be produced into the year 2010.

So, steering commands are no longer transmitted by cables and levers but by electronic signals via thin copper wires to the servo mechanism. This system is not only considerably more precise and easier but also shell-proof and less liable to interference.

However, the whole system has a second function. The F-16 was a deliberately unstable construction, and hence extraordinarily agile, but was only controllable by means of a computer and FBW—at the time of its appearance a sensation in aviation technology.

So that the pilot can better tolerate the high g-stresses in tight turns and air combat, the ejector seat is tilted back 30 degrees. The pilot steers the jet with a mini "steering handle" installed on the right-hand side console that allows for a comfortable hand and arm position.

The cockpit of the F-16 Fighting Falcon. Tight and certainly not comfortable, but functional. The almost frameless cabin hood offers ideal vision and the seat, which is tilted back 30 degrees, allows the pilot to tolerate high g-stresses.

Cabin and wings

The F-16 is a mid-wing airplane in which the wings merge into the fuselage; the blended wing/body functions are aerodynamically pure. This design is based on a harmonic combination of the lift-generating wing unit "wing body"—with the lift-generating wings and the tailplane. The short, swept-back wings, the sharp-edged roots of which are drawn forwards, create vortical aircraft wakes and together with automatic slats provide optimum lift ratios for the wing unit.

In this configuration the F-16 is in the position of flying tight curves with up to 9 g. At the time it came into service in August 1978, this was unique. Theoretically, curves could still be flown in it even with an external weapon load of over 22,000 lb. (10,000 kg) with stresses of 5.5 g.

The MSIP Program

The first flight of the Fighting Falcon, then under the designation YF-16, took place on January 20, 1974. After the awarding of contracts by the US Air Force (USAF), the mass production of the F-16A began on August 7, 1978. Only two weeks later, the first jets were already being delivered. Until the middle of the 1980s, the F-16A remained, together with the F-15 Eagle, the standard fighter of the USAF, but was also used by the US Navy as the F-16N. The F-16B is a two-seat training plane which flew for the first time in August 1977.

With the beginning of the 1980s the USAF published the MSIP program (Multi-Stage Improvement Program). On the existing warplanes and those in development, the all-weather and night-flying capabilities were to be improved. Also, the most modern weapons systems and electronics were to be installed as part of this combat-capability improvement plan in three construction phases. The improved version of the Fighting Falcon arising from this is the F-16C, with a new large wide-angle head-up display (HUD) from GEC-Marconi. Further changes in this series concern the new Westinghouse AN/APG-68 multi-operational radar with improved range and a MIL-STD-1760 databus for the use of AMRAAM and AGM-65D Maverick air-to-air guided missiles. The stealth properties of the F-16C were improved by the installation

of a cockpit canopy specially coated with polycarbonate that reduced the radar echo by 40 percent.

The catalog

As a modern multi-purpose warplane, the F-16 was and is in the position to carry a variety of guided missiles and bombs—alongside the standard weapon of US fighters, the M61A-1 six-barreled rapid-fire cannon with 515 rounds of ammunition, in the fuselage on the left next to the pilot. The whole arsenal of up-to-date weapons and associated systems by Lockheed Martin includes 100 individual combinations, and it is impossible to list them all here.

Intelligent bombs

The F-16 has been considered to be unsurpassed in precision bombing—right from the first combat operation. On June 7, 1981, the Israeli air force attacked the Iraqi atomic reactor Osirak—eight F-16s and six F-15 Eagles carried out the strike. The leading F-16 carried two video-guided bombs ("smart bombs"). Five further Falcons were armed each with a pair of unguided blockbuster bombs developed specially for combating bunker targets with

high explosive force. The atomic reactor was precisely hit and completely destroyed.

In all, 251 F-16s took part in the operations in Iraq, of which most were deployed against Iraqi ground targets.

The hybrid wing combines the advantages of gently and strongly swept-back wings. The flow picture shows the path of the air.

The F-16 can carry additional loads that are as heavy as a whole Second World War fighter

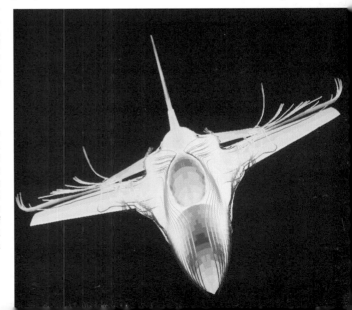

PANAVIA TORNADO

MRCA (or Multi-Role Combat Aircraft) was the name of the joint West European defense project whose beginnings go back to the 1960s. The multi-role combat aircraft developed, the Panavia Tornado, still fulfills the most varied tasks, from air exclusion and close support via reconnaissance to precision bombing. In the air forces of Great Britain, Italy, and Germany, this first successful joint warplane is still serving today.

PANAVIA TORNADO IDS
Multi-purpose warplane
Wingspan: 45 ft. 8 in. (13.91 m) swept-back 25 degrees (fully extended), 28 ft. 3 in. (8.60 m) swept-back 67 degrees (pivoted backwards)
Length: 56 ft. 6 in. (17.23 m)
Height: 19 ft. 6 in. (5.95 m)
Empty weight: 31,973 lb. (14,500 kg)
Maximum take-off weight: 61,743 lb. (28,000 kg)
Power plant: 2 × Turbo-Union RB199-34R turbofan engines each with 9,104 lbf (40.5 kN) thrust without and 16,073 lbf (71.5 kN) thrust with afterburner
Maximum speed: 1,428 mph (2,300 km/h)
Combat radius: 863 miles (1,390 km)
Armament: 2 × single-barreled, gas-operated 1.1 in. (27 mm) Mauser BK 27 revolver cannon with 180 rounds; AIM-9L Sidewinder air-to-air guided missiles; AGM-HARM high-speed anti-radar missiles for suppressing or destroying enemy warning and fire-control radar; TAURUS 350 medium-range high-precision stand-off guided missiles; GBU-24 "Paveway III" laser guided bombs and for sea target combat up to 4 × Kormoran 2 guided missiles with self-steering radar seeker heads, all guided missiles target-seeking "fire and forget"

The Tornado, a joint three-nations multi-role warplane, is produced by the Panavia consortium.

Joint venture

In the mid-1960s, warplanes such as the RAF's Starfighter and the Luftwaffe's Buccaneer that served in the air forces of NATO member states were no longer up to the demands of the time.

In order to be able to bear the development costs of a new weapons system, at the beginning of 1968 five nations joined together in a consortium. In the end, however, only Great Britain, Italy, and the Federal Republic of Germany—where there was strong political resistance to the communal project—were left.

An RAF Tornado converted from a GR1 fighter-bomber to a GR1A spotter—with the electronic eyes under the nose.

The RAF is still flying the Tornado in three locations; one of them is on the Falkland Islands.

Mauser BK 27

In its role as a spotter plane, the Tornado carries weapons primarily for self-defense. One of them—at the time the most modern cannon for installation into a warplane—was the single-barreled BK 27 revolver cannon developed specially for the MRCA project. The single-barreled cannon looked more like a revolver than the American M61A built according to the Gatling system as, unlike the latter, only the magazine revolves in the Mauser cannon. The specifications of NATO were the following: to reach the highest possible speed for the projectile with low weight and an effective range of fire of between 1.2 and 1.8 miles (2 and 3 km). The performance is amazing, the expected service life vastly exceeded the specifications, the projectile weight of 9.2 oz. (260 g) gives it high piercing force, and the impact detonator detonates even when the angle of impact is almost 90 degrees. The much higher fire speed of the American model is compensated for in the BK 27 with a higher caliber. One of the peculiarities of the cannon is its universal ammunition: all seven types of ammunition possess the same inner and outer ballistics and can be fired miscellaneously with the same sight setting. Doing without magazines or belts shortens the time of loading by half.

Maintaining tradition: Two Tornados and an AWACS plane escort an AVRO Shackleton Second World War bomber.

military parlance, the English "reconnaissance" is also termed recce.

Swing wings

If warplanes of the same period are looked at together, it is striking that the geometry of the cabin and the wing are marked by the spirit of the times. The conflict in the use of the planes that still exists—strongly swept-back wings for stable flight at high speeds at the price of poor performance in slow flight and vice versa—was, for a short time at the beginning of the 1970s, solved by the design of the swing wing. Parallel to that, the delta wing was the second most common arrangement.

In the Tornado, three different grades of back-sweep can be set (25, 45, and 67 or 68 degrees), either from the cockpit or, in the ADV version, automatically by the on-board computer.

Flaps with two slots run over almost the whole length of the trailing edge; on the leading edge flaps give lift over the whole wingspan in slow flight. All lift aids can be used up to a wing sweep of 45 degrees.

The steering about the horizontal axis displays a particular feature: the Tornado has no aileron! Instead, the tailplane is swept back and has all moving horizontal surfaces "tailerons" operated collectively as elevators in pitch or differentially as ailerons for roll control.

A Tornado GR1 fighter-bomber of the RAF based in Laarbruch.

The consortium of the companies involved, the British Aircraft Corporation (today British Aerospace), DASA, Messerschmitt Bölkow Blohm (MBB), and Aeritalia SpA/Alenia was founded in 1969 and was given the name Panavia Aircraft GmbH, with a head office in Munich.

Three in one

The model, which was christened MRCA, was supposed to fulfill a variety of tasks—that to some extent contradicted each other.

The basic version was the tactical fighter-bomber IDS (Interdiction/Strike). From this developed the long-range interceptor ADV (Air Defense Variant) and the spotter and electronic warfare (EW) version ECR (Electronic Combat and Reconnaissance) for detecting enemy anti-aircraft radar and attacking it. In

Turbo Union

In the same year in which Panavia was founded, the Turbo Union Company came into being. Borne by thoughts of co-operation in Europe, its business aim was the construction of a jointly developed engine for the Tornado. The founding members Rolls-Royce, MTU Motoren, and FiatAvio (today Avio) developed for the MRCA a new turbofan engine that was adapted to its purpose—for high speeds in low and lowest-level flight with, at the same time, low fuel consumption. The result of this co-operation, the Turbo Union RB199, makes possible speeds of up to 932 mph (1,500 km/h) at altitudes of under 1,000 ft. (300 m); in the extreme case to under 100 ft. (30 m).

Treetop height

The Tornado fighter-bomber's mission is to attack tactical targets, such as radar stations and anti-aircraft positions to name but two, deep in enemy territory. Within the framework of such missions, the performance of the plane in low-level flight—and therefore underneath the ground radar controlled zone—is of decisive significance, that is, on the one hand the engine performance, which in the vicinity of the ground is notably above Mach 1, or the other hand the terrain-following device. With its TFR (Terrain-Following Radar)—in combination with a radar altimeter and the flight control computer—the Tornado can go

independently in automatic terrain-following flight at an altitude of 200 ft. (60 m)—independent of weather or visual range. The automatic stall warning system CSAS (Command & Stability Augmentation System) takes over the flight steering. Under visual flying conditions and with automatic control switched off, the pilot can penetrate

NATO missions

The members of the North Atlantic pact are increasing their responsibility in missions that are not confined to Europe. Both Italian and British Tornados took part in the Gulf War, and German Luftwaffe pilots flew reconnaissance missions over Bosnia and had their first combat engagements during the NATO bombardment in Kosovo. The aircraft operating out of Italy were deployed successfully together with Italian and British Tornados. Even after 25 years, the Tornado remains a capable system in operation and is still being used. After more and more violent resistance of the insurgents in the impassable mountain regions of Afghanistan, in December 2006 NATO asked the German Bundeswehr to send Tornado ECRs to seek out the positions of the resistance movement from the air. The requested Tornados were transferred in April 2007.

The Tornado can be adapted to the different deployment conditions with a variety of weapons systems.

The multiplicity of small bombs and JP233 submunitions pods serve the purpose of destroying enemy runways.

The first prototype of the ADV long-range interceptor is here armed for self-defense with four "Sky Flash" guided missiles.

into opposing territory at an altitude of 100 ft. (30 m)—at treetop height—at a maximum speed of 932 mph (1,500 km/h).

Target locating

The location of the mission target in low-level flight requires a first-class navigation system; without vision the approach would be like groping in the fog. Alongside the main system—a Decca 72 Doppler radar—a Ferranti laser rangefinder with movable map projection provides pilots and weapons systems officers with the navigation data. Steering course and flight position are monitored by a gyro platform. Coupled to this are the TFR and Ground-Mapping Radar (GMR), both from Texas Instruments. A laser targeting device installed in a casing under the fuselage supports the weapons system officer when the target moves nearer.

Signing of the contract—the MRCA in figures

The final contract for testing and subsequent production of the Tornado was signed in 1971.

Under the leadership of Paul Millett (BAC Chief Test Pilot) and Nils Meister (MBB) the first prototype P.01 took off on its maiden flight on August 14, 1974, in Manching/Ingolstadt. The production contract for the first tranche was concluded on July 29, 1976, and the first mass-produced planes were delivered to the RAF on June 5, 1979, and on June 6 to the Luftwaffe. In Germany the planes arrived at the units after the trials of 1981. In total 977 of the MRCA were produced.

Tornado in service

To date (2007) the German Luftwaffe possesses, in four squadrons, 359 Tornados of all variants plus the trainers that are stationed at the Luftwaffe training center in Holloman, New Mexico.

In the RAF, 142 Tornado GR.4s are serving with a range of deployment comparable to the IDS. On the Falkland Islands, the fighter version F replaced the Phantom II from 1992, and alongside them there still exist Model GR.4As for reconnaissance derived from the GR.1, and the Model GR.1B of the Air Naval Wing.

From the original 99 Italian Tornado IDS, 12 were converted to the ECR version and further planes leased by the UK. There, the RAF wants to begin to take the Tornado out of service by 2008. It will be replaced, as in Germany, by the Eurofighter or by unmanned drones.

The only non-European customer, Saudi Arabia, received 72 which flew in Gulf War combat missions.

An RAF Tornado GR1 carries JP233 scatter weapons pods with runway-cratering bombs.

McDonnell Douglas F-18 Hornet

Parallel to the Lightweight Fighter Program of the US Air Force, there was a program called VFAX with similar specifications for the US Navy in the 1970s. The Navy needed a replacement for the F-14 that was less specialized and cheaper, as the procurement costs would otherwise not have permitted a sufficient number of fighters. On the basis of the Northrop Company's prototype, the YF-17 Cobra, McDonnell Douglas, and Northrop jointly developed the carrier-borne multi-purpose fighter F-18 Hornet, whose weapons pylons allowed the combination of the fighter and fighter-bomber variants in one airframe. The result of the co-operation was a strong, flexible, and affordable fighter that is still in the service of various nations today. In a cost comparison carried out by the US Navy the F-18 Super Hornet scored excellently. Thus the costs per flight hour for the F-18 work out at 40 percent of the comparable costs for the F-14, and for repair and maintenance 75 percent less working time per flight hour is needed than for the Tomcat.

MCDONNELL DOUGLAS F-18A HORNET
Carrier-borne single-seat fighter-bomber
Wingspan: 37 ft. 6 in. (11.42 m)
Length: 56 ft. (17.07 m)
Height: 25 ft. 3 in. (4.66 m)
Empty weight: 23,053 lb. (10,455 kg)
Maximum take-off weight: 51,908 lb. (23,541 kg)
Power plant: 2 × General Electric F404-GE-400 turbofan engines, static thrust performance 10,570 lbf (47.02 kN) each without and 15,983 lbf (71.1 kN) with afterburner
Maximum speed: 1,189 mph (1,915 km/h) (Mach 1.8)
Operational ceiling: 50,002 ft. (15,240 m)
Combat radius: 460 miles (740 km) (fighter), 661 miles (1065 km) (fighter-bomber)
Armament: 1 × M61 rapid-fire cannon with 570 rounds ammunition in the upper nose; in total seven weapons stations under wings and fuselage and also at the wingtips for a combat load of 17,000 lb. (7710 kg), such as, for example, 2 × AIM-9 Sidewinders and other air-to-air or air-to-ground guided missiles, auxiliary tanks, laser cameras

The almost round air intake distinguishes the McDonnell Douglas Hornet from other modern fighters

Strike fighter

Originally there were supposed to be three versions of the prototype of the Northrop YF-17: air combat and escort fighter F-18, fighter-bomber A-18, and crew trainer TF-18. High development costs argued, however, for only building one type, and the design showed

Testing

At McDonnell Douglas, eleven test planes were built, two of them in the two-seat TF-18 version (later renamed F-18B). The first of the nine planes of the F-18A series flew on November 18, 1978, and the first TF-18A on October 25, 1979. Mass production began in 1980, and in November of the same year the VFA-125 (Strike Fighter Squadron 125), as the squadron responsible for the mission training with the US Navy and US Marine Corps, received the first F-18A Hornets. The first mass-produced F-18As were then delivered to the fleet in 1982. By the middle of 1984, three squadrons of the USMC were already flying the F-18A, while the US Navy, with a clearly lower priority,

In modern aircraft construction, the flat-designed fuselage is also a lift-creating surface.

itself to be flexible enough. At first McDonnell Douglas was to build the wings, tailplane, and front fuselage, and be responsible for the Navy version as main contractor, while Northrop was to develop and bring to market the land-supported version. As, however, the two companies fell out over this agreement, McDonnell Douglas obtained the rights for all the versions.

The planning of the F/A-18 aimed at the construction of a light carrier-borne Navy fighter.

With the F-18A, the concept of electronic flight steering was rigorously implemented.

The Hornet deployed as a fighter-bomber when it can also be armed with air-to-ground guided missiles.

changed to the Hornet. A total purchase of over 1,300 F-18As by the US Navy and Marine Corps was planned.

Hybrid wings

From a design point of view, the F-18A is a mid-wing aircraft with two tail fins slightly pointing outwards. The prominent leading edge root extensions (strake wings) run like narrow wings and lift boosters up to a level with the cockpit front screen.

The flaps on the leading edge and also those on the trailing edge of the wing are movable. The leading-edge flaps of the wings are extendable to an angle of 30 degrees and produce strong turbulence over the wings, which again provides a strong lift to the wing. The Hornet is capable of flying in sharp curves over a wide range of speeds. The large double-slatted flaps on the trailing edges, that take up almost a third of the wing and provide for lower approach and landing speeds, are striking.

The Hornet in comparison

The superiority of the Hornet lies in its technology (i.e. the structural design), in its easy maintenance, and its reliability. By comparison, the F-18A cannot achieve the same capability as the Panavia Tornado in low-level flight but is first class as a fighter.

Compared with its direct rival, the F-16 Fighting Falcon, the Hornet has one advantage—right from being taken into service it possessed, with the APG-65, a highly efficient multi-modal target tracking radar for air-to-air and air-to-ground deployment with suitable guided missiles. The disadvantages of the F-18A were its limited range and low payload.

Cockpit

The instrumentation was more advanced than with any other combat jet previously in service.

The F-18 was one of the first planes with an almost complete "Screen Cockpit" with HOTAS (Hands On Throttle And Stick = all the important service elements are on the throttle lever and the joystick) and "fly by wire"—steering with electronic signals. In many of the other contemporary warplane models, the steering commands were still transmitted in analog form (i.e. mechanically or hydraulically).

The pilot receives information via three multi-function screen devices that are installed centrally at head height in the front console. Alongside the flight data, the new system also delivers all relevant details about the opponent to be faced, displays the munitions stocks of the weapons, and which of them the computer has chosen for firing. In addition a FLIR (Forward Looking Infra-Red) displays the terrain lying in the direction of flight in real time, even in night flying.

Armament

Like all modern jets, the F-18 can be equipped in its nine weapons stations with a variety of weaponry. An AIM-9 Sidewinder air-to-air guided missile on launch rails with an infra-red target-seeking head against air targets at short distance is usually carried on either wingtip.

Furthermore, the F-18As were able to carry two AIM-7 Sparrow air-to-air guided missiles in fuselage pylons to combat air targets at a range of 31–62 miles (50–100 km). The Sparrow is not a target-seeking missile with active radar but has to be guided to the target by the pilot with the on-board radar. With the Sparrow it was necessary for the pilot to continue flying the F-18 in the direction of the target even after the missile had been fired to "illuminate" its way to the target by means of the nose radar (i.e. to guide it to the target).

By contrast, the AMRAAM air-to-air guided missiles used since the mid-1980s work in the target-self-seeking "fire and forget" mode (fire without further action!) and replaced the Sparrow. The F-18C can carry the Hughes AIM-120A (AMRAAM) guided missiles with independent active radar guidance and thus effectively combat opposing aircraft at medium ranges. The AIM-120A is smaller, shorter, and lighter than the Sparrow and therefore can be carried in greater quantities. As with all "fire and forget" guided missiles, clear target identification has to precede the deployment of the AIM-120A.

The main difference in the model of the F-18 as fighter or fighter-bomber consists of a different combination in the combat payload. As a fighter-bomber, the F-18A does not carry Sparrow guided missiles. Instead, the two weapons pylons intended for the Sparrow on the fuselage are loaded with a laser targeting device.

Further development

Alongside the single-seat F-18A, there is also a two-seat version, the F-18B. In principle

At a short distance above the fight deck the undercarriage is raised after take-off.

enemy target-seeking radar were installed and the night/all-weather attack capability improved. Series C is the single-seat and D the two-seat jet. The latest version is used primarily by the US Marine Corps and serves as an attack plane for tactical air control, as a spotter, and as a training plane. The first F-18s of this series were delivered in 1989.

Its empty weight of only 23,053 lb. (10,455 kg) makes the F-18 a lightweight in its class.

it has the same equipment as the F-18A but carries 6 percent less fuel in the internal tanks. It is used as a training plane or tactical deployment plane.

Normal flight operation had only just begun when, in summer 1984 on an inspection in the US Navy test center in Patuxent River (NATC), cracks were discovered in the area of the tailplane. The causes were determined as air turbulence and lateral forces acting on the tailplane. The whole of the Hornet fleet was temporarily grounded. By strengthening certain structures and retrofitting with a rigid boundary layer fence in the area of the transition wing/fuselage, the problem could be resolved.

The Series C and D of the F-18 developed in 1987 are improved versions of Series A and B. They were given guided weapons of the most recent production such as the AIM-120 air-to-air guided missiles and the air-to-ground or anti-ship missiles AGM-65 Maverick and AGM-84 Harpoon. Furthermore, for self-defense, the most recent electronic devices for jamming of

Slung by the steam catapult, an F-18 Hornet races over the deck of an aircraft carrier.

Super Hornet

In the 1990s at McDonnell Douglas, two new versions, the F-18E and the F-18F, were developed and designated the Super Hornet. The Super Hornet is not simply an improved version of the Hornet but rather more a completely newly designed airframe that only has certain design concepts still in common with the original Hornet.

From September 1995, the first jets of Series E and F of the F-18 were rolled out. As before, the E version is the single-seat and the F the two-seat model. The Super Hornet is today flown by two squadrons on the aircraft carrier USS *Nimitz*.

Operational deployment

In its fighter plane mode, the F-18 had two main tasks to carry out in the US Navy. It served

as an escort fighter and provided fighter
protection for the fleet. It was first used in
1986 by the US aircraft carrier *Coral Sea* when it
flew combat missions against Libyan positions
at Benghazi.

In Operation Desert Storm in Iraq, its dual
role proved useful for the first time. The
F-18 could both shoot down enemy jets and
also cover ground targets with bombs, and all
this during a single combat mission. Thus on
January 17, 1991, two F-18s shot down two Iraqi
MiG-21 Fishbeds. The F-18s deployed in Iraq
proved themselves to be extremely robust
and fireproof. Hornets that were hit by Iraqi
anti-aircraft rockets in Desert Storm not only
survived but could also be repaired at double
speed. Often the jets were already in combat
operations again the next day. Also
in the second Iraq war, Series C and D
were deployed, together with the new Super
Hornet F-18E and F.

*Presence on the deck of an aircraft carrier is extremely
dangerous during flight operations and therefore only
permitted for the highly specialized deck crew.*

The Saab Gripen is adapted to the particular strategic conditions of Swedish national defense.

SAAB JAS 39 GRIPEN

With the Gripen, the neutral and relatively small country of Sweden put into service one of the first "Swing Role" (multi-role) planes of the fourth generation. The Gripen's highly modern weapons system, adapted to the strategic conditions of Scandinavia, bears witness to the capability of the Swedish industry in the categories of aircraft construction and high technology.

JAS—Jakt, Attack, Spaning
These three letters in the name of the Swedish warplane stand for interception, ground target attack, and reconnaissance. The griffin, which

is the translation of Gripen, has the capability of fulfilling all tactical requirements in the conduct of air combat. As a Swing Role Fighter, its capabilities go beyond those of a multi-purpose warplane, and the mission can be changed during flight without refitting, for example from air-to-air to air-to-ground missions.

Tactical requirements
In the 1980s, the obsolete Saab Viggen and Draken of the Swedish Air Force—Flygvapnet—were to be replaced. The Swedish concept of national defense requires from a warplane characteristics that make it difficult for foreign competitors to sell their products in this market. An example is the deployment conditions to be expected: in defense, a Swedish warplane has to remain usable even without intact infrastructure. Take-off and

SAAB JAS 39A GRIPEN

Single- or two-seater multi-purpose warplane

Wingspan: 27 ft. 7 in. (8.40 m)
Length: 46 ft. 3 in. (14.10 m)
Height: 14f ft. 9 in. (4.50 m)
Empty weight: 14,601 lb. (6,622 kg)
Maximum take-off weight: 28,665 lb. (13,000 kg)
Power plant: 1 x Volvo Aero Corp turbofan engine RM12 with 12,139 lbf (54 kN) thrust without and 18,096 (80.5 kN) thrust with afterburner
Maximum speed: 1,320 mph (2,125 km/h)
Operational ceiling: 49,215 ft. (15,000 m)
Combat radius: 497 miles (800 km)
Armament: 1 x single-barreled Mauser BK 27 1.1 in. (27 mm) caliber revolver cannon (underside of fuselage, left), Sidewinder RB 74 (AIM-9L) air-to-air guided missiles on the wingtips, Raytheon AIM-120 AMRAAM, French Matra MICA RB 71 (British Aerospace Sky Flash produced under license), Meteor long-range (out of the vision of the pilot) or the German BGT IRIS-T; SAAB RBS-15 anti-ship missiles, RB 75 air-to-ground missiles (Raytheon AGM-65 Maverick built in Sweden under license) BK (bomb capsules) 90 Mjöl-nir, scatter weapons system DWS39, unguided bombs and rockets

landing must also be possible from makeshift airstrips—such as cordoned-off main roads or motorways—where the take-off and landing strip for the plane is likely to be no longer than 2,625 ft. (800 m). Maintenance must be comparatively uncomplicated: a head technician and five assistants can make a landed Gripen combat-ready again in the minimum time of ten minutes. A further requirement is take-off time: 60 seconds after the take-off command, a plane must be in the air. This specification put the General Dynamics F-16 out of the running, as at the time of the call for bids it needed three minutes to lift off. The F/A-18 Hornet, also US American was quite simply too expensive. The planning department at SAAB did the calculations and came to the conclusion that it would be possible to build a purely Swedish combat plane that would do justice to all the requirements, for a price that was then put at approximately 40 million US dollars.

Export nation Sweden: No other country of this size would have coped with the task of building its own fighter plane.

JAS Gripen, prototype No. 1, during the final tests before the first flight.

characteristics both on the ground and in the air. The Gripen has a total height with extended undercarriage of 14 ft. 9 in. (4.50 m); in comparison, at 17 ft. 7 in. (5.28 m), the Eurofighter is noticeably higher and with a wingspan of 35 ft. 11 in. (10.95 m) over 6.5 ft. (2 m) wider than the Gripen.

Canard

The wing is in principle similar to that of the Eurofighter: a delta wing with a backwards sweep of 45 degrees and canard wings in the front fuselage area. This "head flight control" gives the Gripen excellent maneuverability— and shortens the landing distance. When the canard wings are set almost vertical to the ground they act as air brakes and increase the pressure on the undercarriage; this enhances the effectiveness of the wheel brake. In simulator training it is supposed to be possible to land the Gripen on board an aircraft carrier—without an arrestor hook.

The steering surfaces are arranged as elevons (combined tailplane and aileron) and set on the trailing edge of the wing, while the leading edges display a projection in the form of a dog tooth.

The JAS 39 Gripen is a descendant of famous warplanes from the SAAB workshop.

Unarmed, but fitted with smoke dischargers, the JAS 39 impressively demonstrates its flight performance.

Lightweight

The Gripen is a light warplane with scarcely half the weight of its predecessors the Viggen or the Dassault Rafale. This was possible on the one hand because of the relatively small dimensions and on the other hand because of the extensive use of composite materials. These characteristics contribute to the Gripen producing a relatively small radar echo and displaying excellent operational

The Gripen is not only at home on airfields. The Swedish defense concept also envisages the use of main roads or motorways as auxiliary airstrips.

SAAB

Even though today the Saab Company is more readily associated with motor vehicles, it was founded as an aircraft manufacturer—the name "Svenska Aeroplan Aktiebolaget," Swedish Aircraft Construction Company, makes it clear. Saab was founded in 1937. After a short time as a licensee, production began at the site in Linköping with the company's own developments such as the Saab Draken or Viggen. In 2006 Saab took over from its former partner Ericsson the defense division Ericsson Microwave Systems AB (EMW) and Ericsson's stake in the joint enterprise Saab Ericsson Space AB and, with that, integrated large parts of the avionics production into its own business.

Red Flag

Absolute neutrality is no longer achievable in the 21st century; even the officially non-committed Sweden will, in the case of an attack on a NATO country, have to take its place in the Western defense alliance. That it is in the position to do that was shown in 2006 by the participation of four Gripens in the NATO maneuver Red Flag, which regularly uses an attack on NATO as a scenario and tests out or establishes the joint defense readiness. For the standardization of the common equipment and armament there exists within NATO the so-called STANAG standard that, in the military area, can to all intents and purposes be compared with an industrial standard such as DIN or ISO. In their present form the Gripens are completely compatible with this standard and can be integrated into a common armed service. A surprise for the other participants of the maneuver was the capability of the Gripen to fire laser-guided weapons which were guided by the wingmen or squadron members operating further afield.

The Gripen owes its excellent maneuverability to the canard wings (head tailplane).

Export

The calculation which formed the basis for the construction of the Gripen assumed at least 240 airplanes sold. It is surprising enough that such a small country as Sweden with not even ten million inhabitants can cope with a project such as the development and construction of a high-performance warplane. For a while, the costs of the project amounted to a third of the whole defense budget. Without exports, these amounts could not be financed and it was not surprising that a few countries had to be and were secured as buyers for the system. South Africa, Hungary, and the Czech Republic became customers of the Swedes, and other smaller nations are showing interest. The excellent maintenance-friendly nature of the Gripen and naturally the purchase price make them attractive—even though a plane at just under 80 million US dollars is still a cost factor.

Datalink

The avionics of the Gripen are technically at the peak of development. "Fly by wire," the on-board computer, the most up-to-date target-seeking and high-performance radar—the Ericsson PS-05/A Pulse Doppler Radar for several operational modes—are some of these avionics.

The Swedish model is developing outstanding capabilities in a highly developed defense and data link system. From the ground, from a Saab 340 early-warning aircraft, or from other aircraft of its formation, the Gripen pilot receives comprehensive information by transmission. Even if he turns off his radar in order to remain undetected by the enemy, he still receives at all times an up-to-date overview of the air situation, the positions of friend and enemy, the weapon ranges, and even the fuel reserves of his wingman.

The on-board electronics of the JAS 39 were manufactured by the Ericsson Electronics Company until SAAB integrated the branch of the armament electronics business into its own enterprise.

Communication and weapons systems of the Gripen are 100 percent compatible with NATO standards.

EUROFIGHTER TYPHOON

The Eurofighter is the European warplane of the 21st century and should secure air supremacy for the EU for decades to come. The four-nation project demonstrates the capability of the high-tech future industry located in Europe and has the potential to become an export hit. In the postwar period, Germany had not developed its own warplane but had bought in aircraft—as a rule from the USA, such as, for example, the Lockheed F-104 Starfighter or McDonnell Douglas F-4 Phantom. Then, in the 1980s, an ambitious project was started in Europe—the Fighter 90. From that came the joint warplane of five EU member states—the Eurofighter.

EUROFIGHTER TYPHOON
Multi-purpose warplane
Wingspan: 35 ft. 11 in. (10.95 m)
Length: 52 ft. 4 in. (15.96 m)
Height: 17 ft. 4 in. (5.28 m)
Empty weight: 24,244 lb. (10,995 kg)
Maximum take-off weight: 50,715 lb. (23,000 kg)
Power plant: 2 × turbofan engines Eurojet EJ200 each with 13,488 lbf (60 kN) thrust without and 20,232 lbf (90 kN) thrust with afterburner
Maximum speed: 1,320 mph (2,125 km/h) (Mach 2.0)
Operational ceiling: 55,039 ft. (16,775 m)
Combat radius: 863 miles (1,390 km)
Armament: 1 × 1.1 in. (27 mm) Mauser cannon; explosive ordnance payload maximum 16,538 lb. (7,500 kg) in 13 external stores, twelve of which are arranged for air-to-air and air-to-ground guided missiles such as AIM-9L/I/I-1 Sidewinder, IRIS-T, AIM-120A/B AMRAAM, AIM-132 ASRAAM, Meteor, Taurus KEPD 350, laser- guided bombs Paveway II (GBU 10/16)

A Eurofighter of the Bundesluftwaffe (German Air Force) at Berlin-Schönefeld airport.

Characteristics

The Eurofighter or Typhoon—as the export version is called—possesses the characteristic called "Swing Role." That is the designation given to the capability of changing deployment task during a mission; for example from air-to-air to air-to-ground deployment.

The leading edge of its delta wing displays a back-sweep of 53 degrees and is fitted with canard wings on the fuselage nose. The fighter combines state-of-the-art technology from four nations and will secure the joint airspace of the EU until well into the 21st century.

This aircraft is distinguished by agility and outstanding maneuverability in supersonic flight and in both dogfights and also at distances beyond visual range (BVR) is a dangerous opponent. The flight characteristics speak for themselves: the Eurofighter performs Supercruise—supersonic, cruising speed without afterburner—and a maximum speed of Mach 2 (twice the speed of sound). Unique at present is its capability of flying in the supersonic range with a load factor of 9 g. And the Eurofighter is not bound to intact infrastructures—conceived for deployment on small bases, it needs minimally a 1,000 ft. (300 m) take-off strip.

Screen workstation at Mach 2—the cockpit

The age of dial instrumentation is finally history. On-screen displays show all the flight data. The most important information, such as, for example, target identification, is reflected directly into the helmet visor. The pilot's helmet is multifunctional and, among other things, two image intensifiers function in the dark and the pilot can switch on to track, and attack targets in the visor. If required, the pilot can also see an infra-red image in the visor.

Full thrust.
A Eurofighter Typhoon in a climb with afterburners running.

The Eurofighter prototype DA7 shows off its capabilities.

HOTAS flight steering

According to the HOTAS principle ("Hands On Throttle And Stick") the most important operating elements are arranged on the throttle lever and the steering stick. With this, alongside flight position and thrust, 24 central flight commands can be entered without letting go of the "joystick." With HOTAS the four on-board computers are networked, though in an emergency one of them would be enough.

As the Eurofighter is unstable in the longitudinal inclination—it constantly tends to swing upwards—it is very mobile. For this reason the Eurofighter can only be flown with the help of a highly advanced

computer that interprets the steering impulses of the pilot. Therefore, these are not transmitted directly to the steering surfaces. To carry out a maneuver, the pilot uses the steering quite normally. The computer perceives the steering movements and enters its own steering commands in such a way that the Eurofighter reacts correctly. The optimum manual operation allows a so-called "Carefree Handling," that is the pilot can enter any steering commands in the certainty that the computer will interpret them correctly. This turning capability is maximized and at the same time the risk of deviations or of too great a strain on the airframe is reduced.

Development of the Eurofighter has given the European economy an important impetus in the area of high tech.

commands and even answers. And if, in a dangerous situation, the pilot cannot pay attention to the displays, the Voice Warning System draws attention to problems with verbal warnings.

The sensors—navigation, enemy recognition, and fire-control system

The Eurofighter not only warns of dangers, it takes countermeasures. If the (optional) defense system DASS (Defense Aid Sub-System) recognizes a threat, it initiates avoidance maneuvers, attack, or electronic countermeasures. Thanks to DASS, the pilots can assess dangers according to their priority and automatically or manually activate defensive measures.

An infra-red seeker is installed on the front fuselage next to the cockpit: the target tracking device PIRATE (Passive Infra-Red Airborne Tracking Equipment), with its supercooled sensor, registers differences in temperature caused, for example, by an aircraft engine. By using PIRATE, the Eurofighter can locate, fix on, and attack its target without being located itself.

The main sensor is the multi-purpose pulse Doppler radar Captor (formerly ECR-90). It uses the Doppler effect to separate the signals from the ground and enemy—moving objects reflect fractionally differently from

Austria was one of the nations that bought the Eurofighter weapons platform—after fierce controversy in its own country.

The primary flight steering consists of movable canards arranged on the nose that can be moved in synchrony for steering in the longitudinal inclination and independently of each other for supporting rolling movements. They allow rising and falling without altering the angle of approach; these maneuvers are otherwise only possible with thrust vectoring.

In slow flight, the Carefree Handling already mentioned is automatically secured. If the speed approaches the stall speed of 126 mph (203 km/h), and with it a crash because of engine cut-out, the computer accelerates automatically. The capability of the on-board computer goes well beyond that of an autopilot; the Eurofighter flies itself—on enemy contact the pilot can concentrate on combat—and even fully automatic patrol flights are possible.

His master's voice

Communication with the aircraft also takes place in the Eurofighter via electronic speech recognition and commands; the DVI system understands 200 spoken

The canard wing allows the Eurofighter flight maneuvers at the limits of the possible.

resting ones. What is more, Captor can distinguish friend and foe, set priorities, and co-operate with the automatic weapons deployment to determine the optimum moment for weapons deployment.

And, if that is not enough, the Eurofighter can also be connected with AWACS spotter planes with information received online via data link.

Structure—the materials
The structural surface consists of the most up-to-date materials—70 percent carbon-fiber composite materials, 12 percent glass-reinforced plastics and only 15 percent metal: mainly aluminum and titanium alloy.

For cost reasons, the Eurofighter does not feature real stealth characteristics—yet a very small frontal radar profile was achieved with the choice of materials and skilled shaping—fourth place in the world ranking!

Engine
Drive is provided by two EJ200 turbofan engines (manufacturer: Eurojet). Each engine—eight million Euros each—creates a maximum 13,488 lbf (60 kN) thrust without and 20,232 lbf (90 kN) with afterburner. These two "power stations" allow Supercruise—a supersonic cruising speed without afterburner. At the present time this places the jet in the top flight of fighters worldwide.

The Eurofighter is intended to secure NATO airspace for the long term.

The two Eurojet EJ 200 turbofan engines also came out of a European Union project.

Index

PICTURE CREDITS

All pictures by **Philip Jarrett** except:

Aviation Images: 2 J. Dibbs, 5 K. Tokunaga (left), 9 M. Wagner, 65 J. Dibbs (bottom), 77 J. Dibbs, 80 J. Dibbs, 97 Neville, 110–111 J. Dibbs, 116 J. Dibbs (bottom), 165 J. Dibbs (top), 171 hc (top), 184 J. Dibbs (top), 206–207 K. Tokunaga (left), 224 M. Wagner, 243 M. Wagner (top), 244 M. Wagner, 261 K. Tokunaga (bottom), 262 M. Wagner, 263 K. Tokunaga (top), M. Wagner (bottom), 264 K. Tokunaga, 267 K. Tokunaga, 268 M. Wagner, 270 K. Tokunaga, 271 M. Wagner (top), K. Tokunaga (bottom), 284 J. Dibbs, 286 M. Wagner, 289 K. Tokunaga (top), 291 K. Tokunaga (top), 306 M. Wagner, 310 M. Wagner, 311 M. Wagner, 312 K. Tokunaga, 313 K. Tokunaga, 314–315 K. Tokunaga

Corbis: 13 Bettmann (bottom right), 27 Bettmann, 33 Hulton-Deutsch Collection (bottom), 44 (bottom), 50 Hulton-Deutsch Collection (left), 55 Bettmann, 76 Underwood & Underwood (bottom), 162 Bettmann (top), 165 Bettmann (bottom), 241 Bettmann (bottom), 245 Corbis Sygma (top), 265 George Hall (top), Leif Skoogfors (bottom), 285 Aero Graphics, Inc. (top), George Hall (bottom), 287 Aero Graphics, Inc., 290 George Hall, 291 Roger Ressmeyer (bottom)

Getty Images: 38 Hulton Archive (top), 114 MPI, 172–173 Hulton Archive, 180 Keystone (left), 183 Fox Photos (bottom), 198 John Chillingworth, 199 Raymond Kleboe (top), Fox Photos (bottom), 239 AFP (top)

This edition published by Parragon Books Ltd in 2015
and distributed by

Parragon Inc.
440 Park Avenue South, 13th Floor
New York, NY10016
www.parragon.com

Copyright © Parragon Books Ltd 2008-2015

Original edition produced by: ditter.projektagentur GmbH
Editor: Horst W. Laumanns
Picture editor: Claudia Bettray
Designer: Claudio Martinez
Artwork: Burga Fillery
3D images of the aircraft: www.flight-depot.com
Lithography: Klaussner Medien Service GmbH

English-language edition produced by Cambridge Publishing Management Ltd
Translation: Richard Elliot, Penny Hewson
Project editor: Diane Teillol
Copy-editor: Karin Fancett
Typesetter: Julie Crane
Proofreader: Tony Williams
Indexer: Marie Lorimer

ISBN: 978-1-4748-1867-4

Printed in China

The authors and editors of this book endeavored to reach the greatest accuracy possible by in-depth research. However, since the data vary depending on the source, there may be slight variations in the indicated values, especially as far as the technical data of the airplanes are concerned. In addition, we have rounded up some numbers.